IAN BATEY

ASIAN
BRANDING
A GREAT WAY TO FLY

Prentice
Hall

Singapore London New York Toronto Sydney Tokyo Madrid
Mexico City Munich Paris Capetown Hong Kong Montreal

Published in 2002 by
Prentice Hall
Pearson Education Asia Pte Ltd
23/25 First Lok Yang Road
Jurong
Singapore 629733

Pearson Education offices in Asia: *Bangkok, Beijing, Hong Kong, Jakarta, Kuala Lumpur, Manila, New Delhi, Seoul, Singapore, Taipei, Tokyo*

Printed in Singapore

5   4   3   2
06   05   04   03   02

ISBN 981-235-932-X
ISBN 0-13-066466-9 (pbk)

To my Carolina

CONTENTS

Note: All monetary figures quoted in this book are in US dollars, based on exchange rates applicable at the time of writing.

FOREWORD

By the Hon. Caspar W. Weinberger, Chairman, *Forbes,* **and former United States Secretary of Defence**

The theme of this book is essentially that this is Asia's century and that establishing, developing and using brand names is one of the keys to success for the non-Japanese Asian countries. Many familiar and other ideas about Asian and Western customs and consumers are discussed. There are also many more similarities of Asian and Western consumers found than dissimilarities.

Globalisation is widely accepted as a given and the main point of much of the book is that Asian business and marketing policies need to change, because the international market has changed. Asian brands must be developed and used as Western brand names are and have been used.

"The ways of the West have reached into the heart and soul of Asia, and big Asian consumers of tomorrow are relishing and embracing it all." But "Western values" are hugely diverse, as are "Asian values". Why not "Global values", asks the author, quite reasonably. All this puts a great pressure on modern marketing skills.

Marlboro cigarettes is cited as an example of a brand that has "triumphantly crossed all kinds of cultural and social barriers." Also the author notes, a soft drink commercial that plays well in the U.S.

will usually work in Asia. The opportunities, the author feels, are limitless — "China and India have truly only effectively opened up to brand marketing in the last ten years." Taiwan, Vietnam, Cambodia and Laos are not far behind.

The author worked exhaustively on the Singapore Airlines account and necessarily there is a long account of how Singapore Airlines achieved its coveted lead position by its adoption of a policy emphasizing its superiority in inflight services. The Singapore Girl with her distinctive uniform, her charm and warmth, contributed greatly to the idea of "The romance of travel", the author's invention, and a very successful one.

All of this also contributed enormously to Singapore's reputation as a great tourist destination. After 30 years of skilled promotion, Singapore, despite its small size, now has a tourism industry of over $6 billion. Many countries and industries are now trying the same thing.

Also the current *Foreign Affairs* magazine contains an article called, "The Rise of the Brand State", showing the increasingly wide use of advertising techniques promoting countries and not just businesses. The European Union seems a prime candidate for this kind of help.

There is much more in this book, including a splendid section on how Raffles Hotel in Singapore was saved from destruction to continue as one of the great brand names of the world.

All in all, this is a textbook and a handbook for those who have the responsibility for increasing sales and improving country and industry capabilities. Parts of it will surely become part of the curriculum and assigned reading in many of the best business schools.

Caspar W. Weinberger
September 2001

ACKNOWLEDGEMENTS

I was with a couple of longtime business friends, Geoff Wild and Steve Gray, relaxing in a restaurant in my hometown of Sydney after a fine seafood lunch, and the conversation somehow got round to the several decades I've spent pushing the advertising barrow in Asia. And both colleagues, being disciples of a profession that passionately promotes regular trips to the moon, convinced me that students, marketers and people in my industry would be interested to read my thoughts on the Asian consumer, and how I saw the Asian advertising scene evolving over the next generation, and so on. Thank you, Geoff and Steve, for getting me started on this mission.

I've been told that my best strength is getting other people to do things well, and I unequivocally endorse this opinion in the development of my first book attempt. The team of contributors, advisers and researchers I assembled to put this show on the road performed beyond all expectations.

My deepest appreciation goes to the following personalities:

Sri Lankan Gerry Delilkhan, one of the great Asian journalists of our time, editor of the old *Asia* magazine and former press secretary of President Marcos of the Philippines; Australian Michael de Kretser, my public relations partner, whose creative mind spins and surprises like a brilliant Shane Warne bowling delivery; Singaporean Julian Ng, an original partner in the Batey Group, undisputed media service guru in Asia and the wisest intellectual among us; Indonesian Anggle Sugianto, the youngest member of our team and an amazingly mature researcher; New Zealander David MacKenzie, senior marketing consultant to top agencies in Asia since the 1970s, a goldmine of knowledge and leader of the Batey Research and Intelligence Centre; Australian Jim Aitchison, arguably the most effective creative director in our agency's history and the mastermind behind the structure, writing and compilation of this book. And there's one other I'd like to mention — my personal assistant, Singaporean Irene Chua. During the many months of the development of this production, Irene was charged with the responsibility of collecting all the bits and pieces, obtaining third party clearances, transferring my crude scribbled notes into a sensibly typed manuscript, as well as coping with my impatience. She performed a sterling Florence Nightingale job.

Without Irene, Jim, David, Anggle, Michael, Gerry, Julian and other talented friends, this chronicle would never have seen the light of day.

Ian Batey

Cover Design: Batey Design
Cover Photography: Alex Kaikeong
Cover Photocomposition: Procolor, Singapore

Part one

OPENING SHOTS

INTRODUCTION

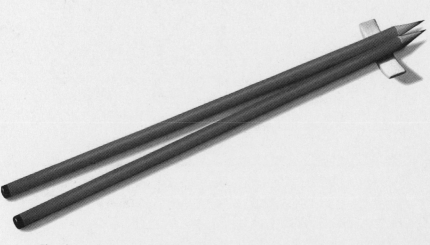

I've been in the advertising game in Asia since 1970 and I've been lucky enough to experience the explosive growth of Asia and the communications industry in Asia from essentially a zero base. I've also been lucky enough to have been part of the success story of some Asian brands. So when the idea came up that I should chronicle something about advertising in Asia, it was not hard for me to accept the challenge.

We all know, of course, that there's a huge gulf between talking the game and walking it. And maybe I'm still caught in between. Because of the way this book has evolved, it is by and large an odd bundle of things that I recall and think are interesting to share with you, mixed with some personal views on how things should be done. Then there are a number of outrageous suggestions on lifting the Asia-based advertising business to lofty heights over the next 20 years. Altogether, a disparate collection of experiences and views, and I confess that if you're hoping for some Einstein-breakthrough revelations, you might not get too excited.

What you will find is my macro view on Asian values and where they're heading in the globalisation game; my support or otherwise for some clever advertising tools invented by others; a stress-related request to all managers in the communications industry to bring some good old-fashioned common sense back into the process; and a call for more respect for established fundamentals in the development of marketing and advertising programmes. Here and there, you might come across the odd touch of madness.

Just in case you find it a bit hard to get any message out of this book, allow me to declare my position upfront on three popular marketing-related issues.

1. Above all else, the 21st century will be *Asia's* century.

2. This century will also be the *consumer's* century, and the branding game will clearly be the most critical game on a marketer's map.

3. The difference today in the buying behaviour between young adult Asian and Western consumers with discretionary income is no more than that between young adult Germans and Americans. And this issue will no longer exist as an issue among just about all middle-class consumers by 2020.

Please keep those points in focus as you digest this book. But first, a fast track read on my advertising years *prior* to my life in Asia.

THE ROAD TO SINGAPORE

My advertising career started in the early 1950s as a despatch boy in the advertising department of a leading Sydney department store, David Jones. I had planned to be a brilliant fine artist and the job provided a wonderful creative environment.

In those days the creators of retail ads were the most talented people in the Sydney communications industry. Not only were they beautiful artists, they were also beautiful-looking people. I was a young greenhorn from the suburbs of London, and their sexiness, sparkle and outrageous behaviour consumed me. All the girls were six to ten years older than I was, but I loved them all, notably a 26-year-old blonde Italian who drove me delirious with her flirting. As time passed I was promoted from despatch to assistant wardrobe-fixer. This meant I'd pick up merchandise and take it to the photographer's studio for still shots. I'd then sit around the studio as slinky ladies undressed and dressed around me with flashlights popping and camera clicking, and at the end of the session I'd take the clothes back to the store. It was fantasyland. And while my desire to be a Picasso gradually faded away, my desire to build a career in advertising grew daily. I mean, no other job on earth offered the buzz and beauty of this business.

After about a year or so at David Jones, I decided to turn adventurous and joined a couple of friends on a working holiday that took us to a special place called Tasmania. This island below the southeast corner of Australia housed the nation's worst criminals during the pioneering days of the continent and at the time I arrived it still maintained a similar reputation, being a sanctuary for hardened criminals eager to escape the law on the mainland. My experience in Tasmania provided an interesting contrast to the slick, sexy Sydney world and reshaped my views on human behaviour. It was a hugely maturing period for me. To earn enough to eat and sleep, I picked apples, cleaned bottles at the Cascade brewery, cut hop vines for a month, and worked in the IXL Jam factory putting apricots into cans.

Somewhere around this time I joined the army. It was obligatory. It was called National Service. I applied to fly a plane.

My academic papers impressed everyone enough to land me in the infantry. It was not a highlight of my life.

Following my military stint, I returned to Sydney at a time of economic downturn, wide unemployment and no dole scheme, I interviewed for all sorts of jobs and finally hit the jackpot as a clerk at a rubber factory located one hour away from my living quarters. To make things more enticing, the daily clock-in time was 7.30 am. Much as I embraced the task of counting rubber parts rolling along an assembly line, I managed to get back into advertising three months later as an assistant to the advertising manager of the same rubber company, Hardie Rubber. At the age of 21, I was appointed advertising manager thanks more to the support of the company's footwear marketing chief, Gordon Walton, than through my natural talent. And I quickly learned that I had as much clout in this position as the uniformed character who operated the elevators of the company's building.

But I tried to play a manager's role. In those days, the four major rubber companies in Australia got together on industry issues on a regular basis. Agreements also applied to advertising, so all the competitive advertising managers met to discuss things twice yearly. It was rather a strange sight to see the four ad managers sitting together. I looked like the nervous nephew among three wise uncles, but I was an excellent mumbler.

While at Hardie Rubber, I was fortunate enough to get heavily involved in the first professional tennis tournaments in Australia's history, with Jack Kramer, Pancho Gonzales, Ken Rosewall and the like. Jack endorsed our tennis shoes. I witnessed the introduction of the first "flip-flops" (thongs) into Australia — yes, the rather Victorian Hardie Rubber surprised all with that pioneering effort. And I helped design and launch the first plastic (expanded polystyrene) kick boards to Australian beaches. Sadly, we didn't capitalise on that initiative.

IN the late 1950s, I decided to try my hand at working in an advertising agency for the first time. So I joined Steele Kelly, a small, *very* small operation where each account executive was a one-man ad band; you serviced the client, you wrote and designed the ad, you art directed the photography, organised the production, planned and booked the media, processed the invoices and chased the payments. Mind you, the ads patently reflected my Jack-of-all-trades-master-of-none skills! My favourite client was the Overseas Visitors Club. This introduced me to the fascinating world of travel marketing. The OVC was owned by some highly entrepreneurial South Africans who met the cheap accommodation needs in London of young backpackers from South Africa, Australia and New Zealand. They had a row of terrace boarding houses in "Kangaroo Valley". At least, that was the start. To enjoy the cheap housing you had to pay a small fee to join the Club. As the Club evolved, so too did the size of the product offering: cheap ground transport and cheap tours around Britain and Europe came on board, and the crowning achievement was cheap sea and air travel from South Africa and Australia to the UK. I embraced the whole concept like a kid chosen to play for Manchester United and the brand owners enthusiastically encouraged lateral ideas to boost sales. Some of the best OVC work was illustrated by a bright young man called Ken Done, the same Ken Done whose signature you see these days on Aussie merchandise around the world.

I also had the dubious pleasure of trying to leverage a media deal with two young Aussies in their fledgling period in the media business. In later years their names would become better known: Kerry Packer and Rupert Murdoch.

About that time I got married, a daughter was born, I got involved in the production of a hi-fi magazine, and bought an Italian grocer's shop in Sydney's Paddington and converted it, with a partner, into a restaurant. From 6 pm to midnight daily I served and washed dishes. When you're young and naïve, there's little you think you can't do. It was fabulous. For three months, that is. While the pressure of work at the office kept mounting, it was nothing compared to the madness in my domestic life and at the restaurant. When you put down 10% deposit on a building and you pay the mortgage at 15% flat p.a., you have a challenge on your hands. When you then borrow another £4,000 (the currency in 1960 was still pounds) to renovate the building and then wait several months before the local council allows you to operate as a restaurant, the financial picture is grim. Then if you add in the fact that you really have no clue how to run a restaurant, and the income from customers hardly pays the gas bill, *and* your wife runs off to be a Scientologist leaving you with your baby under one arm and a pile of bills under the other, well, so much for the restaurant fantasy...

It took me more than three years to pay off all the debts, but being brought up in a proud blue-collar family that never purchased anything it couldn't pay for in cash on the spot, I paid for my stupidity in full. This obligation pushed me to look for a job in a much bigger advertising agency with much bigger salary potential, and I landed a position in the early 1960s at Australia's largest independent ad agency at the time, Jackson Wain. I leveraged my travel industry experience and got an account executive's job on the global Qantas account.

FOR the next seven to eight years I worked exclusively on Qantas in a period that I consider was the greatest in the global ad industry's history. Amazing work was coming out of America, London was starting to do brilliant stuff, and Australian creativity was taking on a new level of confidence and stature. Some work that Jackson Wain did on Qantas in the 1960s was exceptional, but the work done by Qantas' American ad agency Cunningham & Walsh was even better. C&W focused the airline's personality around a koala, a unique and compelling icon. The koala creative was so good we were paranoid that the client would embrace it worldwide, which potentially meant we'd lose a fat piece of business. So at every opportunity we would shoot down the koala icon as a dumb, dozy, useless son-of-a-bear that was an insult to the intelligent, mature, sophisticated person that was Qantas. The client, in their wisdom, supported our views for non-USA advertising.

In international airline terms, the 1960s belonged to Pan Am. It was the huge, all-powerful, supremely confident American service machine at its best, taking on the rest of the world like we still lived in trees. And the Pan Am advertising was equally awesome. It was a mighty global brand. *Where is it today?* You know as well as I do.

The brand owners should be skinned alive for their disastrous management of this noble giant. And this example sends a chill down one's spine because it can happen so easily. The saying goes, "there's nothing more frightening than ignorance in power". All brand owners, take note.

MEANWHILE, back in the 1960s at Jackson Wain the world was bright and beautiful. And full of memorable characters.

A young chap appeared at my desk one morning to say he was the new copywriter and would be doing something on Qantas. He was a strange-looking fellow — thin, with shaggy hair, and one eye that didn't quite have its act together. But the oddest thing was his necktie. In a period when it was fashionable to wear long, thin, plain ties this chap was sporting a tie that was a good 7- to 8-inches wide at the base, and the knot was so large it hid his collar. However, it was the design that really knocked me out — a splash of five or six different bright colours all fighting each other for attention. I looked at this young copywriter in awe. He broke all the rules of the dress code game. At first I thought he was playing a joke; but as the days of different fat, splashy ties moved into weeks of even more spectacular displays, I slowly came to realise that I had met my very first genuine eccentric. His name was Richard Neville. In later years, Richard became well known as an author and personality on TV and radio, and I'm told he still goes to the supermarket in his local country town wearing his very special ties.

Another interesting writer at Jackson Wain worked in the office next to mine, and did he work! For eight to ten hours daily, for months on end, all I heard from the next office was the endless rat-a-tat-tat of the typewriter as he pounded out work. Then one day the noise stopped. And shortly afterwards, a very famous book was released in Australia called *The Lucky Country*. The author was my next-door copywriter, Donald Horne, a clever, no-nonsense intellectual. Donald's message to his nation was essentially this: Despite our lack of productivity and our business incompetencies, we Australians have continued to prosper thanks to our luck of having a huge wealth of natural and agricultural resources. But it was time to get our act together, as things would not be so favourable in time to come.

Sadly, many Australians didn't read this message. Instead, their take-out was that Australians were blessed people. It's a pity they didn't heed Donald's gospel. Since the 1960s, the value of the Australian dollar against the US dollar has declined by *50% or more*.

ON the Qantas front, the airline was expanding its global network and Jackson Wain established overseas offices in London, Singapore, Kuala Lumpur, Bangkok and Hong Kong to support Qantas' communications needs in these markets.

This expansion gave me the exciting opportunity to travel across Asia and Europe quite regularly from the mid-1960s. While the European advertising industry was developed and healthy, the picture in Asia was extremely dark. The game of media advertising in Asia on a planned, regular scale was only taking root in 1965, and it was a common experience for a visitor to an Asian ad agency to walk from the street through a grocer's shop, up a flight of narrow wooden stairs crowded with boxes, along an unlit creaky corridor, then into a tiny office that was also used as a storage room for dried sharksfins and old bicycles. In the pioneering days of the local Asia-based ad shops, the owners often had several diverse occupations. But their enthusiasm for learning the art of advertising somehow transcended their working conditions and environment.

Asia in the mid-1960s was an extraordinary potpourri of newfound energies and newfound freedom. Tokyo was a building site as it constructed overhead and underground highways throughout the city, and future giants like Dentsu were just emerging from the rubble. Kuala Lumpur looked and smelled like the most comfortable country town in the region. Singapore seemed to me like a large, smelly lake with some rather rusty colonial buildings and wooden shacks of all sizes rising out of the water. Very Bogart. Hong Kong was a buzz of crowded streets, crowded neon signs, crowded bars, crowded everything. In this regard, Hong Kong never seems to change.

MY time spent on Qantas was very special and my immediate agency boss, Reg Fountain, taught me the game of advertising. Reg, in my opinion, was one of the best practitioners in our industry, but his gentle, sensitive personality was read as a weakness by some of the agency's management. Of the many memories of my days working with Qantas, one that has stuck in my mind was the way the airline's CEO approved the annual global advertising creative. We focused mainly on print ads and a range of three to four dozen ads, in fairly finished concept form, would be displayed on the walls of a room, much like paintings in an art gallery. The CEO would deliberately not be briefed beforehand on the theme or the strategy. He would walk around the room, and exit within five to ten minutes. As he left, he would simply say, "Good", or "Try again", or words to that effect. And that was it. Four months of creative development and a mountain of work would be judged in a matter of minutes. Amazing as this method may seem at first, I think it was a brave formula. The Qantas CEO positioned himself as Mr. Intelligent Joe Public. He either liked what he saw or he didn't. Very simple. No intellectual waffle. No hypnotising salesmanship from agency smoothies.

Following the CEO's approval of the new annual advertising campaign, the next step was usually to hold a marketing conference in Sydney with some 150 Qantas managers from around the world in attendance and to show them the new advertising to come. In the 1960s, the sharpest state-of-the-art presentation method was to project 35mm slides of the ads onto a large screen. But the innovative, showbiz geniuses of Jackson Wain always wanted to break new ground in presentation techniques, so for the annual Qantas marketing conference of 1968/69, we developed a show that involved about two dozen slide projectors, all electronically programmed to simultaneously project up to 24 different pictures onto a huge screen in an ever-changing, fast-moving manner, everything beautifully synchronised with music and recorded commentary. The result was truly breathtaking. That is, at the rehearsal…

On the morning of the big showbiz presentation, we arrived at the venue about two hours prior to the start of the show, connected everything up, and tested the production. Something didn't work. The projectors kept stopping abruptly about 30 seconds into the show. No need to panic; plenty of time to correct the fault. But the clock seemed to go twice its normal speed on that one morning, and by the time the delegates arrived we still hadn't found the answer to the technical problem. So we hastily organised coffee and cookies in the open foyer next to the conference room, and the 150 delegates waited patiently for what seemed an eternity — about 50 minutes — while the agency technicians fixed the problem. Which they did. So the show started nearly an hour late. And promptly blew up about two minutes into the act. Well, one had dreamed about this sort of disaster, but this was real, and all the agency presenters and top management were too shell-shocked to think of anything sensible to do or say. We froze. Then a chap whom I had always seen as pompous and precious jumped onto the stage and saved the day. He was our creative director, Leo Schofield. And for the following hour or so Leo kept up a great non-stop patter about what the advertising was going to feel like, what it was going to communicate, and how well it would be received. Leo used the advertisement flat boards to support his pitch, but only the front row of the large crowd could see them. So to all intents and purposes Leo just sold a beautiful dream. At the close of his delivery, the Qantas delegates gave him a rousing applause. The appreciation was clearly more for Leo's spunk than for the work. I have to say that Leo's performance left a memorable impression on me. In later years, Leo became a leading newspaper columnist in Sydney and today he does all sorts of creative leadership things for the arts. He is possibly still quite pompous and precious, but now you know that Leo has a lion's heart.

IN 1969, Jackson Wain's Singapore office was going through challenging times with its major client, Malaysia-Singapore Airlines, and I enthusiastically grabbed the invitation to relocate myself and family to Singapore as the account director on the MSA business, charged with the mission of restoring and strengthening relations with MSA management. I arrived in Singapore a few days before the close of 1969. Twelve months on I returned to Sydney, having failed in my mission. The account then moved to McCann-Erickson. Thankfully, some of the MSA management thought I knew something about airline advertising and I was persuaded to move back to Singapore to join McCann's as the top suit on the MSA business several months later.

I originally planned to work in Asia for two to three years, but Lady Luck stepped in and persuaded me to stay a further 30 years and more.

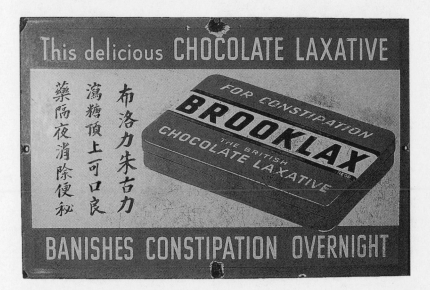

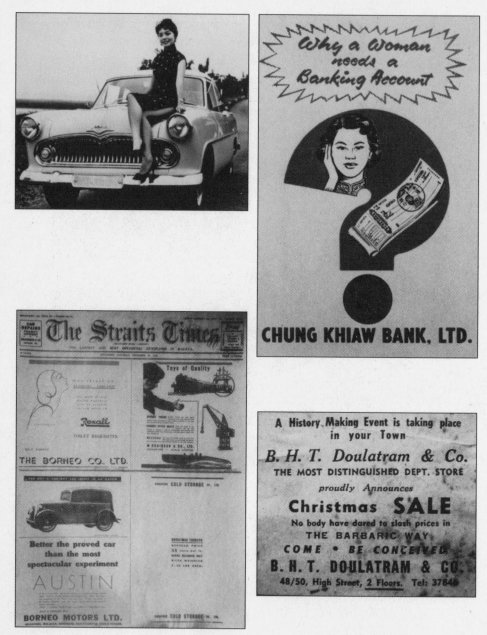

Singapore advertising in the good old days.

The new kids on the block: Batey Ads and friends, 12 months after its 1972 opening.

There have been times for celebration with great brands...

...and times when things didn't pan out so well.

One of Singapore's better known landmarks:
Batey Ads in Ann Siang Road.

Part Two

ASIAN MYTHS AND REALITIES

CHAPTER 1

FACTS,
FALLACIES
AND
FARANG

In order to create effective advertising, we all know it is fundamental to have a sound knowledge of the marketplace and the consumer. To give you the flavour of the very colourful Asian playing field, I'd like to take you through a few things that I encountered in the 1970s and 1980s, and which in some areas can still be encountered even today, and also share with you a mixture of inputs — some eclectic, some eccentric and some pragmatic. As my personal experience has been essentially with Asians of Chinese origin, my scope is mainly Chinese-centric.

FROM CHIANG TO CHANGE

We are all aware that, next to Tokyo, the hottest business hub in Asia for the past few generations has been Hong Kong.

Economist Milton Friedman called 20th century Hong Kong a "one-legged man winning a two-legged race", and there was certainly some truth in that. Chinese blood was thicker than British municipal water and the Shanghai Old Boys Club ran the city like a feudal walled village. They hired those of the same clan. They traded with those who spoke the same ancestral dialect. Patriarchs despatched sons and nephews to the outposts of their ethnic empires. They worked within the confines of family and *kongsi*. Handshakes were binding contracts. Favours were called in through Chinese networking or *guanxi*. *Guanxi* is something you can actually inherit and convey to another. It is a social system built on several lifetimes of trust and intermarriage. This approach is not so much a product of "Asian values" as of a certain stage of capitalist development. Business in Queen Victoria's England was largely in the hands of *three* families. The Chinese model just talks a different language.

It is forged in schools, clubs, clan associations and secret societies. You don't play fast and loose with *guanxi*, which makes it better than a Western legal system. As one of the richest Teochew entrepreneurs the world has ever seen, imagine how much global *guanxi* Li Ka-Shing commands. Imagine how much *guanxi* that tycoons like Malaysia's Robert Kwok and Indonesia's Liem Sioe Liong have at their disposal. *Guanxi* is the lifeblood of the overseas Chinese communities wherever they might be, from Singapore to Sydney to San Francisco. Author Sterling Seagrave calls it an "invisible empire" and quotes from Sun Tzu: "Be so subtle that you are invisible, be so mysterious that you are intangible, then you will control your rivals' fate."

While *guanxi* might be intangible and invisible, its results are not. Today, the GNP of the overseas Chinese, including those in Hong Kong and Taiwan, is around $450 billion. If you added the hoards of gold bullion and ready capital tucked away, there could well be double that figure. Worldwide, overseas Chinese are estimated to control capital of $2 *trillion*. What makes all that money go round is still *guanxi*, but nowadays it is digital *guanxi*. And therein lie the seeds of change.

Without denigrating the swashbuckling talents of Shanghai Inc., they *were* products of their time. Rather like America's 19th century robber barons, the Old Boys Club had things to itself. Government regulations were flimsy. Supervision was minimal. The money flowed because the markets themselves were not exactly sophisticated. But as the New Economy picked up steam, as a younger and often Western-educated generation took the reins, and as the financial crisis of the late 1990s bit deeper, the old business models came under siege. Suddenly, the bad spirits were out of the closet.

Indonesia's Lippo empire, for example, was built by an overseas Chinese entrepreneur, Lee Mo Tie. Adopting the Indonesian name Mochtar Riady, his empire begun with batik and watches and eventually straddled cable television, financial services, retailing and even Chinese power stations. Lippo was a typical Asian juggernaut. In good times it was unstoppable; but when the regional financial crisis worsened, the patriarch's sons lost no time inviting American and Dutch financial corporations to become partners and help weather the storm.

Inviting foreigners into the fold was once anathema to Asian boardrooms. With *gweilohs* came corporate change. Goodbye, smoke and mirrors; hello, transparency. No longer could a *towkay* keep three sets of books — one for the taxman, one for his wife and his business partners, and one for himself. Today, young, Internet-savvy Asian tycoons are becoming modern managers along Western lines. It's not that the clan lines have ceased to exist. Rather, it's a case of getting priorities right. And being pragmatic. After all, despite their fascination with wealth, the Chinese coined the phrase *fu bu guo san dai* — "wealth won't last beyond three generations". The first generation makes it, the second spends it and the third loses it.

The third generation is taking over the shop, but they're hell bent on challenging the old saying.

THE END OF THE ENTREPRENEUR?

America had the Vanderbilts, Ringlings, Rockefellers, Fricks and du Ponts. As the 20th century wore on, however, their dynasties became corporatised. In Asia, too, the rise and occasional fall of great commercial families marked an era that will never come again. There was a time when penniless immigrants could step ashore in Singapore barefoot from a junk and within a generation own a bank and extensive property.

Even today, Asia can still weave great business legends. In the late 1990s, for example, there's a popular story that a triad gang kidnapped the eldest son of Hong Kong tycoon Li Ka-Shing. The gang boss was a formidable character called Big Spender, whose exploits supposedly included the daring heist of an armoured security van ferrying several billion dollars of banknotes to Kai Tak airport. Big Spender was, to be frank, ungrateful. He was an illegal Chinese immigrant allowed to stay on in the colony under Britain's "touch base" policy, which meant that *if* you were Chinese, and *if* you managed to swim all the way across from South China without being apprehended before you touched land, you could stay. Anyhow, when Victor Li was kidnapped, it is alleged that Big Spender turned up in person at Li Ka-Shing's luxurious residence on Hong Kong Island and told the senior Li, "You can have your son back unharmed if you give me one billion Hong Kong dollars in cash. You can't call your bank and you shall not call the police. If you do, your son will be dead and so will you and the rest of your family." With Big Spender's permission, Li then phoned a number of his rich friends and had them deliver the billion dollars in cash to his home. No explanations were volunteered, no questions were asked. It was swift. It was silent. On receiving the money, Big Spender tapped Li on the head and told him, "You have done well. Your son has also been a very good boy. He will be returned to you shortly. Your family will never be harmed again and if you ever need any help let me know. I won't let you down." Victor Li was returned. Li Ka-Shing apparently did not report the encounter to the Hong Kong police, but is said to have contacted his friends in Beijing. Shortly after, Big Spender and most of his gang were picked up in South China. They were tried in a Chinese court, found guilty and shot. Li got all his money back. I'm inclined to believe this amazing story. It's a great example of how efficiently the Chinese network operates.

NO matter how smart an entrepreneur is, however, he's not a match for the presidential palace. The ownership of companies and brands can be swiftly undermined when rulers and their cronies take control of the national economy.

Take the case of Benny Toda. At the time martial law was declared in the Philippines, 22 September 1972, Toda was the president of Philippine Airlines. The flamboyant, canny little Toda ran PAL through a family-held management company. Toda happened to be a crony of President Ferdinand Marcos and his wife Imelda, who wielded supreme power. In those days, PAL was commercially successful and Toda was getting richer by the day. The story goes that Mrs. Marcos had unfettered use of PAL aircraft whenever whim or work required her to make extended trips abroad to the US or the affluent European capitals. Soon, the airline was PAL by name *and* nature. It seemed that Mrs. Marcos disliked travelling in small groups; usually she took a planeload of friends along. Her trips required *two* aircraft; one for her pals, the other to bring home all the shopping. Things were going swimmingly until one day, halfway to San Francisco, Imelda decided that she wanted to go to New York instead. The pilot and crew did not question the order. At first the plane was refused permission to make an unscheduled, unannounced landing in New York. Eventually the authorities relented, but a few days later Benny Toda received a $50,000 fine for one of his aircraft breaching American civil aviation regulations. He sent the bill to the First Lady's office at Malacanang Palace where it landed on the President's desk by error. Ferdinand Marcos flew into a rage, but Imelda came out the winner. Somehow she convinced Marcos that Benny Toda was unfit to run PAL; he was milking a national asset and should be fired. The axe fell. Toda was allowed to retire quietly to a little island he owned and went without a fight. Meanwhile, PAL passed into Imelda's control. She ran it with a bunch of cronies, racking up losses and allegedly using government pension funds to keep the show on the road. When Marcos was ousted, the Philippine National Bank was called in to bail it out. Another Marcos crony, Lucio Tan, took over the reins. PAL remains mired in debt and on its financial knees.

Tan, of course, already loomed large in the beer business. San Miguel, born in the Philippines, is one of the great beer brands of Asia. The Soriano family, which is of Spanish descent, had desperately fought to keep control of their company. Patriarch Andres Soriano resisted every attempt by the Marcoses to put government nominees and cronies on the San Mig board. It was a losing battle and the brand paid a heavy price. Meanwhile, with President Marcos' blessing, Lucio Tan set up Allied Breweries in competition. San Mig was about to launch two new brews, but Tan jumped the gun. Not only did his two new beers beat San Mig to the market; by a remarkable coincidence, they had the same names and virtually identical packaging and advertising.

THEN there is another of Asia's most colourful and daring entrepreneurs, grade school dropout Jimmy Lai. He has given Hong Kong three brands: Giordano, ready-to-wear apparel; *Apple Daily*, magazines and newspapers; and adMart, the cut-price retailer. He has also made powerful enemies. His stand on Tiananmen enraged the Chinese leadership and cost him his retail operations on the mainland. Pro-Beijing loyalists blocked his entry to the Hong Kong Stock Exchange, forcing him to buy a backdoor listing. His Internet-based grocery and electronics home delivery service, adMart, slashed retail prices to the bone, pitting him against

Jardine Matheson's massive network of Dairy Farm and Wellcome stores and the substantial Park'NShop and Fortress appliance chain, both owned by Li Ka-Shing's Hutchison Whampoa. Everyone was bleeding money and determined not to lose face first. Suffice to say that Jimmy Lai and his publishing operations can now be found in Taiwan.

NOT every Asian entrepreneur sails so dangerously against the wind. One such visionary is Dr. Amar G. Bose from West Bengal, long the cradle of Indian literature, music and art. As a young engineering graduate of the Massachusetts Institute of Technology residing in the States in the 1950s, Bose was unable to find a music system with loudspeakers able to reproduce his favourite Bengali music with reasonable fidelity. Drawing a blank, he decided to build his own and began research into psychoacoustics, an esoteric discipline that investigates the relationship between reproduced sound as perceived by people and sound as measured by electronic instruments. Bose patented his new audio technologies and with encouragement from the MIT, created his first audio products. In 1968, Bose downsized his speakers to that of a baseball; unobtrusive, uncomplicated but technically excellent. Within three decades, Bose has become the world's biggest home speaker brand. In 1999, Bose Corporation made an operating profit of $170 million on sales of nearly $1 billion. Dr. Bose is still in control and ploughs back 100% of profits into research and corporate development. His philosophy actually demonstrates a perfect understanding of marketing: *"Audio products exist to provide music for everyone. Music, not equipment, is the ultimate benefit…"*

WILL THE EAST BECOME WEST?

One hundred years ago, if a marketer came to Asia from the West it were as though he had stepped into another universe. He would have had to adapt tremendously from all the practices that were familiar to him in the West. If he came here 30 years ago, he would have seen *half* of those differences erased, but still there would have been quite a distinctly Asian way of looking at things.

The marketer coming here in the 21st century will by and large see a marketplace which, if the consumers have any reasonable disposable income, will be very similar to the one with which he communicates in the West. Business structures and methods are fast becoming the same, too. The world has moved that way. The communication gaps have shrunk tremendously. The education levels have spiralled enormously. Tastes are converging. Everyone is talking about globalisation. People have become much more homogeneous in the way they think and act. Or, to put a finer point on it, they are more homogeneous in the way that they *think* that they think and act.

In 1996, the Arthur Andersen Business Consulting Division and the Batey Research and Intelligence Centre joined forces to investigate how globalisation had impacted on Asian management cultures and practices. With the help of the marketing department of *Fortune*, the views of over 400 senior business executives from Asia, America and Europe were collated.

Western management styles were seen as more open, direct and confrontational, more flexible and creative. Empowerment of workers was encouraged. Decision-making was based on database statistics rather than intuition. Individual initiative was upheld over group consensus. Asian businesses, on the other hand, valued seniority, relationships, family ties and loyalty. They were more likely to be paternalistic and resistant to women in high places. Lifetime employment was supported; hire-and-fire was opposed. Usually, the corporate stress was on quantity rather than quality. *But convergence is upon us.*

According to the study, Asian managers can no longer assume they have an advantage in Asia because they understand "Asian values". Whether they are Asian *or* Western, *the manager who values multicultural diversity will best succeed in an international, multinational business environment.* The clan mindset is out. The Asian economic slump in the 1990s revealed some "old Asian ways" in the banking system and multiple business defects in traditional family-controlled corporations. On the positive side, this economic "correction" has and will continue to help Asia globalise its business methods and thinking.

What also counts these days, said the report, is the ability to anticipate future trends and changes, to manage human resources and harness resources to meet sales and profit targets. Pyramidal structures are being demolished; Asian managers now have more autonomy. Asian patriarchs in vast Asian conglomerates are facing the hard fact that they can no longer make every single decision; yet, predictably, some still refuse to cede. And here's more ominous news for those old male chauvinists: the glass ceiling is starting to crack as Asian career women, upwardly mobile and globally minded, have emerged as a real force to be reckoned with. Information technology will continue to make more inroads. Part-time, project-based staff with flexible work hours will be used more widely.

In October 2000, Hong Kong witnessed an unprecedented public outcry. The chairmen, directors and investors of 23 listed firms ran a full-page advertisement demanding that the government protect them from being swamped by Li Ka-Shing's business empire. Headlined *HELP*, the ad pleaded for a level playing field; government officials, it said, should stop offering preferential treatment to billionaire Li and his son Richard. Earlier, a European Parliament report had alleged that Li's business interests accounted for one-quarter to one-third of the Hong Kong stock market's capitalisation. Li put the figure at just over 15%.

When it comes to marketing though, business traits are less easy to change in a generation. The trader mentality still prevails. In the East, it's buy-and-sell, buy-and-sell; it is still tough to accept a formula that suggests one should build anything like brand equity for the long term. Short-termism has worked well enough for the short term, but when Asian brands look to global markets a completely different mindset is needed. And this will happen.

THE BUFFET, THANKS, NOT THE BUFFETT

Nowhere is short-term thinking more evident than in the stock market. Warren Buffett was voted the best money manager of the 20th century by a poll of three hundred global investment professionals. He amassed a fortune of around $36 billion. Any punter on the planet would do well to pick up some tips from Buffett. For example, his selection criteria. He looks for companies where the share price does not exceed their asset value all that much so there will be a lot of price-earnings growth. He checks their management style. Then he backs his horses with big money, and leaves that money in there for years, even decades. He applies this sensible, albeit conservative, philosophy without exception.

By any standard Buffett's achievements are enviable, or so one would have thought. But in the Singapore *Sunday Times* in early 2000, when Singaporean investors were asked to comment on Buffett's unfrenzied methodology, they were unimpressed. The contrasts were startling. The Singaporean businessman wanted huge growth instantly, in a week. Buffett, for example, had said that he buys shares in great businesses that have great managers; his strategy is to buy for less than the business is intrinsically worth and own those shares forever. The Singaporean investor, on the other hand, said *Forever? You have to be kidding; if a stock goes up 10%, I'll sell.* The preference is to buy and sell within seven days then run, without having to cough up money for his transactions. With on-line trading, he can be in and out of stocks within minutes. The adrenaline charge comes with making big bucks overnight, not over years.

Buffett says most people get interested in stocks when everyone else is, whereas the time to get interested is when *no one* else is. You can't buy what is popular and do well, he says. Nor should you adopt a deliberately contrarian approach; just engage in thinking rather than polling, Buffett tells us. This view earned him a sharp rebuke from Singaporean investors. What about dot.com stocks, they asked. Everyone and his mother have made a bundle on them. Just make sure you get out on time. (*In recent times, many fingers have been burnt in this arena.*)

Buffett advocates avoiding techno stocks. If you don't understand a business well enough to know where it will be in ten years, if you can't predict its future cash flow, if it is too complex or too subject to constant change, stay away. The Singaporean punter takes the opposite view. *Understand the business? That's too much work. Just tell me which ones are the hot stocks before everyone else hears about them, and I'm in.*

While Buffett doesn't want to be involved in 50 different businesses at the same time, preferring to invest meaningful amounts of money in a few handpicked companies, Singaporeans go where the action is. If banks and electronic contract manufacturers are hot, that is where they will buy and sell. If tomorrow construction stocks or shipping stocks are all the rage, so be it. The Singaporean view is, why stay with stocks that are going nowhere fast?

Buffett warns that we should know how business operates, we should understand the language of accounting, so we can avoid mass hysteria in the market and form our own independent opinions. *Forget it,* says the local Asian punter; *just watch the TV monitor. If a stock is moving up, something must be up. If it's coming down, get out. Good bets are IPOs. You can usually sell for a tidy profit on the first day. (These days, this gamble has taken a tumble.)*

ONE upside of thinking short is being able to move fast. And that is the bottom line attraction for the Asian investor. However, when one moves into the marketing arena, expediency often devalues brands in a flash. Short-term thinking applies across most Asian-based brands in Asia, with the exception of Japanese brands. The general understanding of branding is still low. But it is not the Asian businessman's fault.

Clearly, the advertising-communications services industry in Asia has been delinquent. Our industry simply hasn't yet got its act together in educating Asian brand owners on the great upsides of developing positive brand strategies and long-term brand building. Why not? Frankly, just like many Asian brand owners, our industry has also been distracted by short-term thinking and practices.

Here's a snapshot view. Non-Japanese multinational agencies manage the bulk of the ad spend in Asia, excluding Japan. Some are lucky enough to handle prominent local brands, and to service the global needs of an Asian brand is a rare treat. By and large, a good chunk of their business comes from Western brands with their strategic and creative brainpower based in Europe or the USA. A significant focus, therefore, of the local multinationals is in managing the process. And the focus is frequently on price-sensitive, short-term advertising needs.

Against this canvas, we have the multinationals' financial crocodiles in New York or London biting our butts (quite correctly) to deliver bigger profits each year. Then we have the local ad agency CEOs whose annual bonus is linked to profit performance, so they're inclined to think short term. And to complete this tantalising scenario, we all seem convinced these days that the best idea to win a competitive pitch is price.

It's not a pretty picture. But things will change. A mindset leap will happen. There is huge growth potential for both brand-centric Asian companies and Asian-based multinational ad agencies within the next 20 years, as you'll read later in this book.

ARE THE DIFFERENCES BECOMING LESS, OR ARE THE SIMILARITIES BECOMING GREATER?

Stroll around the streets of the big cities of Asia these days and the picture is fairly common: English-language street signs compete aggressively with local language signs, and just about all the younger, prosperous people understand English. You'll see roads crammed with popular Japanese or Western cars, people chatting on tiny phones stuck to their faces, CDs blaring international music on every corner, American-style fast food restaurants on every second corner, trash bins piled high with empty Coke cans, children greeting each other with "high five" hand claps, and just about everyone wearing jeans and flashy sports shoes. But it's the level of human animation that impacts on me the most. The teenagers and their older friends now hang their emotions on their sleeve when their favourite soccer team scores a goal, or when they're enjoying a rock concert. The ways of the West have reached into the heart and soul of Asia, and the big Asian consumers of tomorrow are relishing and embracing it all. And why not!

Some Asian governments are not totally happy with this trend, and are working harder to preserve their social landscapes and cultural ethos. But they're facing a tough, defensive battle, especially when you take on board the expanding dynamics of communications through advanced technology, the lofty education programmes, and the explosive urbanisation of societies and growing prosperity.

Modernisation is the game, and modernisation is a Western concept. Clearly, some Asian governments are concerned that Western values will turn their citizens into clones of everything Western (and there are certainly dark aspects of Western values) and that they will lose their special national identity, whatever that may be. I suggest that the trend is unstoppable, but they should not be so concerned. If you drill down into "Western values", you quickly find all sorts of different cultures and characteristics. While they all eat Big Macs and wear fake Rolexes, a Scot is as culturally close to a Texan as planet Earth is to Mars. If you compare the French to the Germans to the Australians to the Swiss, my goodness — they're all so very much their own unique characters and they preserve their cultural differences with a passion.

I'd apply the same view to "Asian values". The Japanese see life quite differently to the Indians; the Thai is a totally different person to a Filipino, and so on. The "Asian values" label is far too broad, far too obscure these days. Likewise, "Western values" is a foggy term in the 21st century dictionary. In the context of the globalisation thrust, why not replace "Western values" with "Global values"? And instead of using the vague, macro "Asian values" term, why not be more specific and say "Malaysian values" or "Thai values" or "Indonesian values", and so on. After all, the Government of Indonesia, like its Asian neighbours, is essentially concerned only about *its* nation's identity, and about *its* nation's cultural uniqueness and behaviour code. This focus would also help to pin down more specific missions and objectives in the drive to retain and enhance indigenous qualities, while still engaging global free-market forces and all the flair and contemporary dynamics that travel with "Global values" in the 21st century. Just keep spending more and more money on education — the most powerful fertiliser to grow a prosperous nation. On this last point, of course, Asians need no coaching.

Asians are obsessed with their children's education. Asian parents make no bones about their kids studying and getting top marks. However, Japanese anthropologist Mariko Fujiwara says children are now rebelling against parental expectations. The unforgiving Japanese belief that "once a failure always a failure" makes underperforming students as young as 15 feel like losers. Parents send the message to children that they are loved only if they excel in school; as a result, she adds, education has lost its "profound meaning of liberating the mind".

In East Asia, children outperform their Western counterparts in maths and science exams. According to the *1999 World Competitiveness Report*, Singapore was ranked first on the ability of its education system to meet the needs of a competitive economy. Characteristically, Singapore and its Asian neighbours have raised educational standards of the whole population, not just an elite minority. *The Economist* tells us that in 1960, Pakistanis and South Koreans were about as rich as each other. Just 30% of Pakistani children were enrolled in primary schools, while more than 90% of South Koreans were. A quarter of a century later, South Korea's GDP per person was three times that of Pakistan's. In fact, Pakistan has the highest adult illiteracy rates of any big emerging economy; in 1998, 42% of Pakistani men aged 15 and above and 71% of women could not read or write. In the West, America and Britain are looking to Asia to lift their own game. More kids fail at school in the West and when they do, they end up in the unskilled labour force one step from the dole and one step ahead of the drug squad. Why? Are Asians more diligent, more intelligent? The cultural traits, the commitment of family support and the belief that everyone can and should succeed are powerful motivators. The kids work harder in Asia, with longer school days. Yet while the West begins to adopt Asian methods — regular tests are back in vogue in British schools — many *Asian* educationalists are disenchanted with their own policies.

Has Asian education with its tough discipline and learning by rote stifled students' creativity and independence? It seems that it has. Even the president of Tokyo University, Professor Hiroyaki Yoshikawa, has said that employers are complaining that new graduates are unable to think for themselves. If changes are made, the results will not be evident for decades. Singapore, though, has chosen not to wait; from the year 2003, an American *reasoning* test will make up 25% of the university entry score. "Cramming" will no longer be enough. The new test will reveal more of a college student's suitability for university education. And even though the A-level examinations themselves will still be largely content-based, questions will be changed to test students' creativity and thinking skills.

Asians are also perceived as diligent drones. The Japanese are supposedly very subservient, yet apparently one out of every three female Japanese office workers bullies her male bosses. Far from being helpless handmaidens in a male-dominated business world, the average Japanese boss is tyrannised by the girls. The *Yomiuri Shimbun*, Japan's largest national daily, described tactics like adding dishwater to the boss's green tea, increasing the sugar in his coffee day by day, or making crank calls to his pager. Not passing on incoming calls is another subtle punishment. The tactics have not worked any miracles thus far. The status of women in Japanese companies is still low; they are never involved in corporate decision-making.

Asian morals are upheld, in Asia, as something that the West would do well to emulate. Oddly enough though, in 1996, the *Far Eastern Economic Review* discovered that there was still a bias in favour of giving birth to a male child. In truth, it was hardly a bias; 76% preferred a boy while 24% would rather have a girl. Most affluent people in Asia expect their kids to live at home until they get married. Sixty-one percent of Singaporeans would not jump for joy if their kids wanted to cohabit with someone before marriage, whereas 80% of Australians would accept it. Thirty-two percent of Asian executives expect to have their parents living with them in the future, while only 11% of Western expatriates said the same. Hong Kong and Japan, it seems, are going the wicked way of the West — 75% of Japanese interviewed and 68% of Hong Kongers said religion wasn't important; 66% of Western expatriates agreed. Meanwhile, in October 2000, the *China Daily* reported that sex was the big new advertising weapon. Eyes popped when a scantily clad model soaked languorously in a bubble bath in a Hangzhou street; mouths hung open as models in lingerie strutted in a Beijing shop window. Public reaction was mixed. One outraged citizen denounced such tactics as "utterly indecent and detrimental to social values". "Too far ahead of the present social norms in China," agreed another. Others raved positively about such gimmicks as being "refreshing", and praised their "courage to go against tradition". One supporter even said, "If we continue to be prudish and condemn such ads, we won't be able to compete with foreign companies once China enters the World Trade Organisation." Having said all that, Asians are still known for their conservatism in sexual matters, which does not of course explain why Thailand performs more penis re-attachment operations than any other country on earth.

Another "fact" that borders on fallacy: *all Asians are workaholics.* Given higher unemployment rates and threats of downsizing in the West, it isn't surprising to learn from the 1996 study by Arthur Andersen and the Batey Research and Intelligence Centre that more managers put in over 46 hours a week in America, Europe and Australia than their counterparts do in Asia. Likewise, expatriate Western executives in Asia log the longest hours of all; for many, their postings mark a strategic career opportunity within a multinational. If they have regional responsibilities their working hours will be even longer, reflecting working time while travelling and catch-up time on their return to the office.

Perhaps the richest vein of fallacies comprises all those *superstitions* with which Asians apparently love to surround themselves. Often, superstitions were about the only things penniless Chinese immigrants took with them in search of a new life. While these old wives' tales still persist in modern-day overseas Chinese communities, they have long ceased to be practised in China itself. Some ancient myths are perpetuated from the older generation to the younger. We are told that you can't use black — it's the funeral colour — yet you see loads of black-coloured cars, Johnnie Walker Black Label Scotch Whisky is a market leader, and black clothing is highly fashionable among the trend-setters. Superstitions are still around, but after a while they're like an old record playing. In Taiwan, the Chinese calendar is still used to determine the best day and time to do something important. Man, they say, is influenced by the moon and tides. (It is all too easy for Westerners to raise their eyebrows at Taiwanese beliefs; if only they could see themselves through Taiwanese eyes. The Taiwanese view the United States, Australia and Canada as "beautiful sceneries" where Asians will never feel at home or be accepted. You can't make money in such places. They are "immigrant prisons".)

Superstitions, of course, have long been part of the cultural texture of Western societies as well, and were frequently created and nurtured to meet the needs of religious or tribal leaders. Lightly or deeply, I suggest every adult on earth is superstitious. It's part of our spiritual and emotional make-up. Predictably, if you're in the marketing and communications business you need to have a grip on this issue as it relates to your marketing agenda, but this is fundamental research stuff. In the scale of things, I believe the superstition hurdles in Asia are lower than those in the West.

WESTERN MARKETING METHODS:
DO THEY WORK IN ASIA?

Marketing is not science. Neither is advertising. The most one could hope for is to develop one's own models which have been proven to work in a variety of situations. Certainly, a smart marketer in the West would not hesitate to test out various models. After all, what works in New York might not apply so successfully in Des Moines. And logically, if one allows for some quirkiness in the state-by-state marketing techniques across America, the same latitude should be applied in Asia. The main thing is to retain one's core values.

No marketing model should be so rigid that you can't finesse it. No corporate marketing mantra can be so rigid that any change, any flexibility, is *verboten*. Corporately one can say, here's the model we've always used, so let's see if it works in a particular society. For instance, Marlboro has never significantly changed its platform since the 1970s, whether it's talking to men who dig ditches or the men who sit in boardrooms. The brand touches everyone in the same way. But when they get into each individual marketplace, the Marlboro team may have to be very flexible because each market has its own rules and regulations. Strategic guidelines would not change; *tactical* ones would.

Global consistency in advertising has been the cornerstone of Marlboro's power. Because it is visually very strong and simple, everyone can understand it and the values it projects. Wherever local laws permit, they see the brand talking with the same face and the same voice, which builds the comfort zone, builds a bonding. Not a bad effort for a brand that sells well even in many "dark" markets (territories with highly restrictive cigarette advertising regulations). The success of Marlboro among young and old in Asia is a fine example of how a well-established Western brand identity has triumphantly crossed all kinds of cultural and social barriers, and has stayed true to itself in the process — that is, it hasn't essentially changed a thing in its execution and feeling. Once you've got your brand soul and the expression of it pretty right, you're advised to keep the crafting of your brand-building print advertising very simple: a powerful, clean visual, the minimum of copy, and no innuendoes. The same principle applies to electronic media. Frankly, I'd apply this view across the world. There are no walls any more, anywhere.

There is one communication territory that does require some special care and attention in Asia — *humour*. Do you remember the time when British humour didn't get a giggle in the USA? Certainly the German sense of humour needs a few jugs of fine Munich ale in its belly before it enjoys a laugh with Woody Allen. Well, much the same differences in humour apply in Asia. The Thais and Japanese love humour and apply it with enormous skill; other markets have not yet learned how to exploit it so well. If the marketer is selling merchandise like fast-moving packaged goods, and he's talking to the entire market including the very low-income segment, then he has to be watchful and favour humour that has a more slapstick, Charlie Chaplin approach. But if he is selling automobiles or travel, anything that has a reasonable price tag on it, then he can be more adventurous and adopt a similar humorous approach to that which he'd comfortably use in the West — having, of course, taken on board the fact that Asians generally take a more serious view about prestigious, high-ticket purchases. So what's new? I suggest you'd adopt the same differential in Western zones where the middle class is still a young wine and the elite sector is tiny. Another generation from now I figure the sensitivities of humour will not be an issue in Asia.

Turning from humour to other playing fields, talking to the urban youth of Asia is like connecting with the same target audience in California. A soft drink commercial that works well in the USA will usually work well across Asia. Younger Asians enthusiastically embrace the energy, freedom and irreverence of Western youth-focused communications. Against this target market I'm not a disciple of the "think global, act local" sentiment. If you're selling the American dream, don't beat around the bush; just sell the American dream, because that's what your customers want.

MARKETING a global brand that seeks substantial growth across a large group of people should try to follow much the same model anywhere. It's just plain common sense. This fast-shrinking world of communications and the fast-growing movement of people across continents are two reasons for consistency. Another is the need for a consistent brand soul to all people. Even if you're globally selling to a small, vertical consumer base you should aim to retain a common umbrella communications strategy. Life, of course, is not always this simple. Cultural differences and local sensitivities sometimes influence a different attitude. Talking to Mexican labourers in Los Angeles about life insurance will probably not be postured the same as talking about life insurance to the movie community in Los Angeles.

Differing niche communication platforms will always exist, but in the context of big brands with global aspirations the differences are shrinking by the second. That applies to places like China, too, where a *Time* survey showed the under-30 generation loves France and social stability, and bewilderingly voted Albert Einstein their favourite foreigner. Over 5,000 Web users aged between 18 and 30 were polled in September 2000. Forty-three percent had never had sex, 52% spent more than 10 hours a week on the Internet and 83% were extremely worried about the state of China's environment. Thirty-five percent chose Zhou Enlai as their most admired Chinese person; only 16% picked Mao Zedong.

By definition, we all know that younger people up to their late 20s, no matter where they are, will always want a little rebellion. In terms of the marketers, this means taking brands forward in ways that their competitors haven't got onto and attracting the young opinion makers as a result. Marketers should experiment as much in Asia as they do in the West. Asian marketers tend to be much more conservative vis-à-vis their colleagues in the West, while Asian *consumers* are in many ways more daring, more open to new ideas than their sceptical cousins in the West.

The reason is fundamental: many are experiencing their first time in a candy store crammed with loads of goodies. They want everything, and they're willing to experiment if the attraction is seductive. There are many upsides in this marketing environment, but one key downside is evident — *fickleness*. The brand-bonding mission is a tough one. Maybe this challenge has confused and inhibited Asian brand owners. Businessmen in Asia are not renowned risk-takers in an esoteric area like marketing. They are conspicuous by their conservative approach. However, underneath the surface lies an energy that loves to take financial risks at the race track and casinos, so we — the communications services industry — have to find more creative ways to get Asian brand owners to commit to more courageous brand-building programmes.

THE GREAT ASIAN MARKETING EXCUSE: "IT-WON'T-WORK-HERE"

Is it possible to structure a true pan-Asian campaign? According to certain experts, no, it is not; only a series of different campaigns, country by country, will do the job. (The fact that those experts are often advertising agencies with an office in each Asian capital aspiring to earn its own creative kudos and fees is purely coincidental.) The truth is, common sense will always celebrate the similarities not the differences.

Certainly, as modern Asian societies begin to pursue similar lifestyles, they are becoming more homogeneous. As *Asiaweek* tells us, a regionwide sense of cultural identity has awakened, not least because it is in part "a thumbing of the nose at the pushy West".

One thing, however, is sometimes forgotten. The whole methodology of marketing that is practised globally is actually very new to Asia, excluding Japan. Western marketing and advertising only seriously took root in Asia in the late 1960s. The pace of change has been awesome. *Markets like China and India, containing one-third of the world's population, have only effectively opened up to brand marketing in the last ten years.* Taiwan opened its doors to foreign advertising agencies only in 1987. In markets like Vietnam, Cambodia and Laos, Western marketing models are only now taking off.

Marketers need to break down their task according to category.

In the context of a **high-ticket product of high quality**, you can go forward leading it from the centre, in the way that Stuttgart controls Mercedes-Benz. The local distributor in Asia contributes tactical support while the global brand remains in central hands. It makes sense. The local consumers are buying what Stuttgart produces *including* the brand image — the whole aura of German engineering. While Mercedes-Benz is now spreading its wings to capture a larger, more diverse stable of consumers, people still want its European, global, 5-star value. It is interesting to observe that while Mercedes-Benz is adding new dimensions to its brand identity as a result of widening its marketing opportunities, and in certain markets the creative expression for some of its classic sedan models is now stretching the standard advertising guidelines, I feel comfortable that the brand's core values are still in place. Having said this, I sense that the brand's soul could start to lose its way if the diverse creative expressions across the globe are allowed to move further and further away from the brand's core values. Rolex is an excellent example of a global brand that is firmly controlled from the centre, and while it markets a wide range of timepieces to different target groups, it remains impeccably aristocratic and superior.

I'm fairly one-eyed in favour of central control of global brands and I think most brand owners would support this view. However, you obviously need the regular checks and balances to make sure you're scoring well. At the first sign of any brand-relationship decline with consumers, you should bring several actions into play, but more about that later.

The marketer of an **everyday product**, a toothpaste, a detergent, a product that is aiming for the masses, the people in public housing or out in the villages, must take into account the local culture, the local viewpoint. Nonetheless, the central architecture on which the brand was successfully built need not change.

The success of Marlboro or Japan's Mild Seven reinforces the power of consistently promoting one's core branding properties. Wherever legally possible, their brand advertising is universally the same, all over the world, pitched to every socio-economic level. Plainly, cigarettes are bought with a different emotional need, but the fact remains that the Marlboro cowboy has become an international icon in countries where cowboys never existed! Levi's is another fine example of great global brand building from the centre. All young people share much the same universal traits. They are all grappling with authority and coming to terms with their place in society. By concentrating their advertising on the similarities, Levi's overcomes the differences. The more you appeal to the emotions, the more you can transcend the petty differences. The great soap brands certainly understand how to play the global game. Lux is one of them. Wherever it goes, Lux conveys the same aura of luxury and has done so for years. Celebrities, film stars and the most beautiful women in the world endorse Lux. And, as a masterstroke, Lux retains the right to localise its famous celebrities from time to time — such as homegrown Singaporean beauties Zoe Tay and Phyllis Quek. An excellent campaign, famous in Asia.

IN the old days, global brands came to Asia in the hands of a **distributor**. Many still do. The distributor is usually concerned only when the next container load is coming; why should he bother building the brand, especially when it could be assigned to a rival distributor later? Even the Japanese dealt through distributors when they first came to Asian markets. And in many categories it made sense; individual Asian markets were too small to justify the principal setting up his own distribution chain in each centre.

Not all distributors neglected to build the brands they handled. In Singapore, Cycle & Carriage achieved formidable sales and market share for Mercedes-Benz and Mitsubishi while they assiduously helped build both brands. Toshiba office automation products were launched and distributed by a local Singaporean distributor called Data Dynamics; they did such an amazing job against bigger brands like Canon that Toshiba bought into their business when they decided to take over their own distribution. Sadly, however, many distributors left a lot to be desired. As a result, brands could penetrate the market and get sales, but the principals lost brand equity. In some cases the brand would, in time, become just a commodity product.

The lesson here is pretty clear: until such time as a principal takes over from his distributor, he should take a leaf out of McDonald's franchise book on marketing and brand building. The rules the local franchisee has to follow are tight, tough and rigidly monitored. A common brand persona across the globe is never questioned. The trade-off with the distributor, of course, must be fair. Building the principal's brand for a decade and then having the principal take back full control must be balanced by an attractive incentive.

ONE technique of Western marketing that certainly has no place in Asia, or the West for that matter, is **raw concept testing**. In my agency's credo I wrote that a Tasmanian transvestite invented raw concept testing. I'm not quite sure why I mentioned a Tasmanian transvestite other than the alliteration seemed quite nice. Anyway, whether we look at Western or Asian advertising, the whole idea of testing raw creative ideas is flawed. Holding up rough layouts or sketchy storyboards or a scribbled brand name in a mirrored room and asking a group of people to comment on them is akin to madness.

Imagine displaying a number of A4-size flat boards, each showing some crude illustrations. Then playing a soundtrack produced by your in-house team, and using your switchboard operator as the voice-over. The gap between what you have in mind as the finished communication and what you show the focus group is wider than the Grand Canyon. Yet your Joe Public audience is expected to signal whether or not you've got a winning idea. It doesn't work for me. Now, if you start talking about a more highly developed production that projects the emotion, the "feel" of your idea, that's a different story.

Marketing is a new game in the East and the Asians who were trained in the West can be forgiven for being led astray on this research topic. Focus groups testing concepts at a raw stage were in the textbook, so what to do? It is routine, a procedure, whereas the truth about marketing is vastly different.

Great marketing means *anticipating* what the public will want. By definition, if a marketer plans to offer people something beyond their present experience, he can't test it because people can't readily relate to it. *The true entrepreneurial marketer is always looking to be ahead of the crowd, not part of it.* You can't research how to get in first with new ideas. If you want to be first, if you want to be the leader, you must conduct your own homework, shape your own strategy, then take a deep breath and do it. For example, whoever would have believed that the sports shoes worn at the gym would one day be worn to the office or for shopping by smartly dressed grandmothers?

Great advertising ideas cannot be presented in concept form, at a crude stage of development. Only someone very desperate could sincerely believe that lifeless, one-dimensional pieces of paper could elicit a meaningful response from a group of people. Only someone truly frightened to make a decision could hope that such a test would accurately predict the outcome of the advertising in the real world. People in focus groups are not exposed to communications as they are in their daily lives. No allowance is made for the finished production values, the casting, the nuances of real lighting and real sound. People sitting in a room with their peers are all waiting for someone else to say something first. As soon as somebody says something, they can jump in and say, "Oh yes, that's what I thought, too". Of course the research people will tell you, "Oh, we know who the leaders of the pack were and we have factored them out", but the trouble is, the damage has already been done.

Product research is a worthy cause. Raw concept testing isn't. Judging scripts is a specialised craft. Unless they were trained, few people could envision a final building just by looking at the architect's plan. Testing concepts at a crude level *is* crude. Testing a finished commercial is a different issue, providing that it is tested *not* in a testing environment and providing that people are *not* aware that they are giving a reading on it. There are techniques to achieve that. They are among the most sophisticated in the world. *Anything less is a worry.*

In his early years, Steven Spielberg had some embarrassing failures, the kind of flops that might have deterred a less courageous director. I'm told that he developed his own litmus test. He used to do the rounds from one studio to the next with new movie scripts. The story goes that if three studios rejected the same script, Spielberg *knew* he was onto a winner.

One sensible reason to conduct some research might be to establish whether the brand's name is right for Asia. If a famous brand name arrives in Asia, it invariably needs a good Chinese name. Usually marketers obtain a phonetic translation of it by finding Chinese words with nice connotations that replicate the sound of the English original. However, the system has its quirks. When phonetically translated into Chinese, "Mercedes" actually means horseracing track. The illness "AIDS" fared a little better; when translated into Mandarin it comes out as *ai zi bing*, or love sickness. Confucius said, "If your name is not correct, everything else will not be correct, too." The Chinese authorities took his cue. Early in 1996, they cracked down on the irresponsible use of names. For example, unless over 30% of a condominium's area is in fact gardens, the estate can't be called "Gardens". Then the Shanghai authorities ordered restaurant owners to clean up their act, too. Names like Emperor Restaurant were out; please try National Prosperity Restaurant instead. The government feared that exclusive, elitist-sounding names would exacerbate social gaps rather than erase them.

It is still possible to chance upon quaint brand names in Asia, names like the Rising Shirt Company, the Lucky Trouser Shop and the Lee Kee Boot Company, which make perfect sense in Chinese. A stroll through Hong Kong's Wanchai district still brings one to the doorway of a shop selling elegant imported toilets from Europe. Its name is proudly proclaimed: *Eurornate.*

THE WAY FORWARD

Advertising in Asia has received just about all its creative and service methodology from the West. Nothing significant has been originated here in Asia, no advertising techniques of any substance. When advertising took off in Asia in the 1960s, it was predictably quite basic. International names like Grant's, S. H. Benson, London Press Exchange, McCann's, Lintas, Fortune and Jackson Wain were here, but I think one of the best known agencies in the region was Cathay, with offices in Hong Kong, Bangkok, Malaysia and Singapore.

Alma Kelly owned Cathay. According to legend, Alma had been a prisoner-of-war when the Japanese occupied Hong Kong. She had been interned with the business elite of the colony, the heads of the great trading houses and the banks. By all accounts, Alma was a very large woman. If Madison Avenue had wanted to hire a kind of Margaret Rutherford advertising lady, Alma would have got the job. Apparently when the Japanese guards threw their weight around,

Alma threw hers back. She would tell them off in no uncertain terms. She became a heroine of sorts, and so at the end of the war all those British businessmen got together and said, "Alma, we owe you."

Alma decided to go into advertising. She set up shop with all the blue chip accounts of the day. By the late 1960s, Cathay had a trading arrangement with Bates and around 1970 Bates bought her out. Alma was a genuine eccentric. And like the Shanghai Old Boys Club, she perfectly understood the value of *guanxi*.

I'm told by veteran Asian "hands", Peter Cook and David Perkins, that the first Chinese businessmen to seriously enter the advertising industry in North Asia were the Ling brothers. They established two agencies in Hong Kong. One was called China Commercial and the other Ling-McCann-Erickson, the only joint venture in Asia that linked the name of the giant US agency with that of the local partner. The Ling brothers — Ronald, William and Charles — could never have been accused of going out of their way to adopt a sophisticated, Western-style approach to their advertising business. Hence the response of a recently employed Australian creative director when asked how the Ling brothers' methods compared with those that he had been used to in Sydney: "It's a bloody three Ling circus."

Until the mid-1970s, coming from the West to work in advertising in a place like Singapore was like being sent to Siberia. It was a hardship posting, the end of the line. The majority of the expatriate advertising characters had a short-term view of Asia. They wore safari suits and passed their time in bars or tennis courts and put little into the local industry, or into the local bank either if the truth be known.

But there were a few Western crusaders of the advertising faith in the birthing period of the industry in the Southeast Asian region, and I have been lucky enough to have stayed connected with a couple of them. One is Bill Mundy. Bill now resides by the River Thames in England, painting incredible portraits of people on canvas the size of a golf ball. About 40 years ago, in 1960 to be exact, he arrived as a fledgling art director in Singapore to work for Pap, the owner of Papineau Advertising.

The local competitive game was essentially fought between Pap and some of the international agencies mentioned earlier. As there was no television, no quality magazines, no colour newspaper advertising, no direct marketing and no research to speak of, an ad agency's survival rested on its Jack-of-all-trades competencies and salesmanship. The standard menu of services, aside from conventional press and radio advertising, included the design and production of brochures, point-of-sale materials, giveaways, sales promotions, trade functions, staff training, public relations, corporate identity programmes, annual reports, still photography, slide shows, packaging design, being MC at public forums, and driving the client home after a long, intense business session at the men's bar of the Singapore Cricket Club — essentially all and everything that directly or indirectly related to a communication service. At Papineau Advertising, Bill Mundy quickly evolved into a fine craftsman in *all* of the above. But he didn't mind. At the agency he was always surrounded by several pretty young Chinese women wearing *cheongsams*, the standard attire in the 1960s, and somehow their presence helped Bill to stoutly handle the pressures of office work. Being a keen sedan car racing driver, Bill tried his hand in the Singapore Grand Prix and skilfully managed to land himself in hospital with some badly broken bones. On awakening from the operation, the first thing that came into focus was the dark shape of Pap armed with a layout pad and the request to immediately design an urgent press advertisement for VW. But Bill's time in Singapore did have its lighter moments. Bill recalls a popular habit at the Town Club. It was the practice for some elderly members to have a siesta after lunch. They'd stretch out in the comfort of large rattan armchairs having chalked the time they wanted to be woken on the soles of their shoes!

Being a restless young man, Bill moved to Grant's in Bangkok by the mid-1960s and finally ended up the Grant's boss for the region. Advertising in Thailand around that time was about as developed as *tai ji* teaching in Texas. And sometimes it was a case of brain against brawn. On winning the Fiat account from a local competitor called Groake Advertising, Bill and his staff had to physically defend themselves against a sore loser in the shape of

Geoff Groake himself. The rather large Irishman genuinely felt that Grant's had unfairly outwitted him by presenting Fiat with some half-decent layout ideas and some fundamental strategy stuff.

Against all sorts of distractions, Bill still managed to create some interesting creative in Thailand. One notable example was for Mum deodorant. Using the over-crowded non-airconditioned buses where it was normal for passengers to stand and stretch their arms to hang onto the straps, the bus advertisements shouted the message, *Hands down all those not using Mum.* The Thai sense of humour connected with the message. The campaign was a huge success. I have a nagging suspicion that this idea was copied — again successfully — many years later in another Asian market by a competitor. So be it.

Another story, this one about Timex watch marketing in the same period. The American brand owners played to the textbook and they asked Bill to develop and circulate an extensive research questionnaire seeking out the buying behaviour of Thai consumers of timepieces. A big job. Several thousand questionnaires needed to be circulated and completed. The distinct lack of professional research companies or research resources of any respectable dimension compounded the creative challenge for the agency. Bill found the solution. He and his team painfully and personally filled in every single questionnaire — with a clear conscience — but didn't advise the client of this small detail. They believed that they had a good idea of what the independent answers would have been; besides, they rationalised, Thais are always so polite and would only have provided the kind of answers they thought the brand owner wanted to hear. The completed research was then summarised and sent to the local distributor, Hagemeyer, and also direct to Timex, USA. The bottom line? The principal and distributor acclaimed the findings as the best and most professional piece of consumer research they'd ever received from Thailand. More importantly, Timex sales in Thailand grew and grew. There's a message here somewhere.

Another expat advertising pioneer of the 1960s was John Hagley. Actually, John started his Asian advertising career in Singapore in 1958, but his first serious job was around the beginning of the 1960s with Ace Advertising. And like everyone else at the time, John soon expanded his talents from being a commercial artist to a writer, designer, presenter, singer, bottlewasher, you name it. Malayan Airways, forerunner to MSA and SIA, was one of John's major clients and he created the now world-famous *Silver Kris* name and logo, which started life as a special branding for MAL's new Comet service. John, together with close friend and future business partner Brian Hoyle, founded the Singapore Creative Circle in the mid-1960s. Much later on, John opened his own agency and created the all-powerful Courts Furniture branding success in Singapore and Malaysia. John is still around, still stirring things up.

There were, of course, several others in the 1960s trying to lift advertising off the ground in Southeast Asia. Among them was Peter Beaumont, a testy but great brand builder in his day; Jimmy McMullen, probably the best salesman I've known; Alan Green, tough, but knew his game; Bob Seymour, whose Asian secretary referred to him as Miss Bobsie More; and Fred Kent, whom John Hagley describes as "the only real-life gentleman I have ever met in advertising".

Looking to the years ahead some might ask whether the Asian communications industry will attract such colourful characters as those in the pioneering days. You bet it will. Because the Asian ad business, for all sorts of positive reasons, will take wing and become the most dynamic in the world within the next two decades.

CHAPTER 2

THE
CRITICAL
PATH

It was July 1405, almost a century before Columbus. The biggest fleet the world had ever seen set sail from China; 62 large ships and 255 smaller vessels, carrying nearly 28,000 men, made their way out of the Yangtze River. Some of the large ships were 122 metres long. They reached Java, Sumatra and Vietnam. Subsequent voyages reached Aden on the Red Sea and Mogadishu in Africa. The purpose was trade, either willingly or with a certain degree of persuasion. On board were the world's original "marines" — 10,000 of them — ready to encourage access to domestic markets. One could argue that the "marketing director" of China, the three-jewel eunuch Admiral Cheng Ho, had his eye on Chinese dominance of the international market.

Cheng Ho, a Muslim from Yunnan province and a eunuch since 13, stood 2.3 metres (seven feet) tall, with a 1.6-metre (five-foot) waistline. He had glaring eyes, high cheeks and a high forehead, a small nose, and a voice like a huge bell. He described his voyages poetically: "We have traversed more than 100,000 *li* of immense water space and have beheld in the ocean huge waves like mountains rising sky-high. We have set eyes on barbarian regions far away hidden in a blue transparency of light vapours…"

Within 30 years China would retreat from the world and virtually all records of Cheng Ho's epic voyages would be destroyed by Imperial decree. A conservative emperor shut the gate on what might have been China's mightiest brand-building operation in a thousand years. This 15th century decision still hangs like a dark, heavy cloud over boardrooms across Asia. Significantly, with the exception of Japan and Korea (both heavily aided and abetted by the USA), Asia today is still a huge factory for the production of other people's goods and a global provider of numerous commodities, and it is still essentially a faceless marketing exercise. It has an alarmingly small stable of prominent brands. Today, the most valuable financial asset of a company is its brand — so things *have* to change! And with the WTO model spreading its geographic coverage, the timing is right to get going.

TAKING AN ASIAN BRAND GLOBAL

In the context of this chapter, I've defined an Asian brand as being born anywhere from India eastwards to the Philippines, north to Korea and China, and south to Indonesia. I've excluded Japan, which I line up with Western countries as "the competition". *In building strong global markets for Asian brands, Japan is as much an important market to conquer as the Western continents.*

Another qualification is that the Asian brand must be owned and controlled, from a base in Asia, by Asians. (In a later chapter I conveniently include Australia and New Zealand in the Asian brand mix.)

THE FIRST QUESTION:
Are Asian companies temperamentally strong enough, committed enough and financially robust enough to take on the world and conquer it?

Six hundred years ago the Chinese were at the cutting edge of technology. They could print with movable type. They had established a huge iron industry. They had invented gunpowder. They taught the Arabs how to make paper and the Italians how to make spaghetti. *They achieved all that while Europe was still in the Dark Ages.* And then, in the blink of an historical eye, Europe advanced to the centre of the world stage. By the 19th century, propelled by the Industrial Revolution, she dominated the globe. European nations ruled empires that covered vast tracts of the earth's surface. Ancient cultures were trampled beneath Europe's invincible might.

Intellectuals comment that the most painful thing that happened to Asia was not the physical but *mental* colonisation. Many Asians began to believe that they were inferior beings to the Europeans. It is truly astounding that even today, as we step firmly into the 21st century, only one country in the Asian geographical region has reached a level of development that positions it as a serious all-round competitor to the best corporations of Europe and North America.

That statistic is about to be challenged. China now has the potential to overtake the United States and become the world's largest economy by 2020. The surge in gross domestic product across Asia has brought with it higher living standards, improved health and better education, and this pattern will continue. Asians are waking up to the realisation that their minds are as sharp as the best in the West, that it's now a matter of applying a bigger dose of my Three C's Recipe: *creativity, courage, confidence.* The time is ripe to embark on a crusade to build a big stable of Asian global power brands.

Inevitably, the new or upgraded brands going out from Asia will be "Challenger" brands. And as Adam Morgan warns in *Eating The Big Fish,* "One of the greatest hazards of being a Challenger is success. Because success brings with it inflated views of one's importance, and this can turn to blindness and a slowdown in the battle of survival. Best always think like a number two, and keep up the energy and commitment of a person who always wants to be better. Always behave like a Challenger."

Here's a list of some fundamentals I think you need to consider if you're an owner of a popular, discretionary Asian brand and you aspire to make your brand a global power brand.

	Yes	No
Do you see marketing as the dominant driver in your quest for global fame?		
Do you consider your brand your most valued financial asset?		
Have you a brand strategy that you believe will take your brand into the global premier league?		
Have you marketing staff with the experience and courage to match your global ambition?		
Do you have a highly creative ad agency as your communications consultant? (It can be local or multinational, but it needs to be the best.)		
Do you plan to retain firm control of your global brand strategy and the quality/focus of your strategic/tactical campaigns across the world?		
Do you plan to embrace R&D and regular product enhancements with a passion?		
Have you the financial resources needed to seriously compete in the global power brand game?		

If you say "NO" to any of the questions, I suggest that you're not ready to go seriously global and you need to set targets to address and come to grips with each "NO" item on the list. If you say "YES" to all the questions, I think you're in fine shape to take on the world right now...

THE CORE QUESTION:

Does an Asian brand have to have an Asian feel — or should it have a *world* feel?

I think the answer is deceptively uncomplicated. To borrow an old saying, it's essentially a case of choosing "horses for courses".

For instance, New Zealand is globally applauded for its fine dairy produce, and every single New Zealand dairy brand selling in the world milks its New Zealand heritage to the brim. Likewise, Australia's great surfing reputation has inspired global surfgear brands like Billabong, Quicksilver and Rip Curl, and their brand identities leave no questions unanswered about their pedigree. Another example? Stick "France" on your perfume or fashion label and the value of your brand soars immeasurably.

In the global liquor industry, the heritage equity is all-powerful and indicates the brand's personality posture. Guinness is indelibly Irish. Dewars is single-mindedly Scottish. Jack Daniels celebrates its roots in America's Deep South. And if you can't immediately guess where Fosters beer comes from, the brand owner will shoot himself.

A spin on the heritage soul comes from the new popular beer on the global table, Corona. Mexico doesn't exactly win the top-of-mind poll as a beer nation. Mexico, however, does win quick recognition when you say Margarita or Tequila and salt and limes. So some crazy genius decided to take the lime heritage and tag it to the marketing of Corona, starting on the campuses of the USA. It caught on. But the heritage link doesn't work for everyone.

Malaysia does not yet enjoy a strong image for making cars, so the marketing in overseas countries of its very own Proton brand sensibly does not highlight its Malaysian heritage at this stage of its global expansion.

We're all familiar with Japan's "rags to riches" brand-building miracle. Great brands like Toyota, Sony and others had to battle tremendous negative prejudices against "Made in Japan" products in the fledgling years of their global expansion. But they stuck to their guns. Their innovations and engineering excellence, packaged at attractive price levels, finally won them the respect of the world. Japanese brands now experience 5-star quality status, though I might add that I think they still need to get some branding issues sorted out.

For Asian brands (or any brand for that matter) aspiring to go global, the importance of parentage or pedigree is essentially a case of what value such an association adds to the brand's personality, or to its credibility, or both. Think long term in evaluating this question.

KNOW WHO YOU ARE AND WHERE YOU WANT TO BE IN THE MINDS OF YOUR CONSUMERS

While most of the booze brand owners have a fairly good grip on who they are and how they want to be seen in the global marketplace, quite a number of global players are less grounded.

As I see things, the Japanese have gone round and round in circles on this issue. Let's start with Sony, a great brand. Its remarkable R&D engine churns out innovative, cutting edge products consistently. Its advertising is essentially *sub-brand driven*. The feeling, the style of the advertising varies sub-brand by sub-brand, product by product, market by market. The unique proposition alone makes the difference. Excellent distribution and spectacular point-of-sale presence support each product launch. An awesome marketing model. And it works. But I have a problem with it, long term, for several reasons.

The sub-brand advertising often overshadows the author of the communication. The disparate range of advertising has little main-brand ownership or feel about it. Critically, the character of Sony is packaged solely around its greatest strength — product innovation — and the brand is essentially *soulless*. Its bonding with consumers is at best a fickle relationship. There will come a day in the not-so-distant future when the competition will be just as smart as Sony on points of tangible product features; it only takes money and talented focus. And when that time comes, home entertainment electronics consumers — who have become conditioned to buying the latest this or the most imaginative that — will have no compunction to switch to reasonably established competitive brands which offer something seemingly better. Sony needs to drill deeper and explore other, perhaps more gentle values to endear it more permanently to consumers. *Sony needs to find its soul.* The same applies to a host of other Japanese global brands that take on different faces and feelings in different parts of the world. There are exceptions, of course, and one of them is the single-minded, well-disciplined global campaign for Lexus.

The first step in finding out who you are is often resolved by asking: Who is going to buy me? To whom will this brand really matter? Number crunching won't get you there. Neither will pure logic. The marketer needs to understand exactly *where* and *how* the brand is going to fit into people's lives. This seems fundamental stuff. It is. But surprisingly it is often overlooked in developing strategy. If you're selling detergents, spend some decent time in the homes of the housewives and study their relationship with the product and how they use it.

As the great English ad gentleman Jeremy Bullmore put it, you know what you make, but are you certain what your customer is buying? For example, you make expensive pens, but people are buying prestige and personal pleasure. You make laptop computers, but people are buying self-sufficiency, self-esteem and mobility. You sell advertising, but brand owners are buying a bigger spotlight on the stage, a recharge of the brand's batteries and a lasting place in the Hall of Fame.

Another fundamental is, **know what the competition is doing**. Their positions, their ads, their everything in the marketing process. An ad agency should know as much — *or more* — about the competition as the brand owner.

Once you've painted the category landscape, put in some detail. If your new brand were a person, who might it be? What are its characteristics, traits and mannerisms? Remember to take on board the fact that you touch customers at many levels and customers are going to form an opinion about you whether or not you consciously strive to connect with them. Your distribution outlets, the way your people answer the phone, every single thing that a customer sees or hears about your brand is going to create an impression, an image. Bamber Gascoigne goes further and uses the phrase *a consensus of subjectivity*. Each person arrives at a set of feelings more or less independently, but on examination the feelings turn out to be quite close to each other — so much so that we deceive ourselves that we have arrived at an objective truth. But we haven't. A shared brand image, like a shared view of Marilyn Monroe or a Picasso, is not objective; it's a consensus of subjectivity. That is Gascoigne's view, and while it's a bit intellectual for me, I think it makes sense.

Above all, the brand needs a vision. Avoid just selling attributes; they are too narrow, too short-lived, to support your brand structure. Dig deeper. Your customers will. *Customers want to feel the sides of what they're buying.* Think about the intangibles. Your brand soul must be fleshed out.

Once you know who you are, and where you want to be, and your brand-building programme gets under way, you will need **a system that monitors your progress with consumers**. Barometers like market share and profits are worthy benchmarks. But you also need to regularly connect with consumers through tracking studies and group interviews to measure your brand's relationship. People love to be loved, and they predictably gravitate towards brands that know them, understand them, and reach into their hearts. Lifetime bonding is the ultimate lofty dream of all ambitious brand owners.

KNOW WHAT YOU SHOULD LOOK LIKE — AND WHY

Contrary to popular opinion, the most potent trademark of the 20th century was the swastika. Again, contrary to what many people think of the swastika symbol, it started life around 2500 BC in India and Central Asia. The name came from ancient Sanskrit and means wellbeing and good fortune. Tragically, the swastika fell into evil hands and represented unspeakable horrors; even today in the West this symbol is beyond redemption, whereas in Singapore, for instance, the Red Swastika Society is a charitable foundation busily operating schools.

The point of the swastika story is to remind you of the incredible potential power of **trademark symbols**. And leads me to my view on this matter. I'm amazed how graphic symbols are so *under-leveraged* in the creation of brand trademarks.

In this over-crowded, messy communications world you clearly have to take advantage of any and every opportunity to be seen above the clutter, and a brand without a distinctive graphic symbol is to me like a horserace jockey riding without a whip. Just think of the incredible mileage that Nike gets out of its "swoosh"; how Shell leverages its shell-shaped logo; or the way the Mercedes-Benz star is employed so successfully.

If you're a committed, market-driven brand owner and your trademark symbol doesn't make the grade, or if you just don't have a symbol, I would urge you to do something about it. You might shudder at the upgrade cost of the corporate identity exercise, but in the context of how effectively you can leverage your new symbol on the global stage over the next two decades, the exercise could be judged one of your most brilliant investments.

The symbol is one thing; **colour** is another. There is certainly nothing wrong with the desire to try to own one's brand colour, but it pales in importance against the task of creating a strong, distinctive graphic symbol. A brand symbol can be unique, a colour can't. Who owns red — Coca-Cola, McDonald's or KFC? Who owns yellow — Kodak, Lipton Tea or Dunlop? If you are still not convinced, produce the Nike "swoosh" in any colour you want and it still says Nike. You can patent a logo, but you can't patent a colour. You can never truly own a colour.

If brands can be people, then their **packaging** can become clothing. What kind of "clothes" will the brand wear? Modern or traditional, contemporary or timeless, conservative or in-your-face, based on a specific culture or more worldly perhaps? If you adopt the principle that "you are what you wear", your brand packaging will always be true to the character and personality of your brand. Packaging is a key cog, where relevant, in the brand-building programme.

For self-explanatory reasons, those brand owners whose products go into self-purchase outlets are obsessed with their packaging. The liquor industry, the packaged foods industry, the upmarket accessories industry, and the cosmetics marketers patently understand the need for excellent, appropriate packaging. (I think cosmetics packaging is incredible. To stimulate your creative juices, make it a discipline to visit a good cosmetics outlet at least once a quarter — even if you're marketing second-hand bedpans.)

In the home electronics business, however, I think most brands are missing a trick or two in the design of their packaging. The electronics brand that applies more imagination to this important opportunity could, I feel, steal some thunder over its rivals.

KNOW YOUR PLACE ON YOUR PLAYING FIELD

Every brand has its own patch on the playing field. Fundamentally, given that growth opportunities remain encouraging, a brand should not move out of its patch, no matter how green the other fellow's grass looks.

For example, Courts have their patch, IKEA have theirs. Both brands are formidable in Southeast Asia, but Courts essentially sells solid value, conservatively styled furniture, whereas IKEA focuses more on upmarket, contemporary furniture. The bottom line is different target consumers, different styles of advertising, different brand identities. Both brands are immensely successful playing on the same field.

But it isn't always the case. The patch you operate on may well dry up and necessitate a migration to another patch occupied by someone else. Or the pressures of shareholders seeking a bigger return on their investment may drive an aggressive invasion into other parts of the playing field. Then, of course, there's the radical step — a move onto a totally different playing field.

The automobile industry is going through a very interesting brand exercise at this time. Marketing observers are aware that Mercedes-Benz recently made a watershed decision to expand its range of patches on the automobile playing field. As an institution in the luxury and semi-luxury sedan car patch, Mercedes-Benz has invaded the upmarket 4-wheel drive sector, the trendy mini-van area and the young, less expensive small sedan division.

Perhaps the most tantalising issue in this drive down into the bigger volume, mass-market car patches has been the wisdom of proudly branding all the models as Mercedes-Benz. Brand-stretching generally tests the bean counters and the marketing pragmatists, and I feel it's a sensitive, subjective debate at best. Knowing brand-centric Germans as I do, they're usually transparently dogmatic about protecting long-established brand values. To some of the Mercedes-Benz management, I'm sure the very thought of putting the Mercedes-Benz symbol on the fronts of these new types of vehicles was like asking Dame Margaret Thatcher to parade around Piccadilly Circus in a bikini. Anyway, they've stretched the brand envelope, and I think this courageous decision is the right one. It adds a more youthful, dynamic spirit to the brand which is in keeping with the way the 21st century is moving, and customer bonding to Mercedes-Benz can now start at a younger age and be broader-based.

The general consensus is that it's easier to stretch a brand *downwards* — which is the Mercedes-Benz strategy — than it is to stretch the brand up the scale. Toyota challenged this thinking

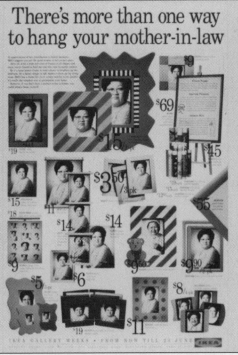

Know your place on the playing field: Courts from Batey Retail,
IKEA from Dentsu Young & Rubicam Singapore.

when they decided to attack the super luxury sedan market, with Lexus taking star billing, and the maker's name taking a back seat. The Lexus brand has worked, thanks to a fine product and a great ad campaign. If Toyota had it all over again, however, I think they'd make the Toyota brand the king and Lexus the sub-brand. As a result of a huge publicity investment and top class product delivery, Toyota *is* a power brand. It should never take a defensive position. I have a thing about never, *never* diluting a strong core brand in favour of sub-brands. It doesn't make sense. Furthermore, in this deafening, fast track world, let's simplify people's lives, please.

The brand-stretching debate, predictably, is never a simple, open-and-shut case. Can you imagine Timex ever launching a watch to compete with Rolex? Or Christian Dior making children's clothes for Marks & Spencer customers? If you applied some lateral thinking, maybe you could go this far. Certainly, brand-stretching has never been an issue for Richard Branson. He takes Virgin onto an amazingly diverse range of playing fields.

In the next 20 years, the seduction of globalisation and shareholder pressures will drive a lot of disastrous decisions, especially brand-related ones.

UNQUESTIONABLY, Asian society currently embraces brands and their perceived values more vigorously than anyone else on earth. The reason? Fundamental human behaviour. About a hundred years ago, economist Thorstein Veblen coined the term "conspicuous consumption"; he presented the theory that the visible display of discretionary income was a means by which people revealed their economic resources and thereby established their social position. How right he was. In the West in the 20th century, we witnessed the explosion of the middle class. Middle-class values rode on the back of economic growth and prosperity. And all those living in that environment were nuts about brands that represented personal success and social standing.

As the middle class matured, however, so did Western consumers' relationships with brands. Renowned sociologist Pierre Bourdieu says that social behaviour has steadily shifted, and now it's not only the "economic class" but also what he calls "cultured capital" that affects consumption patterns. In his view, people acquire cultured capital through family socialisation and educational background, and this cultured capital shapes their tastes and preferences. Taste has become their expression of class position, as do the consumer brand choices associated with it.

By and large, Asian society is still at the stage where it's enjoying the fruits of newfound economic prosperity. Its behaviour is normal in this environment, hence the mad enthusiasm for brands that overtly signal personal affluence and where one stands on the social map. But I smell the "cultured capital" development in the air across Asia. This catch-up will be quicker than many think, stimulated by the high, widespread education standards, IT communications and the new global spirit of Asians.

Leading sociologist Abraham Maslow puts another spin on the topic. He says that human development goes from "survival" to "belonging" to "self-esteem" to "self-actualisation". His theory postures the case of "the more we have, the more we want". He goes on to tell us that the millions of people in developing countries who are enjoying middle-class standards for the first time are now moving into the "belonging" stage and they will quickly fast track to the "self-esteem" stage; the elite in these countries are already doing so. The mounting consumer support for the environment and ecological challenges on Mother Earth makes me feel that Maslow's theory is now outdated in the West. But in Asia, it's likely that the middle class will revel in its new lifestyles for some time yet before settling down to their global citizens' responsibilities for the environment.

BE TRUE TO YOURSELF — WHEREVER YOU GO

Brand building is not for the faint-hearted. David Aaker's book *Building Strong Brands* provides a diagram on how tough it is to get focused on the job, as you will see on the next page.

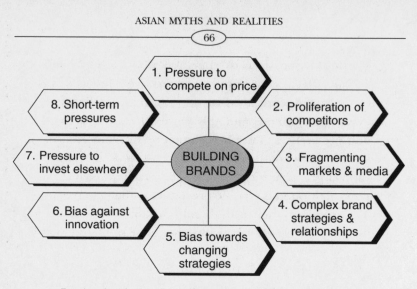

Reprinted with the permission of the Free Press, a division of
Simon & Schuster, Inc., from *Building Strong Brands* by David A. Aaker.
Copyright © 1996 by David A. Aaker.

If you market to a reasonable number of consumers, the brand-building programme is the responsibility of your total organisation because *your brand is the heart and soul of your company.*

In one marketing expert's view, there are eight Cs to observe in your brand-building mission:

1. Customer-focused.

2. Contact — managed across all parts of contact.

3. Control — define everything that you do.

4. Clarity — a clear vision, offer, sense of purpose.

5. Coherence — same tone of voice.

6. Consistency — single message must be maintained across time, geography, media product, ad channels.

7. Commitment — need to have obsessive attitude of mind.

8. Communicate — sell the spirit of the brand among all audiences.

I'd like to add one overriding point to this checklist. *You need to apply a lot of loving.*

Most worthy companies have a sort of brand council to guide the growth path of the brand, to defend it against any erosion of its values, and to protect it from individual executive indulgence and conflicting personal agendas. In gently reminding you that brands are corporate assets that can be wiped out with one inappropriate decision, I'm afraid that this warning is still not getting through to everyone.

According to a 30-month British research project conducted in the 1990s, company boards give nine times more attention to counting and spending cash flow than worrying about where it comes from. Very few boards routinely evaluate their brands, reports London Business School senior fellow Tim Ambler, author of *Marketing and the Bottom Line.* Ambler describes brand equity as the upstream reservoir of cash flow; consumer motivation to buy or to pay more has taken place, but it hasn't yet been translated into actual sales turnover on the company's books. As a concept, it was only formalised about 20 years ago. Although excluded from their financial books, brand equity is by far the most valuable asset of most companies.

The very fact that brand equity is intangible makes the job of protecting and enhancing it that much harder. But it can be enjoyable. Being true to the brand begins by ensuring that the brand owner's staff, distributors, partners and agents understand the brand's identity. They should have a good grip on what the brand stands for — what is timeless about it, and what is not. Any genuine global brand-building effort should include programmes that educate employees — brand manuals, videos, newsletters, Internet communications. Everyone must know and enthusiastically support what aspects of brand strategy *have* to be followed like Moses' Commandments and which ones can be varied to meet local needs. If the brand owner's own staff don't understand and eagerly embrace what he is trying to build, what chance has the public got?

Global brands are naturally obliged to transcend borders; but sometimes those borders are jealously guarded within the company itself. More seminars, workshops, field visits and work exchange programmes will knock down walls. The more employees from different markets can exchange experiences and insights, the faster the "we-are-different" syndrome will be dispelled. A night on the town goes a long way to help one country realise it can learn from the others. Above all, as Eleanor Roosevelt reminds us, you can learn from the mistakes of others; you can't live long enough to make them all yourself.

Cross-border bonding not only nurtures a freer flow of information and cooperation, but also lets a company develop its own marketing vocabulary and templates. Systems can also be put in place to track when brand-building efforts drift off strategy. Getting employees to vote on the ad campaigns they think best exemplify the essence of the brand builds involvement; more importantly, it signals whether employees fully understand what the brand is all about.

Is there one proven effective model in the management of a global brand? It's a question that has and will continue to challenge and frustrate many marketers, and the complexities of different product categories and diverse playing fields are unlikely to ever deliver a common answer. The tendency is to build a brand management structure around the management culture of the company.

I'm personally firmly behind the model that is centrally controlled by a person with final decision-making power. This does not mean that local markets just sit out there and act solely on orders; they have a truckload of tactical trench warfare to fight where the buck stops at local level. The central control effectively means that the local market enthusiastically and rigidly applies the brand values dictated by the control power base.

Scanning some of the current global brand management models, here are a few for you to digest:

1. *Business management teams.* In the P&G model, no barriers to implementing decisions exist because the teams are all top line executives. Their task is to define global brand identity and positioning, encouraging local markets to test and adopt the advertising that will serve the market best. The mighty P&G rarely goes wrong — at least, that's the perception.

2. ***The brand champion.*** (This is my favourite model.) At Nike or Nestlé, he will typically be the chief executive officer. Such is the company's reverence of brands, the top man must have a *passion* for marketing and brand building. He will be able to devote his full organisational power to the task of nurturing the brand assets. He has full authority to veto advertising that doesn't comply with the brand's DNA. He approves brand-stretching. He traditionally carries the respect of everyone in the company. At Virgin, for example, Richard Branson had the original brand vision and continues as brand champion. And he had the last word on taking Virgin from an airline to a soft drink company.

3. ***The global brand director.*** I've found this model to be primarily a case of "two wrongs don't make a right". It starts with a board of directors and/or top operations management that has financial and systems skills rather than extensive marketing skills. So a commercial person is appointed for the brand guardian job, but his autonomy has a low ceiling. The combination of non-marketing central decision-makers and a brand director with limited decision-making freedom is a recipe that should be avoided by brand owners. A positive structure is where the board leaves the brand-management task totally in the hands of the brand director, and this occasionally happens. An even better scenario is, of course, to have the chairman and CEO as a dedicated brand visionary.

4. ***The global brand team.*** The theory is tantalising. An A-Team, the best global talent in the company, champions the brand. Each team member represents a different region or major market, thus providing different canvasses in the development of the brand. Ideally, a crusading global brand manager leads the team. The obvious downside of this concept is that a team is another word for a committee, and committees are a

pain in the proverbial. Even if the brand owner is lucky enough to assemble the right mix of intellects and innovators, this model is patently not effective unless the team leader has huge powers and drives the team like Attila the Hun.

Whatever model is employed in managing the development of a global brand, it's worth repeating that enthusiastic support of the programme at local market level is fundamental. We sometimes forget that the lads and lasses in the territorial trenches are the brand's first line of defence, and attack.

Every brand owner has to find his own way of being true to his brand. Interestingly, in February 2000 when Australian Douglas Daft became only the 11th chairman in Coca-Cola's 114-year history, he embarked on a mission to make America's greatest marketing icon more decisive and agile. His larger plan was to *decentralise* Coca-Cola's management. Regional chiefs were to be moved out of Atlanta and placed closer to local markets. His decentralised strategy came as no surprise; Daft is himself a 30-year Coca-Cola veteran and has worked in the more remote parts of the empire. He believes Coca-Cola is not yet the true multi-branded drinks company it should be. Clearly, Daft is talking about the total drinks business, where local or regional market sub-brand opportunities are also created and driven by field management with limited marketing interference from Atlanta. In such cases, the consumer's knowledge of the sub-brand's link to Coca-Cola may sometimes be as small as a tiny mention on the package.

All this makes eminent sense. What I'm less clear about is Daft's position on the core brand, Coca-Cola itself. So I'll give you my two cents' worth. In the past decade or more, the brand has been flying all over the place, trying to be different things to different mouths around the world. The reason for this has puzzled me. Is it something to do with the tired "think global, act local" battlecry? Or the desire to be seen as more spirited, or hip, or off the planet to combat a general consumer drift away from cola-tasting drinks?

Whatever the reason, the image result has been shabby. True, profits to the corporation have been okayish, the brand's distribution and visual presence is still amazing, and the key competitor doesn't seem to be making any serious inroads. But if you peel back some layers you might find the performance of the world's best known brand is not as good as it should be — that is, its growth rate seems to be declining in mature markets. Can this trend be arrested? Whatever the remedy, it would be useful to get the brand-building media advertising back to a more single-minded focus around the globe. The brand's soul — healthy social values, freedom and the "American dream" — needs to be revisited, too. And the communication drivers of this great brand should be orchestrating the total global programme from a central point. I've recently read that things are possibly moving in this direction. Let's see what happens.

Singapore Airlines has always strongly supported centralised control for its brand-building programme. From the start in 1972, our agency had chosen television as a key brand-building medium in all major markets, and during the launch years in Western markets our media thinking was fiercely debated by our local partner agencies. The facts supported their argument to focus total media funds in vertical print media. The prime prospects — the business travellers — were heavy business print readers and light TV viewers, and the budget we had could only provide scanty TV reach and frequency coverage. We stubbornly held our position, taking the view that it was important to sell the brand's soul and personality, and TV was plainly the most effective emotional vehicle to do this. SIA's central management agreed. Maybe they just liked the idea of bucking convention, of doing something that few others in the airline business had done before. Then again, TV said "confidence" and "leadership" quite firmly. Anyway, the gamble worked.

In terms of TV production, SIA also agreed to our team's somewhat unusual proposal. Conventional wisdom in the 1970s decreed — and still does today — that one should contain TV production costs to a small percentage of the total media spend; you also have to contend with statistical models that influence the number of different commercials to produce in a given schedule.

But in SIA's case, it was common practice in the fledgling years to dismiss the TV production rulebooks and apply one's own judgement on the menu that was needed. We consistently produced and ran a rotation of three to four new strategic *Stewardess* commercials each year on a relatively small global TV media budget, and then we'd annually pop in a further two or three different commercials on tactical product developments. This game plan made SIA look and feel quite different to others; it gave the brand loads of energy and freshness.

The *Singapore Girl* creative work has been well received over the years, but it had a bumpy reception when the concept was first introduced to local SIA management in the Western markets. The consensus of the airline's Western staff reflected good, sound thinking at the time and called for advertising that sold flying experience, Caucasian pilots, convenient flight schedules, solid bricks and mortar stuff. We convinced the central client otherwise. My God, they were courageous.

KEEPING true to yourself and your brand requires eternal vigilance. As Singapore Airlines became increasingly well known across continents, some people felt that the focus on the brand's service soul — the Singapore Girl — did not need so much advertising support. Certainly from the late 1980s onwards, something had to give in terms of advertising as an increasing number of tangible product enhancements and developments of importance took to the stage.

All experienced brand managers understand that a successful brand is a mixture of emotional and rational values, and the weighting depends on how the game is played in one's industry. The balance is always a sensitive issue, especially in airline brands. SIA's position as the airline with the world's most modern fleet has been flagged for many years and it has worked hand in glove with the service promise of the Singapore Girl. As a proud global leader SIA has, in recent years, pioneered superior tangible attributes in cabin entertainment, seating comfort and cuisine, in all classes. All have deserved prominent publicity and their development has predictably taken over centre stage. The airline recognises, however, that the best long-term bonding between SIA and the public is with the brand's service soul, reflected through the genuine, timeless warmth and grace of the Singapore Girl.

When Nicolas G. Hayek, CEO of Swatch, described watches as emotional purchases, he articulated this sentiment: "Emotional products are about a message — a strong, exciting, authentic message that tells people who you are and why you do what you do. There are many elements that make up the Swatch message, *but the most important element is the hardest for others to copy*. We're not just offering watches, we're offering our own personal culture."

THE DANGER OF CHANGE

There is a phrase in the English language that reads, "a creature of habit". There is no phrase in the English language that reads, "a creature of change".

While variety is the spice of life, change isn't. Contrary to popular opinion, I figure that mature consumers generally resist change. On the other hand, many marketers feel change is their salvation. So do advertising agencies. It is conventional to change; it is *un*conventional not to change.

The world is changing so fast, or so we're told. Information technology is upon us, changing us. Everything has to change to survive. It were as though we are all boat-racing down a fast-flowing river, jostling each other to lead the race, with little concern or knowledge of where the river is taking us — and it could well be to Niagara Falls.

You don't have to jump blindly into that fast-flowing river. You don't have to be totally obsessed about change. Sit back and calmly get the perspectives in balance.

Brands are made up of three parts: the body, the soul and the conscience. The body is the change engine; it represents the tangibles of your brand offering, the product developments and enhancements that are an ongoing process. The brand's soul represents the emotional side of your brand offering; it is usually deep-rooted, and mirrors the unique character, personality, and culture of your brand. The brand's conscience represents the company's corporate "pay-back" responsibility to specific target customers or to the public at large. Not all large consumer marketers employ all three brand forces in tandem, but I suggest that if they're serious about global growth for their brand, the three dynamics must come into play.

The mission of the brand body is pretty clear — it is your engine of regular upgrades and innovations. Where things frequently go off the rails for marketers and ad agencies alike is the handling of the brand's soul. They apply consistent change to the look, the feel, the personality, and the underlying compelling core appeal of the brand. Like getting Frank Sinatra to sing like Elvis Presley, and *then* like Pavarotti, just to be trendy. Getting the brand's soul right is not an easy task, but once you've nailed it, it need not essentially change for decades. The brand's soul is the mother of the brand, and like a country's national flag and anthem it should desirably have a positive, long-term place in consumers' hearts. After consumers get the teenage adrenaline out of their system (which means quite a number of years for some), they settle down and prefer things grounded; they're not keen on constant cosmetic change.

The brand's conscience has been an integral part of the game among big global brand owners for generations. As it is more corporate citizen and institutional in character, it should tend to reflect the values of the brand's soul and not be the target of constant change. As the 21st century takes off, this part of the brand's composition will expand in size and commercial value. Asian brand owners (most of whom are not yet embracing this development) should take note to more seriously address this responsibility from now on if they have global growth ambitions.

Before moving off the "change" topic, I'd just like to mention that I've experienced convoluted opinions on what "change" really means coming from the very crusaders of the war cry. The worst culprits of all are advertising creative people who talk up change and the importance of individuality. And yet when you go along to a pub at night that is patronised mostly by the creative people in town, you usually find them all sporting the same black clothes. They seem to prefer the standard tribal uniform and have done for some time. People become the same as soon as they follow someone else. People feel more comfortable with being part of a herd than they are being tall poppies. Once we acknowledge that truth, how do we apply it to advertising? And where does change fit in?

An experienced and respected advertising practitioner gave me his answer to these questions, and here's what he said:

"Great brands are like great women; they are the property of the world. Yet a brand is more than a universal property; it is a highly personal possession. It is the sum of all the beliefs and expectations that we have about that product and how in some way it will fit into our persona and the relationships that we have. What the brand does is important, but how that brand reinforces our own beliefs and attitudes about ourselves is maybe even *more* important. Consequently, a brand is subtly different to every individual. What a brand means to one person will not be exactly the same as what it means to someone else, *because each individual's life experience has been different.* There is however an essential core in a brand that strikes a universal resonance and that becomes the lowest common denominator — or the highest common factor — across the brand. Nurturing a brand is therefore difficult because too many people see a brand only within the framework that is *their* framework. What the brand is to them becomes what they believe that brand is to everybody, when in fact the brand is not quite the same thing to everybody. Some rare individuals have the ability and sensitivity to recognise that. They are aware that they are responsible for something which is very fragile yet very rich in its multi-layering. They can shape and enhance and move it — without actually destroying it."

While I think my colleague struck the right nerve on certain points, his view is heavy going for me and complicates the issues of brand building and "change". If the people who talk the change game are a bit difficult to understand, what chance have others, especially brand owners, in coming to grips with the issue?

Vigilance is, of course, a key watchword. Remember what the

Singapore Girl is. She is the warm, gentle, caring personality in her *sarong kebaya* forever and ever. What, however, does change is that she consistently offers you better on-line booking systems, wider seats, wider aisles, more cocktails, better food, more sophisticated inflight entertainment, and so on. It is equally essential to ensure that the Singapore Girl retains youthfulness and freshness as the years turn into decades. We therefore endeavour to consistently *contemporise the advertising through the story compositions and the production values* — the structure of the content, the styling of the film, the soundtrack, the still photography. Execution can play a big role in shaping a brand's distinctive identity.

It's a recipe that aims to always keep the Singapore Girl relevant and uniquely appealing to consumers.

And there are a couple more ingredients in this recipe. While things happening around the globe are not always positive, the airline feels it is still a beautiful world out there, and always firmly believes in the romance of travel. These two qualities provide the canvas on which we paint the enduring service promise of the Singapore Girl.

BRAND HICCUPS

Fighting for a fair slice of the action in the patch of the field you're playing on is a tough, ongoing battle. And sometimes, to make things more exciting, the patch you're on starts to crumble away. You find yourself trapped in a product category that's steadily losing its consumer appeal. This is an uncommon scenario, but it does happen, and the first natural instinct for brand owners is generally to adopt a defensive strategy that calls for a bigger share of a shrinking pie.

A good example of this scenario is the cognac industry in Asia, a region that for many years contributed huge profits to the coffers of the European cognac makers. In Asia's growing up period, through the 1970s to the late 1980s, cognac enjoyed an important social role in bars and nightclubs. But as things moved forward into the New Economy, cognac's place in Asian society remained static and its image became wedded to that of an old-fashioned, aged uncle versus the dashing, contemporary character of scotch and other trendy drinks. While the volatile Asian economy in recent times hasn't helped, the "old" cognac identity has been identified as being mainly responsible for dramatically depressing total cognac consumption in traditional Asian markets. Will cognac survive in this part of the world? The cognac marketers are now banging the drum about popular and sexy mixes and, of course, China is seen as the great salvation. Whatever the outcome, it seems clear that the cognac marketers in Asia had blinkered vision at a time when they should have been seriously addressing the trends in the marketplace and the cognac brand owners have paid dearly for this fundamental oversight.

CAN A BRAND COME BACK FROM ITS DEATHBED?

Popular consensus supports the view that packaged goods brands have a life cycle, and that the life is governed solely by sales performance. If the brand starts sliding swiftly downhill, funeral arrangements are commenced and something else is invented to replace the dying brand. The big, experienced global marketers practise this principle quite ruthlessly so it must be the right thing to do, I guess.

However, my Scottish blood freezes at the thought of throwing all the brand-building work and advertising investment out the window just because the brand appears to be running out of steam. Maybe it's not the brand but rather the brand managers that are running out of steam.

Cigarette brand owners are renowned brand gravediggers. For every cigarette brand that lives 20 years or more, there are dozens that only survive a quarter of this time. A notable brand enigma is Peter Stuyvesant. It was born in the 1960s and grew into a handsome global brand over the following couple of decades, at which point it then declined into obscurity and essentially became a has-been brand. Several years later, some bright sparks bucked the system by lifting Peter Stuyvesant up from its grave and relaunching it in Malaysia and Australia. They discovered the brand still had plenty of life and equity among consumers.

Another interesting brand revival is Tiger Beer, popular today in Southeast Asia. It was the core brand of its owners in Singapore and Malaysia right up to the mid-1970s when it started to slide dramatically against its new sister brand, Anchor. Finally a watershed decision had to be made: let it continue to slide and die, or do something special to the brand and relaunch it. The Tiger Beer marketing team took the latter route. They developed a strategy that repositioned Tiger as a more expensive premium beer, offering smart, affluent contemporary-minded drinkers a distinctive new labelling and fancy gold wrapping around the bottle's neck. It worked. By the mid-1990s, Tiger Beer had more than 50% of Singapore's total malt liquor market, and strong positions in neighbouring countries. The decision to bring back Tiger Beer from near-death was an immensely profitable exercise for the company's shareholders and demonstrates the kind of marketing ingenuity that I greatly admire. Mind you, the real world made one modest correction to the marketing plan: the prime Tiger drinkers ended up being truck drivers and construction workers, not the bourgeois elite, but who cares?

A classic case on how to get a new spin out of a brand is Doc Martens boots. I think most of you are familiar with this story, so I will not embellish it. Rather, it is yet another example of the many different ways to overcome the hiccups that all brands experience from time to time. The principle of a trusted brand being fed to the worms when it regularly fails to meet targets is, I feel, a reflection of poor, unimaginative brand management.

Best revitalise the brand — or retool the brand marketers.

BUDGETING FOR BRANDS

Let us remind ourselves of two elementary facts:

1. Your brand is your company's most important asset.
2. The fastest, cheapest and most effective way to grow your brand is through advertising.

Now go forth and develop a publicity budget plan, starting with a clean sheet of paper. I would dismiss the established textbook models that follow conventional business practice. You're in an entrepreneurial game, so think and create an imaginative budget plan.

The launch of the Apple Mac broke all conventions. A huge budget was spent on the TV production and the famous *1984* commercial ran once on the Super Bowl telecast. It is still frequently voted one of the top three television commercials ever created in America. Apple also bought an entire issue of *Newsweek*, and every single ad from cover to cover was for Apple Mac.

When Rank Xerox launched in the UK, they used television right from the beginning and their budget was determined by what was needed to make the brand highly visible. Here were these massively expensive machines that only a few corporations would be buying, but by going on TV they were able to get an unbelievable impact.

When the First Direct bank launched in Britain, they ran two different commercials on two different channels at exactly the same time. On one channel the commercial gave the optimistic view of the new product, a bank without branches, with an invitation to switch to the other channel for the pessimistic viewpoint. The media buy idea dictated the level of the budget.

At the time Singapore Airlines launched in the USA, they broke all the rules. California was a critical market. Even in that state alone, it takes a lot of money to achieve an acceptable basic exposure. SIA invested about 10% of projected revenue for the full year on advertising. (At that time, the industry norm was 2–3%.) It was not a decision taken lightly. It was based on the aim to quickly establish a firm footing in West Coast USA, not just a beachhead.

A budget level should desirably be arrived at as a result of intelligently analysing and calculating what you wish to achieve against your target audience in a given period, in the relevant competitive environment. And then you add creative flair.

When it comes to pinpointing the weight (the frequency) of your advertising there are endless models to guide you, but allow me to give you a view on this topic. Brand building is like building a relationship with a friend. If you connect fairly regularly you stand a good chance of nurturing the friendship. If for some reason it declines to a chat once every six months, then once a year, then maybe you see each other once every two years, you'll gradually forget each other. It's the same thing in advertising. If you're serious, you've got to keep up a regular dialogue; you've got to keep nurturing the relationship. You've got to get your customers interested in you, bonded to you. Even when times are tough and business is slow, somehow you've got to sustain a level of contact that signals your genuine desire to retain a relationship with your customers. If you cut off the connection over an extended period, the downside could be extremely dark and life-threatening for your brand.

An ambitious ad budget is usually influenced by an ambitious marketing plan. And anything ambitious has a decent amount of risk investment attached to it. Sadly, "risk" is seen by some as frivolous and irresponsible, whereas "risk" should be seen as a brave, inspiring word and liberally applied in any budget planning document.

The seemingly outrageous financial risk of the Apple Mac launch in 1984 represented but a fraction of the mammoth business revenue it generated. The inroads made by SIA in its first year in the USA as a result of a large advertising investment put SIA years ahead of its competition in terms of reputation and appeal.

So long as you have a good product and distinctive communications material, the model of AMBITIOUS PLAN + RISK = SUCCESS is a sensible budget rationale. This opinion relates especially to high profile national, regional or global consumer brands that have ambitions to hold a large market share in their industry, or to sharply improve their sizeable market position. In the context of these highly competitive playing fields, strong ad budgets should not be an issue and calculated risk-taking should be an integral part of the standard agenda. There is, however, an important caveat to all this — it's called accountability. While success should be rewarded, failure to achieve targeted results should mean financial punishment for the authors of the budget. A worthy risk!

Of course, "risk" is probably one of the most bandied-about words in marketing. Everyone talks the game, but very few people have ever risked anything in their lives. *The real risk-takers are those who know and have experienced the worst. They're not afraid of it.* But the concept is not easy to embrace for some. Younger Singaporeans, for example, are very comfortable, and have been all their lives, and can't imagine what it would be like to have nothing. They're prone to be risk-averse. Whereas if you've been through a failure or two you probably accept that it was a cross you had to bear, it was something you had to experience to understand the real world better, and you're prepared to take risks again in your desire to achieve your goal. Success in those conditions also toughens one's spirit and character, the kind of entrepreneurial stuff that helps build stronger nations.

CHAPTER 3

THE HOLY GRAIL AND HOW ASIAN BRANDS CAN FIND IT

Brand management has become a game that everyone is talking up. Brand strategists are emerging from advertising agencies, the big conglomerates and the big advertisers, the specialist brand communications groups and the big business service entities like Accenture. Once people talked sales, then marketing; now they talk brands. Planning, positioning and brand building have always been part of an advertising agency's stock-in-trade, just delivered under other names and usually without pomp or ceremony — just part of the standard service.

"Positioning" was invented as such in the 1960s. From having a simplistic sales increase as its objective, advertising was suddenly tasked to position the product in a certain way, aided and abetted by its unique selling proposition. Advertising agencies crusaded positioning campaigns, followed by repositioning campaigns when the positioning didn't quite work first time round. In those days no one talked brands. People talked product or corporate or theme advertising, using words like trademark or image.

Marketing only evolved in the 1960s. Before that, there were no marketing departments, just the sales department. And the sales director worked closely with the ad agency. It was a given that the agency would supply marketing intelligence without actually getting any extra income — the agency's service fee and media commission covered those duties. Agencies played the role of brand manager and marketing consultant long before those titles had been defined. Agencies had a powerful role in the growth of those companies at a time when marketing wasn't identified as the major weapon in most consumer product companies. The companies themselves saw to it that they had good disciplines at factory level and good distribution setups. From time to time they enhanced their products. And that was acceptable in the immediate post-war years because the world was starving for anything new that came onto the market. Companies couldn't meet the demand for new consumer goods. Choice didn't exist. Anything half-decent met with good sales. A classic example was the radio set pre-Sony; they were made from a brittle substance called Bakelite, one of the early plastics. They were crudely designed, like a crouching cat, until Sony came in and brought quality, sleek design and a new global standard.

People were in awe of post-war technology. Every year brought forth some wondrous new invention like Samsonite, Fibrolite, Everlite, Globite or Masonite. And in that post-war period, from the mid-1950s to the late 1960s, the best advertising of the 20th century was done by such legends as Bernbach, Burnett and Ogilvy — advertising driven by adventurous thought, personal intuition and great emotional creative expression.

But this utopia for the ad industry didn't last too long. As the 1960s swung into the 1970s and the Western economies mushroomed, global consumption appetite became more ravenous, competition stimulated choice, small businesses exploded into big businesses, and big businesses ballooned into awesome corporations. Very quickly, marketing emerged as the driving force of industry and growth, and life in the communications business became more frantic and exhilarating. But this shiny picture would not be complete without some dark clouds. And they came in the shape of bean counters and rational analysts.

As larger revenues and bigger profits appeared more frequently on financial reports, so did shareholders and company management feel the need to protect their mounting treasure more vigilantly. They became more scientific about the employment of expenditure, and ad spending in particular. Nothing wrong with this attitude; it's pretty normal business behaviour, but it sadly influences a climate that challenges the spirit of entrepreneurship. Intelligent brand owners have already come to grips with this issue, but there are still scores of good brands out there fighting battles with spreadsheets rather than with spirited creative leaders.

Despite innumerable attempts by clever intellectuals and statisticians to transform marketing and advertising into something that can be summarised in structured boxes on a computer screen, *the art of the game shall always prevail.* It is an ever-changing, ever-moving target that can't be pinned down on charts and graphs.

The most important rule in coming up with those great ideas that become the international legends is *not to have any rules.* However, like an architect designing a unique and beautiful home, you need to build the creative idea on solid foundations and you need to shape your idea with the help of some plans and handy tools. But all these tools, all these checklists, are not exclusive. They are not Holy Writ. Formulae can be cobbled together as a result of studying the theories and work of the great advertising gurus. The danger is, ultimately, *all formulae become formulaic* which is why they should be constantly challenged.

BATEY BRAND BALANCE

All brands have a body and soul. The Batey Brand Balance is a tool that helps to more clearly identify where the brand's body and soul are today, what we all want them to be, and what the long-term core appeal of the brand should be. I might just mention that this model is an extension of a method created by a worthy brand-building competitor.

The grid is a yin-yang equation; or, if you prefer, a left brain-right brain structure. The key emotional brand values are lined up on one side, and the major rational brand values are lined up on the other. The combined assets are then summarised through a brief statement that reflects the brand's enduring core appeal.

(I'd like to quickly add that while the Batey Brand Balance is a useful tool, in the hands of amateurs it is capable of producing nothing more exciting than a big yawn.)

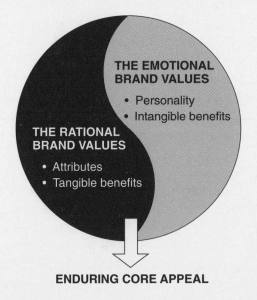

Definitions

Rational (The Body)	**Attributes:** What is the product (not the brand)? What are its functional product features and physical characteristics?
	Tangible benefits: What will it do for me? What are the functional consequences of these attributes that make the brand desirable?
Emotional (The Soul)	**Personality:** If the brand were a person, what kind of person would it be?
	Intangible benefits: What feelings are evoked by the brand? What are the end emotional rewards I can expect from using the brand?
Enduring core appeal: A fusion of the key rational and emotional values of the brand into a bedrock promise. A succinct phrase or sentence that captures the very essence (core) of the brand's appeal. The most compelling reason to buy the brand — now and for the foreseeable future — in the minds of consumers.	

Special note: In an earlier chapter, I talked about the brand being made up of three parts — the body, the soul and the conscience. The third part — conscience — is still a tiny part in the brand-building model. But expect it to grow in importance as environmental, ecological and community responsibilities spread their influence. In the context of developing your brand strategy, however, you should treat "conscience" as a kind of sub-brand of your soul.

The Process

First, using the Brand Balance grid, audit the brand as it exists today. This is ideally a joint client-agency exercise. The toughest part is often pinning down the enduring core appeal of the brand as it is currently perceived by consumers. If you emerge with a clean bill of health, fantastic. Frequently, however, the first audit is likely to reveal defects in the balance between the rational and emotional core values, with a negative impact on what the enduring core appeal should be when you look into the future. Which means going to the next step.

Secondly, address the *desired* Brand Balance. Refine the attributes and benefits on both sides of the equation until you achieve a healthy, positive balance and arrive at the enduring core appeal that you firmly believe is right for the future.

What is the desired Brand Balance in the communications

programme? Should you add more weight to emotional values? Or strike equal weight for both emotional and rational values? It depends on the brand category, the competitive pressures, the consumer-buying environment, market trends, and so on. Research may influence some of the appropriate dimensions. You are looking into the future and by definition, it is an exercise in good common sense and courageous thinking. The critical thing is to let creative exploration manage change and not, as somebody once said, let change create you.

Because the world of marketing moves at a breathless speed, the Brand Balance analysis should be revisited once each year in conjunction with an annual review of the brand's advertising strategy. This action ensures that everything, including the enduring core appeal, is always in good shape in the minds of consumers.

There is so little difference in what most companies can offer in the rational sense that the emotional side of the equation becomes the separator. Insurance salesmen are a good analogy. They come at you from all angles with all kinds of different ploys and invariably they're all the same — the same proposition, from all the different companies. In the end, if someone asked why you went with Mr. X and not Mr. Y, it's usually because you felt you could relate to him better than the other guy. Somehow you liked his nice, generous, engaging manner, or you liked his cool, conservative manner. And that applies not just to selling life insurance, but to selling most brands today. There isn't much difference in the rational offer; the emotional side is increasingly more important in relationships with brands.

In 1972 the client and our agency jointly wrote a positioning statement for Singapore Airlines: "To present Singapore Airlines as a competent, modern, international airline of Asian origin, offering the best inflight service in the world." And it hasn't changed significantly in 30 years. Attributes like reliability, experience, modernity and internationalism are conventional ambitions. The Asian roots underpinned the credibility of the service promise; the key difference was the best inflight service promise.

Some brands, of course, find it tough to shape a distinctive emotional difference out of their pedigree or company culture. In such cases, they should explore other ways to address this need. For example, it could be how a proprietary look is built up, the style of cinematography, maybe the music, and sometimes they all evolve into a personality difference.

The brand builder's job is to build those differentials. The most successful brands are the ones that are not only emotionally strong with you, but are also seen in your mind as providing *a strong rational advantage* to you. Interestingly, a brand can live through its history, like Levi's, the originator. It gives people a very strong rational argument, which they can internalise; *oh, they know what they're doing.* There's a lot of substance in Levi's. The pedigree of Levi's underpins a lot of its values.

Another global brand I admire is Rolex. I think this brand is one of the most successful marketing exercises of the last century and will continue to do well. Essentially, they put a lot of expensive metal on their product, but there hasn't been anything exceptionally technically superior vis-à-vis other brands. They marketed it at a price above the second most expensive popular watch and then went out into the marketplace and consistently kept on pushing that particular position. Over the years Rolex gradually moved from being a well-known, admired brand into what all brands aspire to be — an institution. Rolex invested 30 to 40 years of consistent brand building in order to institutionalise their brand. They haven't changed their core brand platform in all that time. Even when the economy is tough, their advertising programme is relentless. They communicate 6-star quality. They have always had a strong endorsement programme: the great intellectual achievers, the people who do so much for the world, great explorers, great singers, and always the more lofty names. Some people say the ads are unexciting and unchanging, but I think their strength has been their unchanging, focused view of the way life should be. They've been consistently tasteful and conservative, like all aristocratic Swiss should be.

Once the Brand Balance establishes the brand's enduring core appeal, the blueprint exists for the communications programme.

From our advertising agency's perspective, we have always started from the stance that *the consumer is our client and the advertiser is our business partner.* We sweat blood to know more about the consumer than the advertiser does and, as such, we — rather than the advertiser — feel we best know how to connect with the feelings of the consumer.

Just keeping up a basic connection is an art in itself. As the consumer travels around, he sees the brand at the airport on posters, he sees the brand in magazines, he sees it on neon signs. The Japanese are masters of sustaining the basic connection. You often see huge outdoor signs with just the word "SANYO", and nothing else. And when you first see them you think, shouldn't the message work harder? But the more you see them, the more you feel their presence and power — like mammoth flags of confidence shining brightly on the skyline. Their identity reminds everyone that "SANYO" is there for them wherever they go. It's all part of the brand's strong global connectivity exercise. The Japanese have taught the rest of us a trick or two when it comes to putting the brand regularly in front of consumers. They've been less impressive, I feel, in their bonding skills.

EVERY AD IS A BRAND AD

Everyone is talking up the brand game these days. While still at fuzzy talk stage for many Asian brand owners, the importance of the brand and what it means in the marketing programme is now on the table — which is great for communications service consultants.

What is less clear is what the word "brand" represents in the total communications programme. To many practitioners, it is the new label for strategic/image/awareness-building advertising, and another title is given to communications that sell specific products and specific propositions. Why do we like to complicate things? Your company name, your company trademark, is your brand. Whenever you put your company name/trademark in a communication you are conveying a brand message; you are doing brand advertising. So *all* ads are brand ads. Which means a commitment to upholding the brand's values across everything, no matter whether you are selling a rational or emotional story. *Propositions can vary. The media can vary. But the brand's voice should be "family".*

It certainly doesn't help matters when brand owners, marketers and agency folk get their terminology twisted. As Jeremy Bullmore says, "The word 'brand' has become so fashionable that we've stopped thinking what it means; we now use it almost interchangeably with the word 'product'." On that basis, reckons Bullmore, we can see a great deal of advertising that fails to epitomise clearly defined brand values; it is content to be simply product advertising — the style of the ads is not the style of the brand. *In good advertising, every single executional decision is taken consciously and for a good reason.* The voice-over, the casting, the colour of sets and costumes, the prose style, even the length of the commercial combine to strengthen the brand's particular competitive personality. It is that personality that makes the brand our friend and inspires our respect.

Some brand ads are tasked to reach out to consumers, offering a relationship with the brand, or reaffirming the one that already exists. Called strategic brand advertising, they connect with consumers, talk to them on a deeper level, and build up a relationship. Then there are ads that say, look, if you come in today you will get two bottles for the price of one. Now that is *still* a brand ad. The only difference is that it is a brand ad trying to get some fast, direct response, a quick sale, that's all. Over the years though, we have broken all that down and given each type of ad a different label. One type is *strategic*, which is long-term brand-building advertising, while the other is *tactical*, therefore it is short-term and not brand-building. Unfortunately, the semantics have got in the way of common sense. We can call them different things if we wish, but the fact remains that *every* ad with a brand logo in it is doing the same thing; it is contributing to the building of the brand.

The implications for brand builders and creative people are clear. They have to be a little more sensitive and disciplined about the way they talk to consumers. Say there's a need to run a print ad promoting flights from A to B at *50% off.* One of the creative options might be to do a "retail" looking ad, an "urgent" looking ad, something that visually conveys a "bargain basement" feeling — quick, hurry or you'll miss out. But the fact that the airline's logo is in the ad means there is still the brand's quality and stature to uphold. *Even if those tickets are 50% off, the ad is still offering the same brand.* The ad has to pull in the consumers, of course, but it still has to speak with the attitude of the brand. It still has to uphold certain core values. It still has to convey certain personality traits. Despite the fact they live or die by immediate response, IKEA speaks with the soul of their brand in every ad. They preserve their style and humour, while their distinctive art direction delivers an unspoken message about the quality of their furniture.

Tragically, many brand owners and their agencies don't bother to craft *all* their communications. Agency people tend to abdicate on this issue; they say, oh, that's a product ad, or that's a tactical ad, or that's a promotional ad. Oh, don't worry, that's just a sale ad, it will only run a few times, then everyone will forget it. Famous last words; after the ad has run for the tenth time, everyone begins to wonder when someone is going to wake up and stop it before it does any more damage. *As far as the consumer is concerned, every piece of communication they see is a brand ad.* That is why brand owners need to establish systems that stop different people with different judgemental abilities approving the so-called tactical work, while a different group with a different agenda and abilities controls the strategic. There is no such thing as having A grade ads, B grade ads and C grade ads. *The same people, charged with building the brand, should approve every ad.* Once you adopt this thinking, you'll find that your marketplace presence will become dramatically more synergised and distinctly sharper.

A GRID FOR PLANNING THE MARKETING COMMUNICATIONS WAR

(Applicale to sizeable discretionary consumer brands in popular, highly competitive categories)

Category	Type	Programmes	Programmes
STRATEGIC BRAND	Image/ Corporate	• Major brand identity campaign	• Showcase the brand's personality and core promise across a broad front. This brand-building, bond-building exercise should invade consumers' minds three to four periods of the year. (Furthermore, the value of this advertising to foster strong staff loyalty/bonding is enormous and should be recognised by the brand owner's management.)
		• Corporate citizen/ environment campaign	• Establish and consolidate a position of high stature among the nation's leaders and population through generous support of special community and/or environmental programmes. *A growing responsibility.*
TACTICAL BRAND	Product Range/ Services	• New product launches and/or product enhancement campaigns	• Mount dramatic surprise attacks about three times yearly. Must be breakthrough stuff. Make a lot of noise. Penetrate enemy lines and secure enlarged market share. *Builds business and leadership respect.*
		• Sustaining product/service campaigns	• Mount regular proposition-led assaults through the year. Vary the weaponry. Don't go into battle without a competitive proposition. If it's hard to identify a superior tangible angle, create one that gives you perceived superiority. *Builds business and reinforces brand's delivery.*
		• Retail, price-led campaigns/ special promotions	• Sustain a consistent, year-round barrage. This is tough, hand-to-hand fighting in the ditches. *Market share builder, but attracts many low-yield, low-loyalty customers.*

Clearly, all worthy brand warlords have powerful intelligence resources to handle the ongoing checks and balances, as well as the timing and weighting between the strategic and tactical brand programmes.

HOW TO PLOT YOUR MARKETING COMMUNICATIONS WAR

It is alleged that Napoleon Bonaparte once said that military generals had the skills to be the best businessmen in the world. Certainly there are many similarities between planning and executing a military campaign and a marketing one.

While the strategies and tactics for each battle can vary considerably, a model I like for addressing *wars* is on the facing page. It is predicated on the needs of a prominent discretionary consumer brand, in a popular product category, competing nationally, regionally or universally against formidable opponents.

HOW TO WRITE A GOOD *TACTICAL* BRIEF

If I had a dollar for every book or article written on this subject...! For the student of advertising, the creative briefing models can be a bit too fussy and fuzzy.

As it is, the majority of account service people get far too much waffle from their clients when taking the brief in the first place, and then deftly pass on much the same waffle to the creative people. The tedious task of actually getting to the core of the brief is frequently left in the hands of the creative team. Not only do they end up writing the real brief themselves (once they have cracked it); they then have to write the ads, usually in the space of a few days. In recent times, agency account planners have eased this problem, but the challenge of writing a good creative brief — historically and essentially an account service responsibility — remains a sizeable issue. And because the vast majority of briefs relate to short-term tactical needs like new product offerings or retail messages where turnaround time is minimal, it is critical to outline the job in the most helpful, least confusing way possible.

A model that I personally like appears on the next page. A fictitious example demonstrates how simple the guts of a good tactical brief should be:

Client: Premier Golf Clubs

Why are we advertising? To increase market share by 5% by convincing consumers that Premier's new range of irons drive the ball further than any other golf irons on the market.

Who are we talking to? Golfers who take the game seriously. They expect their clubs to improve their performance. Predominantly, men of 40 years plus, with above average incomes and education.

What would we like them to think? "With these new Premier irons, I'll really be able to nail the ball."

Why is this believable? Premier's new irons have shorter hosels to maximise the power of each swing. That is, they put more weight behind the ball. Tested and proved by leading golf players to drive the ball 15% further than competitive golf clubs. They also have a patented PowerPin, which provides a feel that is unsurpassed in a cast club.

All the other important information like the brand strategy, the Brand Balance, competitive frame, media selection, budget, and so on should be on hand, but as separate references and addenda.

HOW TO JUDGE CREATIVE WORK

Assume we are working on the launch of a strategic brand-building campaign. We have done all our homework and the brand communications strategy feels brilliant. Next, the brief is turned over to the creative wizards to bring everything to life in a stunning fashion.

The bottom line, of course, will be to achieve the great creative idea, an idea with the power to be the central force of a brilliant, enduring brand campaign — a *got milk?*, a Tango Big Orange Man, a *Just do it.*

While no checklist will ever exist (*thankfully!*) on how to create "the great idea", I focus on four fundamental points in judging the creative development work of new strategic brand campaigns:

1. *A unique, relevant, compelling proposition.* This is consistently the toughest component in the mix to get right, as tangible competitive differences are generally marginal. And even when there is a unique story to tell, the delivery may not turn on the consumers. Furthermore, there are different interpretations on what defines a proposition. Clearly, a proposition is not a proposition unless it presents a compelling benefit of relevance to its target audience. If there isn't a good proposition in the advertising, the campaign will be functioning on wobbly legs and could be history in no time.

2. *A unique visual statement.* This can be *anything* visual — the layout or the typefaces in print ads, the filming technique on television. The idea is to create a visual look that sets the brand apart from others but, in doing so, it must be comfortable and complementary with the brand's personality. The execution will contribute significantly to the success of a great idea. Indeed, I support the view that a great execution could very much be the central idea.

3. *A unique icon or property.* It's unlikely that the Marlboro Man will be bettered as a visual icon, although some of the world's most successful campaigns have *not* had a graphic icon in their communications. I just happen to believe that a compelling, *exclusive* graphic entity is a huge asset in this game and that this ingredient should be firmly on the agenda in developing new brand communications programmes. Apart from graphic characters, there are numerous other properties that can be employed *exclusively* to the brand's advantage. A unique wordsmith style is one, the quintessential slogan is another. Then there are catchphrases that potentially become part of everyday language — *Does she or doesn't she?* for example, or *got milk?* Or, squeeze more life out of the trademark symbol like Nike has done. For me,

creating and massaging exclusive brand icons or properties is an essential prerequisite in a brand-building exercise.

4. *A unique, appealing personality.* Imagine stepping into a boardroom and presenting a staff pension plan to a group of people. They're getting a bit tired and restless as they've seen presentations by several salesmen in the previous two hours. Your plan is only marginally different in tangible benefits from your competition. And yet *you* win the contract. Why...? *It was your personality.* Somehow, in some way, your audience took a liking to you. Maybe it was your youthful spirit, or your ready laugh, or your genuine humility, or your straightforward professionalism. Whatever you did, you connected with your audience and given that everything else was just about parity with your competition, your audience chose you. Which is why we can never underscore too much the importance of creating a unique, compelling personality for every brand. And once developed, that personality must filter through *every* piece of communication the brand delivers — classical advertising, relationship marketing, public relations, and so on. And patently, the *same* personality must drive the culture *within* the brand's organisation.

Against this background of some key things that I look for in judging new brand campaign creatives, I hasten to add that this sensitive, critical area of an ad agency's skills is often a minefield of conflicting emotions and egos.

Some people evaluate creative ideas with a mental slide rule that works like this: "Well, it might get a silver award at the One Show, and a gold at New York Festivals." Others have a little scale that weighs up the ideas like this: "Now, I know the brand owner hates too many words in headlines, and I know they don't like big pictures, so I won't show them those ideas..."

For some advertisers, judging a creative presentation is a large committee exercise and a case of ticking boxes on a formidable questionnaire sheet. How right or wrong are they? There'll never be a clear direction on this issue. A few great clients and their ad agencies will continue to consistently roll out outstanding creative, *whereas 90% of all advertising everywhere will consistently continue to be remarkably forgettable.*

At the times when I've found myself in two minds about a new creative concept, I've had pretty good results using what I nicknamed, for some odd reason, my "quickblink" test. I get experienced brand managers in the agency who don't work on the brand being critiqued, and get them to react to the creative like a consumer. In other words, they get no pre-sell, no advance details about the objectives, or the proposition, or the idea. The creative concept in its naked form is just put in front of them with one simple question: "How does this grab you?" I would underscore that this game should only be played by seasoned brand-building practitioners, people who can mentally translate a line-drawn TV storyboard into a brilliant Ridley Scott production and who also have a good understanding of the character and psyche of the relevant consumer.

I have a feeling that this was much the way creative ideas were judged in the era that produced the world's best advertising. I'm against raw concept testing among consumer groups for reasons explained earlier in this book; instead, I'd love to see the re-emergence of skilled ad people having the final say on creative concepts, just by looking at the work through the eyes of the consumers with no pre-sell inputs. After all, consumers never know the brief when they see the ad.

Brand builders need a mental filter that will recognise the right brand communications when they see them and reject the ones that do not speak with the brand's voice. It is not rocket science; we should be able to train ourselves to look at ads and say, *is this our brand talking to us or is it some alien voice that our brand would never use?*

Brand builders must be firm and focused. While nobody likes to reject ideas, it goes with the job. Too many creative directors become overly protective of their teams. The truth is, rejection will harm them less than prevarication. Still others admit there is always "another way" of doing something and therefore if the ad is not totally off strategy, tend to give people the benefit of the doubt — "I-might-not-have-done-it-that-way-myself-but-hey-you-can't-reject-work-on-the-basis-that-it-is-not-what-you-would-have-done". *There are no half measures building a brand.* If an ad isn't right, if the language is wrong, if it is not the brand talking, say so. It is a tougher call than most people think.

Evaluating is intuitive; you can tell by the look and the words that it will or won't cut through, that it is clear or obscure. However, sometimes in advertising we get too clever by halves. On one occasion, a television commercial destined for the Taiwan market had music specially scored for it in Sydney. The end result was like looking at a European movie, a Fellini film, or one of Ingmar Bergman's mystic pieces; it was all very macabre, dark and sinister. It appealed no doubt to the darker side of the Aussie creative spirit, but what about the young, new-world Asian enthusiasts watching it in Taipei?

If all else fails, at least make the creative look terrific and keep it simple. We've just finished the 20th century and if you took the one hundred best ads from that century, at least 75% of them *weren't* done in the last 15 years. There were beautiful ads sculptured from the mid-1960s through to the early 1980s. If you ran the work that art directors like Neil Godfrey and Helmut Krone were doing in the 1960s in tomorrow's paper, it would still look classic. We talk about things of great beauty and great strength in our world, the great classic music, the great operas, the great art, the things of beauty which have survived centuries and will continue to survive as long as man lives; the same will apply in advertising. There are communications of such great simplicity and originality that age and change will never diminish their appeal.

MIND YOUR BRAND LANGUAGE

In Jeremy Bullmore's book *Behind the Scenes in Advertising*, he talks about the issue of hard sell versus soft sell in advertising. "There are two ways to sell a Rolex," he says. "The first is from a dodgy barrow on the high street... You do not pause to calculate possible damage to long-term brand values and corporate reputation. You will never see these punters again. You will hit them hard." The other way to sell a Rolex, Bullmore says, is the way they sell them in real life: "Politely and assuredly, with a style and grace to match the merchandise, conscious as always that *every ad should be making a small investment in the brand's eternal worth.*" Jeremy believes that a great deal of advertising does not, and should not, seek an immediate transaction. Instead, its purpose is "maintaining and building brand relevance or value".

What all consumers seem to want, we're told, perhaps because they're only human after all, is quality and value (low price). The factor of price, which is measurable, remains a negative, restricting factor. *"There are few consumer markets in mature societies where the cheapest brand is also the brand leader."*

IN advertising, **brand language can be visual as well as verbal**. The notion of investing in style and grace, "the brand's eternal worth", is anathema to many Asian brand owners who still tend to talk coldly to their consumers. If they aspire to have a serious global brand, they will need to change their brand's tone and manner. About the only people who can be aloof to their audience are the French brand owners. The French say, we're French, we're clever French, we're superior French, no matter where we are. And everyone loves it because they're buying that Frenchness. Their advertising has a lofty attitude. People say, ah, that's the impossible, irresistible French for you. If they tried a warm and cozy tone, the world would dismiss them as frauds.

Brand language is directly related to brand personality. Sometimes, global advertising tries to be all things to all people and that means a lot of it is doomed before it even begins. Theodore Levitt claims that the needs and wants of the world's customers have become "irrevocably homogenised". Others think this view is too narrow. An advertiser who sells beauty to women, or rebellion to teenagers, or masculinity to smokers, or luxury to business travellers can successfully use common stimuli to evoke a universal response. Gurus like Jeremy Bullmore believe it is the coded tribal message we should increasingly look at with respect. "Talking" visually and verbally, in a way that touches a global audience, is very much a function of the brand's personality. I fully agree. Mercedes-Benz can deliver a message about its German passion for engineering to a global audience and be immediately understood and welcomed. McDonald's can portray its Ronald McDonald universally and evoke a successful response.

Production values can never be discounted from brand language. Production craft impacts immediately on consumer perceptions of the brand. Well-crafted messages imply manufacturing craft in the brand. The subtleties of lighting, set design, camera angles are picked up by consumers; they can't articulate *how* it affects them but it does, another reason why crude drawings and storyboards are a flawed way to test television concepts which ultimately will draw their power from their finished production values. Intelligent brand owners nowadays are employing production values as brand differentials. They respect what the subtleties can deliver; they are prepared to invest in them. As short-sighted marketers talk down their brands with cheap production, a new league of brand builders has recognised the value of having a variety of top-quality, well-crafted executions. It all depends on where a marketer wants to be in life.

When executional standards fall, when our craft gets sloppy, when mediocrity becomes the norm, brand owners and agencies are selling themselves short. The old truth still stands: *the best advertising is done by the best brands, the worst by the suspect brands.*

MUSIC can also be indelible brand language. Contemporary music particularly crosses all cultural and racial borders; it seems that every Asian can relate very comfortably to Western-style popular music. Music dissolves differences. The karaoke craze showed us how normally reserved, inscrutable people in an office during the day can break out and sing at night. Inhibitions vanish. In fact, the Asian is more likely to get up and sing whereas his Caucasian companion might hold back, which reminds us once again how the right environment (and, by association, the right emotional buttons) can open up the heart and feelings of all people, of all races and cultures. The music that the incredible composer, lyricist and singer Pat Aulton wrote for Singapore Airlines has always remained part of the brand. It has been rearranged and woven through dozens of different commercials. It has played across the whole, integrated platform of SIA communications, right through to trade shows. Even on board the aircraft, you will hear the song. Interestingly, it has *always* been sung in English. It has never been translated. It sounds true to the soul of the brand without being overtly "Asian".

IN my experience, the majority of advertising creative directors have an aversion to jingles in TV commercials. The reasons are unclear, and I can only guess that they somehow think that the jingle technique is too mushy or old-fashioned. My personal view on jingles is simple — I love them. A good jingle can provide the best mood and communication energy, while lyrics consistently score the best ad recall for a brand.

While popular music and song reach out and connect with all societies in Asia, they take sound to its limits in India. If you want to score well at the movie box office with the one billion Indians, your movie — no matter whether it's high drama or comedy — must include several song and dance renditions.

"Buying" a famous song has long been an advertising technique to catch audience attention. The theory is everyone knows the music, and you don't have to gamble on a new composition that may or may not click. I'm not keen on this route — a unique brand should have its own unique music, I feel, and financially it makes more sense. There have been exceptions, the most whistled being Marlboro with the *Theme from The Magnificent Seven*. For years Cathay Pacific licensed the rights to *Love's Theme*. That piece of music was arguably the single most enduring element in their advertising.

If a marketer has a lofty ambition and wants his brand to be seen as the best in its category *in the world*, it is more appropriate that everything to do with the brand is new and original. *If the music is an original composition, it can't be associated in the consumer's mind with anything other than the brand.* There are no rules governing the style and form of the music. It is a matter of taste and appropriateness, though you certainly need to be true to the soul of the brand. A traditional Chinese medicine would be hard pressed to use the Rolling Stones, whereas Acer global advertising would sit more comfortably with Western music rather than classical Chinese strings.

HOW TO PUMP MORE ENERGY INTO A BRAND'S PRESENCE

Marketers know how crowded it is out there in the media. An expensive but sometimes appropriate way to be seen or heard above the din is to spend more on advertising. Buy a bigger schedule. Put more X's in media boxes. As mentioned earlier, don't be bashful about pitching for bigger exposure, so long as you observe the tough accountability rule. Predictably, of course, a bigger budget is not necessarily the best solution. Nor do you always need the heavier weight if you produce creative work that stuns everyone. The great campaigns that everyone responds to are the dream of most marketers and advertising agencies. Apple Mac's *1984* commercial — where the girl destroyed Big Brother — was so powerful it only had to run *once*. Which is fine, but as we move into the new century we have to seriously question whether the one great creative ad every so often is enough.

The growth of information technology and the knowledge economy has accelerated the pace of our lives. We are eager to travel more frequently, and see and achieve things faster than ever before. This heightened buzz and energy are now part of our business and social agenda. While the playing field still responds strongly to a great ad, consumers increasingly empathise more enthusiastically with brands that entertain them with more energy — brands that present them with not one, but a *menu* of great executions every year.

Some marketers would argue against this idea, expressing the view that their advertising production costs would become extremely unbalanced and wasteful. With media costs rising, why throw money away on more and more production? There would be no money left to air all the new commercials anyhow! The whole thing would just be an exorbitant indulgence. And they are right to an extent. *What they really have to calculate are the risks of merely following industry norms.* If marketers follow the conventional production-to-media ratio, generally placing a 10–15% cap on production costs, they risk being just like everyone else — especially if they have an average-sized budget within the category.

The classic example of creating more energy and impact as a result of a great series of advertisements is Absolut Vodka. How many different ways can you present the same bottle? The brand just keeps doing it, to everyone's delight; great variety, great energy. People talk about the ads; they compare favourites, like they compare soccer heroes. *When you can make your consumer's lips your advertising medium, then you know your brand presence is dominant.* The same goes for Nike; hundreds of different commercials are created annually and they relentlessly keep up the pace. The *got milk?* campaign follows a similar strategy, presenting one entertaining scenario after another. Just when you think you've seen them all, another one comes along.

Absolut, Nike and the California Milk Processor Board broke the rules when their budgets were relatively small. So did Singapore Airlines. When the airline began building its global presence, a stable of *Singapore Girl* commercials was shot each year.

IBM discovered the same Holy Grail. Some very bright people at O&M have taken IBM from a huge, dull, cold brand to a huge, very smart, very human brand in no time, and an important ingredient in their success has been their extensive menu of commercials. Even though the key message is basically the same, there is a lot of entertaining variety and loads of energy.

If a brand owner aspires to have the predominant brand in his country, or globally, he has to move into the fast track. He can't afford to limit his thinking in terms of the norms and the averages — otherwise that is where he will stay. The days of relying on one or two strategic brand commercials to last 12–18 months are over. Variety, which translates into energy, is a hugely persuasive ingredient. If this calls for 20–25% of the total budget being applied to the production of a good stable of ads, so be it.

(Those in retail advertising need not waste their time reading the foregoing; their energies are running in top gear every single day to attract more store and e-traffic.)

HEAT TREATMENT:
EVERY BRAND NEEDS IT

Brand building, like a woman's work, is never done. A friendly warning from Rich Teerlink: "The day we think we've got it made, that's the day we'd better start worrying about going out of business." Teerlink is worth listening to. He was formerly president and CEO of one of the most famous brands the world has ever seen: Harley-Davidson.

The pressure on brand owners is unrelenting. Brands are being challenged every week, every day, every hour. In the young days of Asian advertising, the ad agencies were recognised Idea Factories for a lot more than classical advertising, and their ideas on product enhancements, pricing, distribution — on anything to do with growing the business — were enthusiastically encouraged by the advertiser. And why not? The brand owner and the ad agency were a team!

For several reasons, this relationship in Asia has sadly declined and become more distant over the past decade or so. In a later chapter, I'll attempt to address this issue in more detail. Meanwhile, in the context of the real world today, I think ad agencies should get back on deck with a commitment to helping the heavily pressured brand owner with more and more free, "out-of-the-box" ideas. They should try adding some heat to their delivery.

At our shop we've been practising what we call a Heat Treatment programme for several years. I'll briefly take you through its delivery. Its strength is its simplicity, I feel. It costs nothing to operate. It requires no training. It involves the commitment of every single person in the ad agency's account service team to think and contribute ideas on a lateral front, on a regular basis.

With the Heat Treatment, the principle is that any new idea counts.

Present every single brand owner on the agency roster with *one new proactive idea* every single week of the year.

The Heat Treatment idea could be as small as sticking a tyre brand logo on the foreheads of all taxi drivers, or as big as having King Kong scale the Eiffel Tower wearing a Rolex watch. It could be as strange as selling ice cream to commuters on buses, or as delightful as promoting *Playboy* subscriptions to the clergy. The brief pushes everyone to be inventive and crazy in any dimension. Just be enthusiastically proactive. And take on the tough discipline of doing it every week. Make the client feel the heat — of your enthusiasm.

THE BRANDING IMPERATIVE
FOR EAST ASIA

The challenge I'm posing as an imperative is to pioneer and build a large range of Asian-owned, Asian-managed brands into powerful global power brands over the course of the next 20 years. Asia, in the context of this programme, excludes Japan but includes Australia and New Zealand.

Given that the central power and advertising creative factories of a big stable of Asian global brands would be located in Asia — and this caveat is essential — success in the world theatre would monumentally change the character and the dynamics of the communications services industry in Asia, to put it mildly.

Today's measured global advertising spend is close to $340 billion a year. Come 2020, I'm projecting that this figure will be trebled — to more than $1 trillion, reflecting the war between emerging Asian power brands and their Western and Japanese counterparts; it will be the first world branding war, so to speak.

The global carrot is patently gigantic, but the task for Asian brands to achieve global popularity is equally formidable. Currently, if you delete the national airlines and national tourism organisations of Asian countries from the equation, the cupboard of today's Asian global brands is essentially bare compared with the abundance of Western brands. This great divide also prevails even when you narrow the focus down to the Asian region. Plainly, the global journey for Asian brands will be long and tough, but like the incredible trek by Mao Zedong and his people in the late 1940s it is doable, I believe. The target I have in mind is to see 20 or more Asian power brands in the World's Top 50 Brands by the close of 2020.

In a later chapter, I'll sketch out scenarios for some Asian brands and industries that I think could score great global triumphs in the specified time frame. An underlying concern, an old chestnut, is the view among many Western critics that Asia will not get its marketing act together until it breeds a lot more entrepreneurs, and that such characters can only materialise in a liberal, free-thinking, creatively stimulating environment. And, because several Asian governments are not comfortable with such social reforms, my dream of lots of Asian brands conquering the world will always remain a "fantasy".

There's certainly substance in this Western commentary, *in the past tense.* The critics are not quite up-to-date, in my opinion. Today, Asian societies — fuelled by forces such as IT dynamics, the needs of globalisation, and the rising number of energised, internationally-educated 21st century Asians — are clearly coming to grips with the creative environment issue. But, quite correctly, they'll do it their way.

Singapore is an excellent example of focus and commitment to the agenda of developing a social and business environment where creativity sings and flourishes. It's not an easy journey. Singaporeans are deeply rooted in conservatism, and the nation's amazing growth has been heavily led (and some even say spoon-fed) by strong-willed, top-quality government leaders. But Singaporeans are a determined lot and the entrepreneurial game is now gathering momentum. Many government-controlled organisations will be steadily privatised, corporate and personal taxes have become highly competitive with Hong Kong, the excellent local universities are introducing entrepreneurship components to appropriate degree courses, the R&D programmes and budgets in technology and the sciences are the envy of Asia, and life in the arts world is looking more beautiful each passing day. Add all these initiatives to an infrastructure that has the best civil service, the best highways, best telecoms, best golf courses, best-looking parks and trees, and the most exotic cuisine experiences in the world, and surely you have some potential for creative stimulation.

Not quite. Foreign business visitors remark that Singaporeans, notably the younger business people, are too full of their own importance; they're more inclined to lecture rather than listen. This "know-all" attitude is not appealing to sensitive creative minds and somehow needs to be corrected. I'm inclined to see this arrogance as short term.

What's more important, surely, is a more open, engaging, egalitarian spirit that encourages emotions to be freely expressed. And Singapore and some of its neighbours are working on this. Emotional electricity generates creativity, whereas equivocation is negative. When a creative presentation in Asia is greeted with silence, it often means acceptance of the creative. If the same presentation took place in New York, the response would be wild cheers or a healthy debate on the work. An emotional connection takes place. Creative people and entrepreneurs live or die by their egos, and emotional stimulation is a critical force in a healthy, exciting, creative environment.

The process of shaping an appropriate creative environment and breeding and fostering large numbers of entrepreneurs across Asia is, I sense, a 5- to 10-year programme. In the short and medium term, hire or steal the best talent from other parts of the world to crusade your global ambitions.

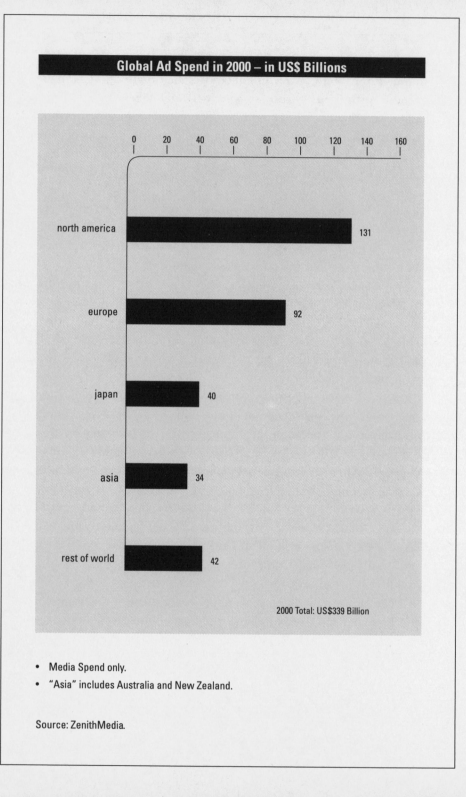

Global Ad Spend in 2000 – in US$ Billions

north america — 131

europe — 92

japan — 40

asia — 34

rest of world — 42

2000 Total: US$339 Billion

- Media Spend only.
- "Asia" includes Australia and New Zealand.

Source: ZenithMedia.

Asian Ad Spend in Year 2000 – in US$ Billions (excludes Japan)

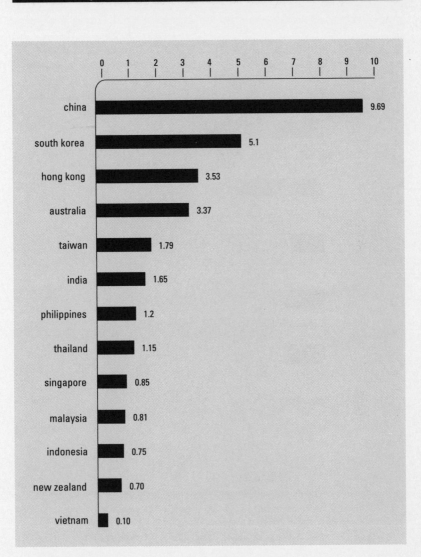

	0	1	2	3	4	5	6	7	8	9	10

china — 9.69
south korea — 5.1
hong kong — 3.53
australia — 3.37
taiwan — 1.79
india — 1.65
philippines — 1.2
thailand — 1.15
singapore — 0.85
malaysia — 0.81
indonesia — 0.75
new zealand — 0.70
vietnam — 0.10

- Media Spend only.
- As Hong Kong is an important advertising centre, it is separated from the rest of China.

Sources: AC Nielsen (except Taiwan); Rainmaker Research (Taiwan).

A Conservative Global Ad Spend Projection for Year 2020

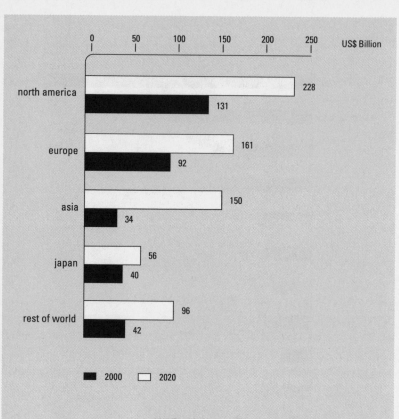

US$ Billion

	2020	2000
north america	228	131
europe	161	92
asia	150	34
japan	56	40
rest of world	96	42

■ 2000   □ 2020

2020 Total Estimate: US$691 Billion (104% increase on 2000)

- Media Spend only.
- "Asia" includes Australia and New Zealand.
- Based on a linear projection of actual Ad Spend figures from 1988 to 2000 for all regions except Asia. The growth of China and India will, I believe, increase domestic Ad Spend in these countries a minimum of ten times between now and 2020 and impact positively on the Ad Spend in the rest of Asia – hence a significantly boosted projection for all of Asia in this "conservative" chart.

Sources: World Advertising Research Center (1988–1998); ZenithMedia (1999–2000).

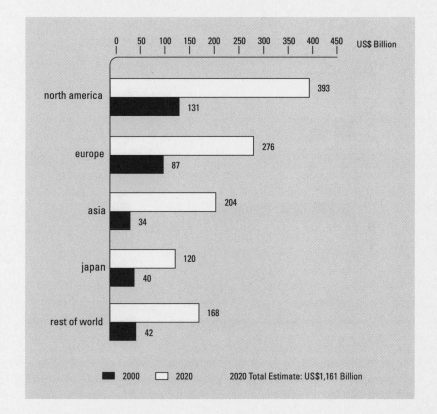

A Bold Global Ad Spend Prediction For Year 2020
(More than three times greater than Year 2000)

This projection assumes:

• Affluence in 2020 will be surging in the mighty domestic markets of China and India.

• There'll be a huge growth of Asian brands in established "Western Brands" world markets.

I'm therefore comfortably predicting a three-fold Ad Spend growth over 2000 in the mature advertising markets of North America, Europe and Japan and twice that in Asia. (I'm also picking the Rest of the World to grow four times over 2000, fuelled primarily by growth in Latin America.)

US$ Billion

	2000	2020
north america	131	393
europe	87	276
asia	34	204
japan	40	120
rest of world	42	168

■ 2000   □ 2020   2020 Total Estimate: US$1,161 Billion

• Media Spend only.

• "Asia" includes Australia and New Zealand.

A Bold Global Ad Spend Prediction for Asian Brand Owners in Year 2020 – US$400 Billion

This projection is based on several assumptions:

- A global Ad Spend in 2020 of US$1,161 billion.
- Asian companies owning close to 40% of the popular global power brands in 2020.
- Asian companies driving/controlling the marketing of their global brands from Asia.

Total global Ad Spend of Asian brand owners in 2000 is estimated to be around US$20 billion.

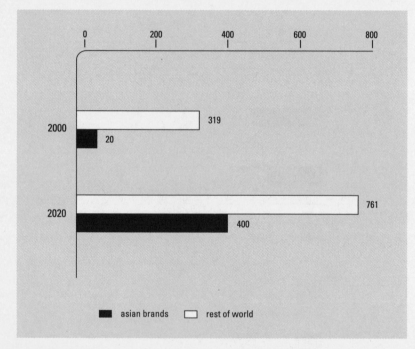

The implications of this scenario are many, but the most obvious one is that the Asian advertising industry in 2020 could be more than three times the size of today's USA advertising industry. Think about it.

Part Three

ASIA CONQUERS THE WORLD

CHAPTER 4

THE
SINGAPORE
GIRL

Before Malaysia and Singapore went their separate ways on their national airlines in 1972, there was Malaysia-Singapore Airlines. I worked on this advertising account with the Singapore-based management of MSA.

Some key brand identity seeds that subsequently manifested

The **Singapore Girl** *... the service soul of Asia's most successful airline.*

into Singapore Airlines were sown during the MSA period. The service culture was built around the inflight stewardess. Pierre Balmain designed her famous *sarong kebaya* uniform. The slogan, *A Great Way to Fly*, first appeared in the MSA ads, as did the memorable tagline, *Inflight service even other airlines talk about*. Many basic ingredients were there, and we were keen to repackage them as part of the Singapore Airlines promise, so long as the brand owner was supportive.

INVENTING THE SINGAPORE GIRL

Around the time Singapore Airlines was preparing to take to the skies, the closest cabin service competitor was arguably Thai International, which focused on the romantic experience of Thai service. If Thai International had sustained this platform, they would have been a very serious opponent. (Many believe they still are.)

Following convention, the Thai airline — like other international Asian airlines with rich, credible quality service pedigrees — bowed under the pressure of the popular global commentary and consumer research in the early 1970s. Both firmly called for a communications strategy that highlighted modern technical skills, modern aircraft, international experience, network size and Western pilots. There was nothing wrong with this thinking at the time; it was safe, conventional wisdom supported by substantial research data. It was (and still is) the marketing bible for most airline brand owners.

My experience working on the Qantas business in the 1960s had taught me many things. What registered most was the lack of forward thinking on consumer desires in an industry that was about to experience massive growth as a result of burgeoning world economies. Looking ahead, this growth would clearly trigger bigger, faster, more economically-operated aircraft, ever-expanding flight frequencies and networks, sophisticated technical maintenance and training, and increasingly cheaper airfares; which in turn would attract hordes of new business and holiday customers and transform travel into just about the world's biggest industry! The mechanics of this scenario were reasonably well-understood among airlines in the early 1970s. What was far less understood and murky was what would appeal to consumers as they evolved and matured into regular air travellers. What features of an airline's promise would be most important to travellers in 10, 15, 20 years' time? Would there be different appeals to different types of travellers?

Thinking ahead about the attractiveness of next year's product enhancements, or next year's trends or changing habits, is something you might be able to pin down through appropriate research. Thinking ahead 5 to 20 years is *not* something you can shape as a result of today's consumer inputs. Yet I think that projecting long-term consumer behaviour patterns is a desirable scenario to address in building your brand temple. If you get the foundations right, your temple can stand firm and proud for a long, long time. If you only think short term, it's likely that you'll need to rebuild your brand temple every few years — a costly, confusing, culture-sapping saga. So, for the SIA challenge, our team looked into the crystal ball and made a number of predictions.

First, that *all the national airlines of note would become increasingly homogeneous in terms of hardware benefits* — modern aircraft, networks and schedules.

Secondly, while reliability and modernity were important to customers, such attributes would eventually become basic "givens" and *the distinctive differential would increasingly relate to what goes on during the flight — the onboard travel experience, the personal service and the service-related comforts.*

The initial response from SIA marketing management to the "service" core appeal scenario was positive and lined up with their thinking, but the issue was debated for some time. We were repeatedly reminded that the airline had lofty global ambitions, but it represented a country which, in 1972, was seen in the West as a Third World city-state with creaky trishaws and flooded streets rather than a place that could produce a highly competent international airline. (Traditionally, the image of a national airline is only as strong as the image of its country.) It seemed more professional, more appropriate to build a communications strategy around the airline's experienced people, its fairly modern fleet and useful network — a safe, defensive strategy. On the other hand, the inflight service platform would play to the existing built-in strengths of the brand, and certainly differentiate SIA from Western competitors. The airline's marketing management fought tooth and nail for the service communications strategy and they prevailed. It was a brave, historical decision by SIA.

Another courageous decision by SIA was choosing my totally new, small, somewhat eclectic Singapore-incorporated company to handle the advertising for the nation's totally new and most important international brand. Numerous soul-searching sessions took place with the airline prior to them reaching their decision, but the one that still remains crystal clear in my memory 30 years later was a meeting at which I was quizzed by the airline's board of directors. They were a formidable bunch, all powerful leaders of Singapore Inc. I felt like the proverbial lamb waiting to be slaughtered. But my nervousness steadily faded away as they posed questions in a polite, dignified manner. Until the final question: "You have never run a business before, so why should we trust you to competently run our large, complex advertising business across continents?" I was stumped. I didn't have a rational answer. As a kind of knee-jerk reaction I blurted out, "Just give me a 12-month contract and if I don't perform to your satisfaction in that time, I'll rebate you all the commission that I've earned from the airline." The board members exchanged glances, stood up and silently exited the room. A few days later I got the news — Batey Ads had won the business and the client agreed to pay full commission. Even today, I still shake my head in awe at the guts of those 1972 airline decision-makers who entrusted a tiny team of youngsters to crusade their global advertising battle, rather than taking the safe route with a large, experienced world agency.

The airline launched in October 1972 as the Singapore successor of MSA and vigorously pursued inflight service as its core promise, leveraging the properties of the Balmain-designed *sarong kebaya* stewardess uniforms, and an adventurous "let's-stretch-the-envelope" spirit. From the start, a special persona was shaped around the natural, positive qualities of the stewardess.

Physically, she has the attractive, natural looks of most young Asian women, and her trim figure is ideal for the distinctive *sarong kebaya* uniform. Character-wise, she mirrors her Asian heritage — natural femininity, natural grace and warmth, and a natural, gentle way with people. For all of us working on the flight stewardess' persona — both the ad agency and the SIA marketing team — this young woman represented the essence, the soul of the airline's unique style of service, and we all got to work, enthusiastically and patiently, to build her into a very special global symbol, an icon for the airline. Following the launch period, one of the first things we did in the advertising of the flight stewardess was to *take her out of the aircraft cabin* and place her in beautiful locations across the world, usually enjoying the company of all kinds of interesting local people, young and old. There were a few reasons for this somewhat (at the time) unusual scenario. For a start, we felt it useful to spread the message that SIA was a growing global brand. Secondly, it gave us a more beautiful, more flexible canvas against which to project the natural charm and warmth of our flight stewardess and went a long way to fuel one of the airline's future cornerstone claims, *We believe in the romance of travel.*

While this plot was one expression of a different type of airline, execution saw yet another exciting opportunity to express the brand's special qualities. Some say that we were the first brand to consistently employ soft focus techniques in our still and moving pictures. I'm not sure about that, but we certainly attempted to create a visual feel that stood out from the crowd. Arguably, however, a more memorable dynamic in the early years was the soundtrack of the TV commercials. What the genius of John Ashenhurst gave to the images, so too did Pat Aulton create with the soundtracks. And it was through Pat's lyrics that *Singapore Girl* was born.

While the brief was to create a clear Singaporean identity for the flight stewardess in the soundtracks, the phrase *Singapore Girl* was initially introduced very much as a "let's-try-it-and-see" experiment. And it was left to find its own level of appeal without any hype or special PR support. The consumer playback was slow in the first season of its introduction, but we persevered with the idea. The day a rather reserved senior Singapore Government official told me that he liked what he specifically called the "Singapore Girl" TV spots, I knew the phrase was on its way to becoming a highly valuable commercial property. And consumers have happily embraced it since.

The airline's *Singapore Girl* advertising and, for that matter, all SIA advertising has never been researched before release. And the same strategic brand advertising creative always travels the world. Maybe the formula of large pictures in print, simple plots on TV and modest use of copy in both has helped us connect easily with all global tribes. We'd like to think that the advertising has the kind of personality that *touches all hearts*. In a sense, the same warm feeling everyone experiences onboard an SIA flight, wherever in the world it goes.

Not that the *Singapore Girl* advertising has not had its antagonists. Some feminist groups in Europe and the USA have taken swipes at the advertising from time to time. Their view is simple and dogmatic: the sexual attraction of the stewardess is being exploited to sell seats. The airline management is extremely sensitive to any consumer complaint, no matter how small, and they diligently address the so-called sexual issue in their vetting of all flight stewardess advertising. I personally think they are sometimes too tough on themselves in this matter. What you see in the advertising is a genuine, unabridged reflection of the inflight service personality. All the stewardesses you see in the productions are genuine SIA flight stewardesses at the time they are filmed. This policy of using only authentic cabin crew has been religiously applied since SIA took to the skies. These young women are naturally attractive Asians, with an inbuilt natural grace, charm and femininity that comes from being Asian. If the Western feminist critics toured SIA's home region and seriously connected with young Asian women, I think they'd retract their views about the airline's *Singapore Girl* advertising. However, if the critics still stand firm on this issue, so be it. I'm not going to push the barrow on the thought, "evil they who evil think".

Coming back to the fact that every single Singapore Girl you see in the advertising is the genuine article, this strict ruling has had its challenges as well as its virtues. The fact that the girls are genuine amateurs means that in front of the camera, they are usually nervous performers. And that nervousness often creates exaggerated expressions, stiff model-style movements, and too many toothy smiles. This can happen despite having carried out extensive interviews and screen tests beforehand to narrow down the choice of stewardesses. I think we can all sympathise with the young stewardess who is filmed in a foreign environment for the first time in her life, surrounded by strange production people and huge camera equipment, knowing she is the central figure in a TV commercial that will be screened across the world. It's all very overwhelming. It's only natural for her to be nervous. Our film directors are aware of this, and they patiently work on relaxing the young stewardess and shooting plenty of footage at the same time. Another technique is to move the camera crew some 100 metres or so away from the girl herself and film her with a long lens. This often relieves the tension; sometimes she doesn't know the film is rolling and we capture more interesting, spontaneous moments. It is also a practice for another stewardess to go on the film shoot with the chosen girl. Having a friend along helps relax things, and sometimes it works better to change the script on the spot and film both girls interacting to achieve the desired result. Our agency has produced containerloads of TV and print advertising for SIA since October 1972, and I take my hat off to the courage and selfless commitment of the people who made the advertising look so good — the Singapore Girls.

One other point. There's always a lot of drama going on in the world and the media tends to consistently bombard everyone with events that are negative and dark. In our tiny way, the *Singapore Girl* advertising attempts to say that the world still has a lot of positive things to offer. Indeed, we think it is a beautiful world, and it shows, we hope, in the style of the advertising. Let me share with you the lyrics of one of my favourite *Singapore Girl* soundtracks...

Everywhere I go I see you.
I feel I'm at home.
Every different road I travel
I'm never alone.
'Cause you have a gentle way about you
All around the world.
It wouldn't be the same without you,
My Singapore Girl.

Every city seems to know you,
And they want you there.
Everybody's pleased to see you
'Cause they know you care.
Such a gentle way about you
All around the world.
Wouldn't go away without you,
My Singapore Girl.

Singapore Girl, you're a great way to fly.

PUTTING THE SIA AD BRICKS TOGETHER

From the very first days of SIA, several things were clear in the mind of the brand owner: the airline was determined to be a highly profitable brand, a worthy global brand, and the best airline brand in the aviation industry. Quite a modest mission, would you not say, for the airline of one of the world's smallest nations!

To make matters more interesting, the traditional foundations on which an ambitious national airline brand is launched were a bit wobbly for SIA. Traditionally, international airlines have strong home markets to lean on. In many cases, the home traffic delivers 50% or more of the total global business. SIA's home customer traffic was projected to provide a somewhat lower percentage. Traditionally, too, the stature of a national airline is only as strong as the stature of the nation it represents. In the early 1970s, and arguably through to the mid-1980s, the image of Singapore was somewhat foggy to most people residing outside Southeast Asia. Indeed, Americans popularly perceived it as a city somewhere in China! So perhaps it is not too difficult to understand why SIA initially did things that defied traditional thinking and challenged the rules of the aviation game. Free drinks and free headsets were introduced in MSA time, but when SIA spread its wings to other continents, competitors heatedly pressed for the "free" element to be removed from SIA's agenda. Sorry, said SIA, we're in the business of providing the best service there is — and the freebies became part of SIA's unique promise. As the years rolled on, the outgoing, inventive, high-energy spirit of SIA pioneered a host of inflight services firsts and it didn't take long for the brand to become popular across the world. *Clearly, this is an unusual case of a national airline brand successfully helping to shape the global stature of its country, rather than the reverse!*

The pioneering SIA culture spread like a powerful, jasmine-scented breeze across its advertising; the challenge to do things differently and with flair embraced us all. And we loved it.

In those fledgling years our creative team in Singapore was a bunch of Asians and Caucasians led by Australian Peter Hutton, a highly sensitive, excitable chap with an incredible knowledge of Asian cultures and the Oxford Dictionary. His art director was a young New Zealand lass who had never worked in an ad agency before; she had previously designed brochures and window displays and I just hoped her great taste and madness would be right for what was needed. She eclipsed my wildest dreams. Her name is Faie Davis, a rare and beautiful talent. The art studio, acknowledged by learned locals and foreign visitors alike as Asia's best, was made up solely of Singaporeans and managed with an iron rod by Tan Keng Seng. The chief accounts person was C. K. Teng, a gentleman who had never been in advertising before. Faie nicknamed him "Terry" because his smile revealed a distinct gap between his two largest front teeth, just like British movie actor Terry-Thomas. C. K. reminded me every week that he couldn't understand how we could ever make a dollar as we ran the business like a disorganised kindergarten and that he didn't think he could stand it for long. He stayed for about 15 years.

The account service people, our infantry so to speak, were led by the trim figure of Rick Scott-Blackhall, unquestionably one of the smartest, nicest gentlemen in the universe. (Rick has shouldered the responsibility of leader on the SIA business through several decades.) Then there was the resolute Henry Lim and a bevy of beautiful young Singaporean ladies. Shortly after we started, important contributors to the growth of the airline's advertising came on board: the likes of Patrick Seow, a tough, highly disciplined manager; art director John Finn, a superb craftsman; Norman Kerr, a Scotsman with a fine pen and wit; and Banu Nathan, identified by many as the best "mother" of the SIA account.

We all worked in a building that would be generously described as a bomb shelter. The place only had one window where you could check the weather outside, but the excitement of the brand and the encouragement of the brand owner transformed our shelter, in our eyes, into a beautiful botanic garden.

In those times, neither the brand owner nor our ad agency had the luxury of much time to get things done. Long, protracted meetings on strategies and ideas were rare. The lean management crew of SIA was flat out running their expanding business and shaping new product ideas, and the ad agency was flat out providing advertisements and tabling off-the-wall product concepts. Gut judgement made decisions on creative, not research; creative approvals or changes were fast and incisive.

Mind you, not everything was always plain sailing. The airline's very active and visionary chairman, J. Y. Pillay, was also very particular about the art of the English language, or so it seemed to me. Every now and then he would query the syntax or the sentence structure of the advertising copy, and our answer never changed: "Advertising licence." On one occasion, Mr. Pillay politely mentioned to me that he didn't quite understand certain aspects of the *Singapore Girl* advertising and I sensed he was seeking a response of some intellectual depth. I recall nervously replying, "Have faith." And, thankfully, he did.

THE SIA CREATIVE TEMPLATE

Right from the outset we were single-minded and disciplined. Compared with the big global airline brands our budgets were lean and our ranks of brand builders thin.

An agency-produced document called *How We Play the Game* became the route map for everyone at the agency involved in SIA advertising, centrally and across all our associate agencies around the world. While several parts of these 1970s guidelines have long been superseded, the advertising template is an interesting historical reflection on how the creative fundamentals of the brand have been protected over time.

EXCERPTS FROM THE 1970s GUIDEBOOK
HOW WE PLAY THE GAME

Corporate Positioning Statement

"To present SIA as a highly modern, top-quality international airline of Asian origin, offering the best inflight service in the world."

The Style of SIA Advertising
The way we look. ,

Whenever possible, we go for an uncluttered expansive visual look. The number of elements should be kept to the bare essentials. We're big-picture oriented. In spaces less than a full page we favour a picture that fills nearly all the area, or a composition that allows a substantial amount of white space around the elements.

At all times, one element should dominate the presentation.

For the bulk of tactical programmes, the headline typeface should be standard: *FUTURA BOLD CONDENSED*.

For strategic advertising, the headline typeface is generally gentle — a *serif face*. The style of the face is subject to variation each year.

For the one-off "event" style of ads, complete flexibility is allowed in choice of the headline typeface and structure of grid.

The way we talk.
We're Asian and therefore essentially humble. We try to say things in a simple manner, sometimes with humour, sometimes quite straight, never smugly.

When we have a competitive hardware fact to talk about, we're inclined to tell it like it is, but restrain the headline voice visually against the power of a strong picture.

When we talk about our software, we always keep the superlatives to a few meaningful words and our copy voice is visually soft.

Overall, we don't believe in talking a lot. We try to keep headlines short and body copy down to the essential facts.

One of the few overt embellishments we allow ourselves is to tag general tactical print ads with the line "...enjoy a standard of inflight service even other airlines talk about", with optional extra "...from gentle hostesses in their *sarong kebayas*".

We never indulge in "Knocking" ads.
It's simply not compatible with our personality. Besides, why spend money advertising competitive brands?

We always think big.
Talking in a fairly humble voice is one thing. Looking impressive is something yet again. While others may think single colour pages, we think colour spreads; while others may produce six cheap mailers, we target to produce one expensive-looking piece that upstages them all. The same principle applies to sales promotions.

We always go first class.
We have always believed in turning out on parade looking like a million dollars. We will enforce this view with even greater resolve in order to achieve a stronger exclusive stance in the way we present ourselves to the public, both in media and non-media materials.

An ad selling cheap fares should reflect a sale for Mercedes-Benz cars; an inexpensive mailer must look like it cost a heap more.

When we judge our media and non-media creatives we must ask ourselves: "Is this right for the world's most exclusive airline?"

Taking on an even stronger exclusive posture, however, does not mean a more stuffy or cold attitude. Indeed, we must make every effort to preserve a distinctively engaging, warm personality.

We always look after our Singapore Girl with kid gloves.

Other than promotional fare and the one-off "event" propositions, the Singapore Girl appears in just about all media passenger advertising — sometimes as the centrepiece, sometimes as the small sign-off picture.

She is always beautiful in her Asian way, and we try to preserve a natural warmth and charm that is an integral part of her personality.

She is slightly Baptist in the type of people she mixes with — we never see her with young bucks or older men who think they're young bucks.

While she's a very caring person, and laughs and smiles quite frequently, she never gets overtly familiar with passengers.

Being an elegant and serene person, it's only natural that our girl is never caught in an inelegant pose.

Planning the Media Advertising

First, where do we stand in terms of advertising power? In the more developed countries and regions served by SIA — USA, UK, Europe, Japan, and to a slightly lesser degree, Australia — SIA is and will remain a moderate ad spender until such time as SIA starts selling soft drinks instead of airline seats.

To relate the strength of SIA's spending solely to competitive airlines' spending is narrow thinking. In an advertising context, SIA is fighting for attention against all other advertisers, and this point is of critical importance in the development of SIA advertising programmes.

For example, a schedule of five weekly TV spots for four weeks might look good vis-à-vis competitive airlines' activity, but if such a schedule gets drowned in a sea of other products' TV spots screened in the same period, the schedule is perhaps just not good enough. When we advertise we must attempt to be highly visible against all others singing their praises.

The following guidelines are interrelated. They must be assessed in tandem.

The key is concentration.

(a) Communications concentration

The marketing objective could be extensive, so too could be the range of advertising objectives.

To develop media advertising to serve all the needs can often be self-defeating because no one task achieves sufficient exposure. Indeed, media advertising is not always the right answer for certain tasks.

Identify the objectives in order of priority, both long-term, medium- and short-term.

The airline's long-term (strategic) identity is woven round superior inflight service, reflected through the Singapore Girl personality. This is our unique difference. And we must continue to nurture this difference through media advertising so long as we can uphold the promise.

The value of strategic advertising in meeting short-term sales goals is difficult to pin down. But without it, short-term sales targets will become increasingly harder to achieve.

In markets where SIA still has a formidable identity job to perform, and/or where SIA has little or no other appealing competitive communications to impart, strategic advertising should dominate media spending. This could mean strategic advertising getting as much as 70% of the budget.

In markets where SIA's identity is strong and it also offers highly competitive capacity, frequencies, promotional fare programmes and the like, strategic advertising must still nonetheless retain a fairly prominent presence — minimum 35% of total consumer media budget.

Having established what should be placed against the long-term (strategic objective), then move on to the next priority — the key medium- and short-term (tactical) objective and assess the level of media weight needed to satisfy this particular task.

Then move on to the next most important tactical task, and repeat the exercise.

Depending on the size of the budget, you might find that in order to achieve the desired levels of impact, the consumer media budget may be employed to serve just the top two or three tactical objectives.

So be it.

The other nominated objectives will simply have to be served at trade media level and/or in below-the-line (non-media) activities. Some of them might even end up with no advertising support at all. That's the way it works.

(b) Geographical concentration

While sales offices might stretch right across the country, the consumer media advertising should be geographically concentrated with the aim of achieving a good weight of exposure in those cities/regions providing the best revenue potential.

Identify the key market centres in order of priority.

Take the most important centre and evaluate what level of advertising activity is required to generate good exposure. In one city, for example, 30 half pages a year in the leading paper might achieve a big presence; in another city this schedule might reflect a small advertiser.

Then assess the second most important market zone in the same manner.

If the consumer media budget permits sound advertising exposure in, say, the two top market centres only, that's the way it has to be.

As you consolidate and grow, so too should the advertising budget, allowing you to steadily expand the geographical concentration approach to more centres.

(c) Media concentration

We believe in talking more often to a smaller but strong prospect group rather than attempting to talk to everyone less frequently.

This means employing a slim but powerful stable of media.

By ploughing the funds into a tight range of communication vehicles, you obviously achieve a more desirable level of frequency against the prime prospects, plus the opportunity to project a little more theatre at times, e.g. topping up a 30-second TV spot schedule with a few 60-second spots, running some full pages as well as half pages, and so on.

In the key market zones it is probable that the travel prospect universe for all the various propositions will be fairly high. Such being the case, a media reach of 60–70% of the target prospects should provide an adequate cover in line with SIA's marketing ambitions.

One other point: media facts and figures are great, but don't let your head totally rule all media selection decisions.

A TV spot might give you 70% wastage but its kind of theatre outsings most other media combined.

Research might tell you nine out of ten prospects read tiny bus tickets. Forget the tickets and run a massive message right down the side of the bus — even if there's no research to support the quality of viewers.

In the choice of media, let your entrepreneurial gut judgement also have a say.

(d) Scheduling concentration

The principle is to schedule in a "burst" pattern, as opposed to spreading the exposures right across the full year. For example, instead of running one press ad every week for 52 weeks, run three ads a week for 4-5 weeks at four periods of the year. And run a good TV schedule in the same periods, plus a radio schedule on top, etc. If the press burst is selling flight schedules, and the TV is selling the strategic message, and the radio is selling a package tour, no problem. One rubs off on the others. The total effect should feel big.

What Should We Realistically Expect to Achieve from the Various Forms of SIA Advertising?

With the exception of a small percentage of the travelling market (essentially the regular traveller segment), brand loyalty is not common. Even if you've heard favourably about SIA, or experienced a good flight with SIA in the past, you'll switch to another known airline if it matches your schedule better, and/or its aircraft are perceived to be better, and/or its flight is faster, and/or the price or incentive deal is more attractive.

The most effective advertising in the world can't help prop up an airline's revenue if the product does not meet the varying needs of the flying public.

This point is stressed because some people believe that good advertising will save the day for a suspect product.

Fortunately, in the case of SIA, the product is competitive in many areas of consumer wants.

But even in this situation, advertising should not be expected to perform miracles.

Advertising that promotes a very appealing flight schedule or price benefit, etc., that no other airline can match should produce an immediate response. But such advertising is not common.

The game in the airline industry is such that tangible differences of the nature described are usually marginal. A good percentage of advertising is therefore in the reminder-cum-awareness area and, at best, it can only be expected to build a favourable image for the airline, and thereby create a receptive attitude towards the product at the time the prospect decides to travel.

Predictably, a few local territory managers are not too happy about spending funds in advertising that does not directly assist in achieving short-term revenue targets. One of your key jobs is to persuade such managers to more fully appreciate the roles of the various forms of advertising.

Strategic Advertising

It does the main ongoing image-building job for the airline, and focuses on the Singapore Girl. It's a long-term investment, and we are unshaken in our belief in the value of this investment, even in rough market conditions.

There are mixed views on the weight of advertising that should be given to this category. However, strategic advertising has and will continue to be given reasonable exposure.

General Frequency/Route Advertising (Tactical)

Here we refer to communications that mainly impart flight schedule information.

While generally perceived as a means to assist short-term sales, general route advertising is perhaps the most controversial in regard to its short-term effectiveness.

In addressing itself to regular (mainly business) travellers it is clearly of low interest to a big percentage of newspaper readers.

Furthermore, a good number of communications are reminder messages, and/or do not offer a superior flight schedule benefit, and therefore, against the fairly discriminating regular traveller, the advertising effectiveness in terms of generating immediate sales could be argued.

With the exception of those ads that do have a significantly appealing flight benefit (in which case, an immediate favourable sales response is probable), it is believed that general route advertising essentially assists in steadily building more awareness of SIA's size and network, and that its key value is medium term.

This assessment could lead to some rethinking.

(a) Only use general frequency/route advertising when we have a highly superior (and appealing) benefit to sell. Which probably points to a drop in general frequency/route ad spending, or

(b) Continue along the lines already established, but fully recognise what we can expect from this form of advertising.

The size of the ad budget, awareness levels and marketing priorities should dictate which course to take.

Price-oriented Advertising (Tactical)

Package holidays, excursion fares and the like come under this category.

The potential customers usually do a lot of shopping around before they buy. Quality often gives way to price.

It's fairly essential advertising in markets where SIA has a lot of capacity to fill.

As it's primed for direct response, it's the type of advertising that can be measured for effectiveness with a reasonable degree of efficiency.

Its big defect is that it's low-yield income.

HQ client continually stresses the need to improve yields. In line with this directive, the weight of advertising and marketing energy given to price-oriented programmes must be evaluated carefully.

Special Product/Route Campaigns (Tactical)

When we want to build stronger share-of-mind for a particular product, a new product service, or a certain flight schedule, etc., we give it the clout of a full-scale (sometimes systemwide) campaign extending over several months. Most recent examples include the Business Class and First Class campaigns.

As the prime role of these campaigns is to steadily build greater awareness of specific products/specific services, the sales rewards are more medium term and the advertising should be measured in this context.

Of course, clearly defined and more easily monitored campaign propositions such as the daily London–Australia service should be expected to help improve the airline's market share fairly quickly, and the effectiveness of the advertising can be judged accordingly, given that all other things are equal.

News/Event Advertising (Tactical)

We define this to cover the announcement (only) of a new destination, new aircraft or increased frequencies, and/or a new product service feature.

It's essentially flag-waving advertising, it usually gets limited exposure and generally does little to boost immediate sales. However, it is considered valuable in helping to build the airline's stature (so long as the piece of news is formidable, and not a navel-gazing exercise).

Every now and again, however, a new story emerges that is specifically related to boosting short-term sales. One such story was the introduction of non-stop London–Singapore flights.

Further excerpts from the agency's 1970s Guidebook, *How We Play the Game*, may be read in the Appendix.

SIA — THE ETERNAL EXPLORER

Captain Kirk of *SS Enterprise* would be in his element working at SIA, because from the day they were born they've been tireless in their mission of exploring and bringing to their customers a continuous stream of new, breakthrough service ideas. It's all part of the airline's enduring core appeal to provide a unique travel experience.

Such a mission, of course, involves risk. Back in the late 1970s, at the time the airline placed one of the biggest aircraft orders in aviation history, some critics declared them crazy. History has shown that SIA made an incredibly astute decision; the new aircraft were more economical to operate, yields improved, and SIA suddenly had the most modern fleet of all international carriers in the world. This efficient aircraft "roll over" programme is now part of SIA's business culture.

When SIA got its first 747s, however, these aircraft were already in service with leading competitors so wasn't it a kind of "me too" story? Not quite. The aircraft may have looked the same from the outside, but the experience on the inside was something else. SIA promoted the largest drink menu in the skies, the largest complement of cabin crew, and the most comfortable seats. Interestingly, this campaign was launched six months before the 747s arrived to pump up the airline's stature during the early SIA days. And it worked. Later, an upper deck cocktail bar and "Slumberettes" were pioneered with the support of substantial advertising funds. We all firmly believed in beating the drum loudly with advertising that presented breakthrough propositions.

Innovations kept flowing out through the years, from food to beverages, from "live" onboard entertainment to onboard poker machines. Some of them were successful, some of them were failures. And most of them were enthusiastically supported by healthy advertising budgets. The service image of SIA grew and grew in stature. At the introduction of the bigger 747-300s — the ones with an extended upper deck — SIA was about the first to fly them so we decided to build a strong identity around the aircraft. The agency came up with the name BIG TOP. This proposed name received a divided response from SIA — some hated it, some thought it was great. The marketing chief had the casting vote and he bought it. SIA took BIG TOP to market with much fanfare, and while there were some initial negatives, the name quickly gathered positive support and BIG TOP gave the SIA brand a great boost on the world stage.

The same attitude was applied to the launch of new destinations on the network. Somehow the advertising weight and the creative combined to make these occasions wonderful, exciting celebrations for all — and I think consumers thoroughly enjoyed the entertainment.

Every year it seemed like SIA was always doing something new and bold. SIA steadily evolved to entrepreneurial status in the world aviation industry, a leader among leaders, with the Singapore Girl gently steering the way.

SUCCESS has its challenges. Once you become a global brand leader in both profits and reputation, there is a tendency to move to a defensive strategy, to protect your treasure, to look for safeguards, rather than retain the adventurous spirit that won you fame and fortune in the first place.

In SIA's case, you can bet your last dollar that, while they have enjoyed amazing success, they will never waver in their tireless commitment to provide consumers with the best air travel experience in the world.

IN a strong relationship between a brand owner and his brand-building advertising consultants, it is a very natural thing for the consultant to be an ideas machine across a lot more landscapes than media advertising. Our agency has been fortunate that SIA has provided us with a creative environment that has encouraged us to do this. Over the years, we've put up many silly ideas, and a few good ones. Frankly, we haven't always seen eye-to-eye with SIA on concepts, but it is sometimes healthy to have differing views. Critically, the airline understands our fragile egos and even our rejected ideas get a "nice try" score.

Of the number of off-the-wall ideas we have dreamt up through the years, one of my favourites related to a special anniversary. The 21st birthday of the Singapore Girl was coming up, and we wanted to do something a bit different to celebrate this event. Putting ads in the newspapers was too conventional and public relations too easy. Besides, the self-congratulatory tone would be hard to avoid, and no one wanted that. One of my ideas partners, Michael de Kretser, hit the jackpot: "How about getting the Singapore Girl displayed at Madame Tussaud's in London?"

It was a wild dream. SIA loved the idea. In all its illustrious history dating back to 1835, Madame Tussaud's had upheld a strict policy of displaying only world famous individuals and *never* any commercial icons. And certainly, Tussaud's had never displayed any personality from Southeast Asia before. Anyway, we somehow convinced the Madame Tussaud's people to break with tradition. And so the Singapore Girl entered the history books of this world-famous establishment as the first commercial identity ever to make an appearance there. It was a memorable 21st birthday for this young lady.

I would urge all ad agency consultants to engage more vigorously in non-advertising, brand-building ideas with their clients. It makes the game so much more stimulating.

The **Singapore Girl** *makes her debut in 1972.*

Strategic brand advertising in the 1970s.

A FEW HOURS GRACE BEFORE THE MADNESS STARTS ALL OVER AGAIN.

In today's business world you must put time aside to slow yourself down.

And one place you can do that is in the privacy of our Business Class cabin. Relaxing in an exclusively-designed seat some airlines would be pleased to call First Class.

Here, as you stretch out in an area roomier than you imagined, decisions are deliberated at your leisure.

It's your prerogative to change your mind over the choice of drink, or whether to have Lobster Newburg, Rib Eye Steak or Szechuan Fried Fish. It doesn't matter that those extra

documents made your baggage heavy. Our Business Class allowance is thirty kilos.

And it was good to find that we reserved your favourite seat when your secretary booked the ticket. And that our Premium Accommodation Plus service has your hotel confirmed well

ahead. But from this height, as you leisurely consider another brandy offered by our gentle hostesses in sarong kebayas, any problems on the ground are starting to look a little *SINGAPORE AIRLINES* insignificant. aren't they? *BUSINESS CLASS*

IT'S NOT ONLY OUR INFLIGHT SERVICE THAT OTHER AIRLINES TALK ABOUT.

Fly from Singapore via Bahrain to London in just over 9 hours. Any Tuesday, Thursday, Saturday. On our supersonic Concorde. Return flights depart London for Singapore on Monday, Wednesday, Friday. *SINGAPORE AIRLINES*

SIA Concorde operated in association with British Airways.

Tactical brand advertising through the 1970s and 1980s...

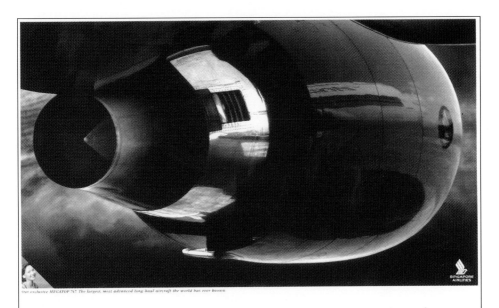

Our exclusive MEGATOP 747. The largest, most advanced long-haul aircraft the world has ever known.

THE WORLD'S YOUNGEST, MOST MODERN FLEET.

MAINTAINING THE MOST MODERN FLEET IN THE WORLD
REQUIRES A HEALTHY SUPPLY OF DOM PERIGNON.

As our inflight service sets the standard that even other airlines talk about, it should come as no surprise that we are celebrating our recent acquisition of over a billion dollars of new aircraft with nothing less than Dom Perignon.

Gentle hostess in your sarong kebaya across four continents of the world's most modern fleet. Singapore Girl, you're a great way to fly.

SINGAPORE AIRLINES

Strategic brand advertising in the 1980s and 1990s...

All around the world, Singapore Girls give a great way to fly.

SINGAPORE AIRLINES

1947-1997

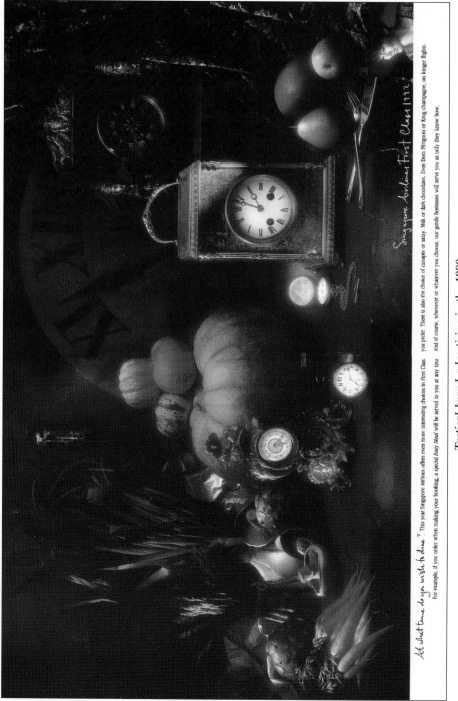

Tactical brand advertising in the 1990s.

WHERE WOULD YOU EXPECT TO ENJOY THE TRANQUILITY OF A DESERTED ISLAND FROM THE SHADE OF A COCONUT PALM?

AND EXPLORE THE SIGHTS OF A BUSTLING CITY FROM UNDER A TRISHAW CANOPY?

TO SEE CLOTH DRAGONS FLUTTER IN THE FRENZY OF A CHINESE PROCESSION?

AND AN ENDLESS PARADE OF EXOTIC GEMS AT DUTY-FREE PRICES?

Singapore

THE MOST SURPRISING TROPICAL ISLAND ON EARTH

WHERE WOULD YOU EXPECT TO SEE BEJEWELLED INDIAN GIRLS BEGUILE YOU WITH SPARKLING EYES?

AND SAMPLE MARINATED MALAY SATAY UNDER A STAR-STUDDED SKY?

TO FIND ANTIQUE CHINESE BUMBOATS STILL PLYING THEIR TRADE?

AND BUY FUTURISTIC TIMEPIECES AT PRICES FROM A BYGONE AGE?

Singapore

THE MOST SURPRISING TROPICAL ISLAND ON EARTH

One giant picture. No more than 60 words of copy.

Evolution of the **Surprising Singapore** *theme.*

A new theme is now in place: **New Asia Singapore.**

The mother of all brochures is now a collector's item.

CHAPTER 5

BRANDING A COUNTRY

Numerous disparate dynamics obviously contribute towards the brand identity of a country, and the negative effort of just one small part can seriously upset the good work of all the other parts. That's life. In the context of this chapter, my focus is just on the part that I have a bit of knowledge about — tourism branding for Singapore.

Booming global economies from the late 1960s onwards predictably fuelled huge growth in world tourism. National and state tourism organisations materialised overnight to try to net a decent share of this very attractive bounty. For some, the task has been relatively easy. Britain and Spain historically have strong tourism reputations, awesome tourism magnets, good infrastructures, substantial inbound air and sea services, and so on. On top of all these assets comes the icing on the cake, with the world media consistently providing a generous helping of free publicity about these popular places.

Singapore, like many of its Asian neighbours, has had to battle harder to pull in sizeable tourism traffic. But it's worth the effort. In 2000, for example, tourism contributed nearly $6 billion to Singapore's economy.

When Singapore seriously got into the tourism business at the start of the 1970s, it didn't have a whole lot going for it. And lack of money was one reason why. So a clever colleague of mine at Jackson Wain, the ad agency I worked for at the time, allegedly helped convince the Singapore Government to introduce a small tax on all hotel and restaurant bills at tourist-related establishments. This tax revenue underwrote the growth and development of the Singapore Tourism Board. Interestingly, the scheme created a chicken-and-egg dilemma. The Tourism Board had to attract more tourists to get more money to attract even more tourists, if you know what I mean.

Several other challenges faced Singapore in the early days. First, its image ranking as a holiday destination was low and vague in most Western countries which, at the time, were the stronger markets to address. Secondly, the nation's more exotic characteristics, while attractive to Westerners, were like "selling coal to Newcastle" for Asian visitors, with the possible exception of the Japanese (but they were relatively small in numbers in the early 1970s). And to make matters even more exciting, the government's urban modernisation agenda didn't exactly match the promise of the "unique foreign experience" that tourists generally seek.

Against this, Singapore's strategic location was a huge plus, and Singapore was clearly the best duty-free shopping warehouse in

Southeast Asia. These two things appealed to all visitors.

As the 1970s moved aside for the 1980s, our agency got involved with the Tourism Board's global advertising campaign for the first time. The main emphasis was against visitor traffic from selected Western markets. We put everything behind the multiracial character of Singapore and created the umbrella tagline, *The most surprising tropical island on earth.* I would rank this campaign among the best our agency has ever produced. It did a number of things that were a bit unusual at the time. In print, we developed five different large-space colour ads and rotated them in popular magazines in a series of bursts throughout the year. The method proved successful in generating high recall. Somehow, the readers felt we were talking to them every week, whereas in reality the ads ran on a cycle of five consecutive weekly issues (with a different ad each week) followed by 12 weeks off, thus giving us three bursts a year. The TV commercials followed much the same pattern.

Undoubtedly, however, the most unusual development was the creative work itself. Standard research dictated that consumers love to get loads of tourist destination information, which pointed to long copy. Our creative people had no problem with the need for information, but questioned the need for long copy. Instead, taking on board the media plan, each of the five advertisements carried no more than an average of 60 words of copy and the 60 words embraced four different tourist subjects. Which meant a healthy menu of *20 different tourism topics* was promoted in each advertising burst. The graphic energy of using just *one* giant picture in each advertisement also challenged convention — tourism advertising generally calls for a gallery of pictures in each advertisement. The end result was an egoistic and commercial triumph for both the brand owner and the ad agency.

But this fairy tale was short-lived. The reshaping of Singapore into a smart, pristinely clean, contemporary place where things worked like a Swiss watch was casting an increasingly longer shadow over the rustic, traditional, multiracial expressions that drew Western visitors to Singapore. On the flip side, this reshaping started to attract more and more Asians to the city-state, with the Japanese (the largest of the Asia pack) caught a little in between.

The older, less urbanised Japanese visitors tend to favour things more modern, whereas the younger, educated Japanese bend more towards what the Westerners looked for in Singapore. On all fronts, the most critical visitor magnet — duty-free shopping — was steadily losing its "great bargains" power as a result of the strengthening Singapore currency. It was time to be more aggressive, said the new brand managers at the Tourism Board, as they got out their scalpels and magic markers.

The tagline, *The most surprising tropical island on earth*, was slashed to *Surprising Singapore*. Strategic print ads had a mandatory eight or more pictures in each advertisement. (The Tourism Board Chairman at the time made it a discipline to only approve ads with this number of pictures.) Different campaigns were developed for Japan, the rest of Asia, and Western markets. Other short-term tactical measures were introduced to harness more tourism interest.

It was an impressive demonstration of energy, but was it going in the right direction? Some experts called for full focus on selling Singapore as a sole-destination package, other people felt a short stopover proposition was the best story, while characters like me favoured the hub concept, selling Singapore as the capital of an exciting holiday region. All these marketing routes were worthy strategies, but all had different appeals to different international travellers. A clearer map needed to be drawn. But an even more critical question was then put on the table: what exactly should the Singapore Tourism product be all about? Should it try to be all things to all people, appealing equally to the Japanese, the rest of Asia and Westerners alike? Or should it try to be more attractive to the bigger-spending Japanese or the more upmarket Western tourists? The scenarios were numerous.

Then some bright Singaporeans stepped forward and said something like this: "It's time to get our priorities right. Tourism is big business, but what's more important is to evolve Singapore into a place that's the pride and joy of its citizens for generations to come. So let's try to shape a physical environment for a Singapore of the future that will have long-term appeal to Singaporeans and, at the same time, will also be a highly attractive tourism product for Asian and Western visitors alike."

Not long after, a Tourism Board-led committee released a paper that mapped out a future landscape for Tourism Singapore, keeping firmly in mind the lifestyle aspirations of Singaporeans, their growing interest in historical Singapore, and their bonding with their multiracial cultures. The fruits of this carefully crafted landmark paper have steadily transformed Singapore into a vibrant, cosmopolitan global city, with a distinctive multiracial character. The twin agendas of satisfying Singaporeans and attracting more visitors have been successful, but the architects of Singapore are not renowned for resting on their laurels. They're consistently focused on the task of making things even better. Looking ahead, this challenge appears quite daunting. The home population is targeted to grow from 4.1 million to 5 million by 2030, and arguably the present annual visitor numbers of 7 million will double over the next 30 years. It's a tiny island, but somehow I think they'll work out something.

Now, I'd like to go back a bit in time and share with you a few more campaigns and ideas we created for the tourist promotion of Singapore.

THE MOTHER OF ALL BROCHURES

At some point in the 1980s we asked ourselves, what do people want when they're looking for a place to go? Everyone looks for a brochure. So we said, let's create the mother of all brochures!

To start with, it had to be larger than life. So we made it 14 inches deep and each spread ran some 21 inches across. No two spreads in the book were alike; each had a holiday in terms of graphic freedom and structure. And the mix of different styles of illustrations compounded the overall potpourri delivery. And then we got someone who creates kids' books to shape some of the spreads into cutout, flip-up, flip-down dimensional interactive experiences. The brochure was a success. More than 100,000 copies were distributed. It has since become a collector's item.

The graphic energy of the brochure overshadowed, to a large

extent, the contributions made by the writer of this piece. And it was brilliant copywriting, I feel. Here are some extracts:

The hotels are monuments to their architects, the shopping emporia such that the islanders dress up to visit them.

*

"CONTINUING HOT."
(End of weather forecast.)

*

Island of many faces.

The Monkey God, the legend goes, was once only King of the Monkeys until corrupted by ambition he stole the elixir of immortality. Consolidating it with a peach of eternal life from the trees in Heaven, he next apprenticed to a sorcerer and learnt not only how to translate himself into any form, all-seeing and all-hearing, but to turn every hair of his body into a replica of himself to confound his enemies. He then stole, for a fighting staff, the iron rod which controlled the tides and learnt how to somersault 6,000 leagues. Finally he challenged the Jade Emperor of Heaven, was crushed in spite of his extensive insurance and obliged in penance to join the Pig-Headed God and a Patriarch in bringing the teachings of Buddha from India to China, overcoming on the journey 999 mortal obstacles. Ho ho, you say, believe that and you'll believe anything. But if you should happen to be in Singapore over either Festival of the Monkey God's Birthday, attend it. You will see a medium possessed by his tortured spirit, his held-down body flailing as the drum beats climax and the incense fills the air, his blood flowing as he gashes himself with a proffered sword. Dressed by assistants in the Monkey God's clothes he then runs amok, leaping and cartwheeling over the altars until eventually he falls silent and inscribes, on 4 pieces of paper placed before him, 4 ambiguous figures which fortunehunters will use every arcane skill to decipher. Finally 5 men in Monkey God costumes and in a state of trance, long spears driven through their cheeks, lead a procession in which a sedan chair, untouched by human hand but now itself possessed, rocks wildly in a frenzy of its own. Now see if you ho ho quite so loudly.

The Singaporean enjoyment of food verges on preoccupation....

Peking Duck is alive and well at several highly recommended establishments, and what the Hainanese chefs can do with chicken it would be unkind to dwell on.

And for something utterly different, you must try a "hawker centre". Overheads being almost non-existent, the prices make you wonder how it's worth their while... and if hygiene worries you, it needn't.

In Singapore, cleanliness runs godliness the closest second in the business.

*

What can you do in Singapore that you can't do anywhere else? An evening cruise in an ancient Chinese junk, supper served by lantern-light as the famous skyline dissolves into the dusk? Coffee on a Sunday morning at the slightly dotty Birdsong Concert? Have tea with an orang-utan as fond of a joke as the next man....

*

Chinatown you must see, dusty and private, a fabulous Indian temple rubbing shoulders with the rather alarming consulting rooms of Nelson Ho Kwok Wah, Physician in Eye Cataract, Sprain, Rheumatism and Fracture...

*

Illuminated glass lift capsules dart their passengers silently up giant stalks from polished-marble promenades half the size of football pitches. And these are average hotels...

*

Be caught with drugs and your flight home may be delayed by 30 years. Be caught with a serious quantity and you might as well get a refund on your ticket for your next of kin.

*

The author of those words, Duncan Sinclair, worked on an old typewriter. None of the letters lined up with each other. When his copy came in you'd see words that had been crossed out on the typewriter. He found it difficult to articulate a view verbally, perhaps because he had a nervous stammer. And when you praised his writing he always displayed surprise. I've found that genuine creative souls like Duncan are rarely satisfied with their work.

The brochure scored high marks among Asians as well as Westerners, yet another demonstration that a strong, simple idea can transcend racial and cultural differences. It also pleased its creators by winning critical acclaim in global advertising contests, notably a Silver Pencil at the London D&AD awards. A copy of the brochure is lodged in the permanent archives of the Victoria & Albert Museum, London.

THE MOTHER OF ALL DIRECT RESPONSE ADS, MAYBE

Having done the mother of all brochures, we wanted the mother of all coupon response ads to help circulate it. How best to do this? We felt we needed to create a series of print ads that were more immediate, more newsy in character. We also felt that we needed a large variety of them to run in tightly packed media bursts.

The media thinking nearly gave the available budget a heart attack. But the solution was soon identified: forget costly full colour ads in favour of black-and-white ads; dismiss insertions in glossy travel magazines in favour of the hard news section of daily newspapers. The direct response daily press campaign took off like a rocket and coupon response for the brochure was good, but not for long. We didn't keep to the recipe; the variety of ads gradually got thinner, the frequency of insertions steadily faded from high to low gear. Here was a sad case of not sticking firmly to one's guns. Thankfully, the brochure kept circulating well under its own steam — it was a creative giant.

In 1891, they began clearing some of the densest jungle in Singapore. Needless to say, they were making room for the first golf course. Under the tropical heat, colonial sportsmen worked their way round to the 18th hole with only the occasional interruption from wild boars, monkeys or pythons. And then it was on to evening cocktails at Raffles Hotel. As it still is today. Only now, Singapore boasts a wealth of golf clubs, tennis clubs, windsurfing and waterskiing clubs and facilities for every sport under the tropical sun. Where every day of the year, the warmth of the welcome is only matched by the warmth of the weather. And to give you a taste of what else awaits you on a holiday in Singapore, we have produced an exciting, colorful book that does more than capture the flavour of the island. It will give you a glimpse of the exquisite fare, the exotic festivals, the irresistible shopping and the tapestry of cultures that make up Singapore. Send off for it now. It could do wonders for your handicap.

Three bogies, one birdie, two eagles and a rather nasty python on the last hole.

Singapore

Please send me your free book on Singapore so I can drive myself crazy wishing I was already there.

My Name

My Address

Town/City   Zip Code

Send to: The Singapore Tourist Promotion Board, P.O.Box 67D94, Century City, California 90067 USA.

P.S. For the uninitiated, Singapore is only 3 hours north of Australia.

The mother of all direct response ads. The campaign defied convention by running black-and-white in newspapers.

Looks like your dinner's in the drink again.

Who wouldn't be, after being drowned in half a bottle of brandy? Which is how you cook Drunken Prawns, one of Singapore's more flamboyant local delicacies. Or if that's not your tipple, why not try something a little more old-fashioned like Hundred Year Old Eggs, for instance? Then for the more adventurous, there's Fresh Sting Ray, or when you're really hungry, there's nothing like sinking your teeth into a mouthwatering Fish Head Curry, Bacon and Eggs? No problem either. But why not go the whole hog? Roast Suckling Pig's a Singapore specialty too. In fact, there's very little here that isn't a local favourite. Singaporeans love their food, and to prove it, boast some of the finest chefs in the world as well as the most tantalising array of Chinese, Indian, Indonesian, Thai, Malaysian, Japanese and Western foods. Would you like to see the menus? No problem. Send off the coupon for our free colourful book that will more than whet your appetite for a holiday in Singapore. For starters, it shows you the scenery, the shopping, and the hotels, with the jungles, the wildlife and the festivals to follow. To say the least, it's somewhat intoxicating.

SINGAPORE

Please send me your free book on Singapore so I can drive myself crazy wishing I was already there.

My Name

My Address

Town/City   Zip Code

Send to: The Singapore Tourist Promotion Board, Suite 1604, Level 16, Westpac Place, 60 Margaret Street, Sydney 2000.

What some people feel like first thing in the morning in Singapore.

You'll soon wake up when you realise who you're having breakfast with in Singapore! Ah Meng, the most delightful orangutan you've ever shared a tea-pot with, entertains a select group of visitors every morning at the Singapore Zoo. She's particularly fond of buttered croissants and freshly-squeezed orange juice. Yours, normally. Or for other people, breakfast with the birds is more their cup of tea. Exotic singing birds entertain with a delightful melodic concert every morning in the peaceful setting of the Jurong Bird Park Tea Garden. And as for the rest of the day? There's no end of surprises around every corner in Singapore. Parrots on bicycles, Chinese fortune-tellers, festivals for Hungry Ghosts, Monkey Gods. You'll find them all in the lavish, colourful book we have produced on holidays in Singapore, that is yours for free. Send off for it now. It'll certainly open your eyes.

SINGAPORE

It's not a UFO.

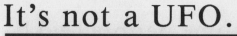

Twisting and twirling through the air it orbits the chef's head at lightning speed. And in a flash, it whistles down to earth for a perfect landing on your plate. Spicy minced lamb folded in a paper-thin pancake, served with a bowl of steaming hot curry, a murtabak from Zam Zam restaurant is a meal in itself. But is it as good as Indonesian Nasi Padang? Or as succulent as Chinese chilli crab at Choon Seng? There's only one way to find out. For starters, send off for our lavish, colorful book on Singapore. Feast your eyes on the menus

It's a Murtabak from Zam Zam.

of our many different, and exquisite, Malaysian, Indonesian, Indian and Chinese restaurants. Drool over the tropical islands, the steaming jungles, the exotic festivals and irresistible shopping that are all part of a holiday in Singapore. It's free, and it's yours when you send off the coupon. Do it now if you really want to whet your appetite.

Singapore

P.S. For the uninitiated, Singapore is only 3 hours north of Australia.

THE SAVING OF RAFFLES HOTEL

Its owners would say that a visit to Singapore is incomplete without a tipple or two at Raffles Hotel. Nestling like a proud Victorian duchess among the steel and glass of surrounding skyscrapers, Raffles is recognised worldwide as Singapore's best-known landmark. However, it would have been history, so to speak, but for the dogged determination of the Singapore Tourism Board.

As far back as the 1960s it was apparent that Raffles needed a huge facelift to keep it looking stately and appealing to travellers. No money was forthcoming. Raffles continued its decline and by the 1980s it faced the distinct possibility of the death sentence, with the extremely valuable government-owned land on which it stood being converted into a massive commercial skyscraper block.

This is when the local Tourism Board stepped into the fray and saved the Grand Old Lady. But it was by no means an easy victory. The battle had all the trappings of a big court case. The prosecutors — the government bureaucrats — strongly argued for the demolition on several grounds: more efficient land use in tiny Singapore; the commercial development would boost the country's business infrastructure agenda; more riches for the Treasury; and who needed to keep a dying old colonial relic anyway!

The defence — the Tourism Board team — went straight for the heart and soul, but also dangled a long-term financial carrot. Their platform: Singaporeans were becoming increasingly bonded to historical Singapore; Raffles was a unique gem in the world; a beautifully restored Raffles would (once again) become a treasured tourist icon; and the restored building would also send out a positive signal about the sensitive, artistic side of a maturing global city.

The final decision rested with the Cabinet, notably the Minister for National Development at that time. The Tourism Board was instructed to produce its proposal in document form and to submit the document to the Minister's office several days in advance of an official meeting between the two parties. We had about a week to put the whole thing together. Our agency excitedly got immersed in the creation and production of the document, which ended up as a rather lavish full colour, 20-page hardcover coffee-table size production. Each page was meticulously designed, all the text explaining the concept was immaculately typeset, and many pages featured illustrations of what the restored Raffles would look like. We burned the midnight oil, about a dozen copies of the document were printed, and half of them were delivered to the Ministry for the relevant people to read prior to the meeting with the Minister himself. Everything seemed to be going to plan. A team of about five of us rehearsed what we should each present at the meeting. We agreed to keep our slide presentations short and sweet, essentially summarising our proposal. We certainly didn't need to talk in detail about the proposed concept as that was well chronicled in the document sent days earlier to the Ministry.

The venue for the meeting was a large, cold room in a hotel. The seating arrangement reminded me of an old cowboy movie where you'd see the sheriff and his posse hunched together on the judgement bench, directly facing several defendants sitting behind a long wooden table about 15 feet away. As is customary at meetings of this kind, our team arrived about 60 minutes before the scheduled start. We tested the slide projector, the carousel drum, and the slides — no problems. And then we waited.

The Minister and his entourage entered the room, right on the button. They sat down and our first presenter went straight into his talk and slide show. Things went smoothly for three minutes at which point the Minister himself raised his hand and quietly said something like:

"Excuse me for interrupting, but I think it would be more useful to know the strategy and concept details of the proposal before you give us the summary points."

A stony silence filled the room. We sat there in shock. Eventually one of us bravely spoke up: "Minister, the document explaining everything was delivered to your Ministry last week."

The Minister immediately eyeballed his colleagues and as one they disavowed all knowledge of having seen our prized document.

I'm not sure if there's a crisis management course on what to do in situations like this, but I do know that I was looking for a big hole to hide in. Thankfully, our team leader had the strength and composure to quickly verbalise a picture of the core thrust of our proposal. We left the meeting feeling a bit depressed.

Shortly after, the government made its decision. The Tourism Board's proposal was approved. And Singapore's Grand Old Lady was restored to her former glory.

THE relaunch of Raffles Hotel took place in the early 1990s. I had a phone call from the brand owner asking if we'd like to handle the communications programme. They wanted to inform the world about the rebirth and there were a few other things to address such as the hotel's logo and major in-house literature. The task was made somewhat more exciting by the size of the worldwide budget — $200,000! Under normal circumstances, one would advise a client with this budget and brief to either rethink his game plan or rethink his publicity budget. But Raffles was like family to us, and for family we just had to bend over backwards.

The richness of Raffles Hotel's soul needs little explanation and establishing the brand strategy was not exactly a test of one's creative skills. The *real* test was how best to employ the limited global publicity budget. The expenditure breakdown ended up close to this: logo design/in-house literature, 15%; small, eclectic-style ads in vertical media like *New Yorker*, 25%; public relations, 60%. The logo and literature design work was handled by our design department; the PR by a member of our group, MDK Consultants.

The tiny ads did a fine job, I'm told, spreading the Raffles message, but by far the most potent of our weapons was public relations. Here we managed to get a number of great global columnists with extensively syndicated columns to come and stay at Raffles, and then to write about their experiences. (One columnist, for example, was syndicated across 200 newspapers in Europe and the USA.) This idea proved to be immensely successful and the excellent editorial coverage enjoyed by Raffles has still a knock-on value today. It's probably fair to say that Raffles Hotel has now achieved "institution" status, not bad for a brand that was on its deathbed not so long ago.

SHE WAS, HE SAID,
AN ARISTOCRATIC EIGHTY YEAR OLD

French lady and he loved her with a passion that bordered on the physical. The young receptionist reached for her pen. The caller went on to explain that he would be coming to Singapore during the first week in March. And his travelling companion would be arriving a few days earlier. Could arrangements be made to look after the old lady in his absence? Despite her impeccable French pedigree, he said, she was liable on account of her great age to be a touch cantankerous. The receptionist explained that the hotel was always delighted to look after elderly ladies, cantankerous or otherwise. Let's hope so, the caller added. She was the one true love of his life and had survived all three of his marriages. Somewhat taken aback by this demonstration of gallic candour, the girl inquired if the gentleman had any particular suite in mind? Just put her in the garage he said. When she finally arrived, the gleaming 1908 Peugeot quietly excelled all expectations in the Singapore to Malaysia vintage car rally.

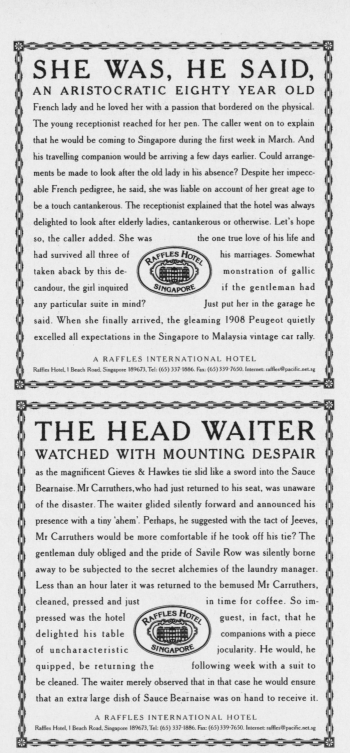

A RAFFLES INTERNATIONAL HOTEL

Raffles Hotel, 1 Beach Road, Singapore 189673, Tel: (65) 337-1886. Fax: (65) 339-7650. Internet: raffles@pacific.net.sg

THE HEAD WAITER
WATCHED WITH MOUNTING DESPAIR

as the magnificent Gieves & Hawkes tie slid like a sword into the Sauce Bearnaise. Mr Carruthers, who had just returned to his seat, was unaware of the disaster. The waiter glided silently forward and announced his presence with a tiny 'ahem'. Perhaps, he suggested with the tact of Jeeves, Mr Carruthers would be more comfortable if he took off his tie? The gentleman duly obliged and the pride of Savile Row was silently borne away to be subjected to the secret alchemies of the laundry manager. Less than an hour later it was returned to the bemused Mr Carruthers, cleaned, pressed and just in time for coffee. So impressed was the hotel guest, in fact, that he delighted his table companions with a piece of uncharacteristic jocularity. He would, he quipped, be returning the following week with a suit to be cleaned. The waiter merely observed that in that case he would ensure that an extra large dish of Sauce Bearnaise was on hand to receive it.

A RAFFLES INTERNATIONAL HOTEL

Raffles Hotel, 1 Beach Road, Singapore 189673, Tel: (65) 337-1886. Fax: (65) 339-7650. Internet: raffles@pacific.net.sg

Small eclectic ads in vertical media relaunched Raffles Hotel.

BOWING TO PUBLIC PRESSURE, RAFFLES HOTEL OPENS A SINGLES BAR.

Which immediately presents us with two problems.
The first problem first: Young men, eager to cohabit with lithe members of the opposite sex are not encouraged to invade the Bar & Billiard Room.

(Well, having said that, let us hasten to add they are most welcome to attempt enjoyment of the prime purpose of this advertisement.)

Which raises the second problem: We are offering you tonight an unbridled opportunity to explore some of Scotland's finest achievements.

means that the youngest of the whiskies has been aged for at least 12 years, whilst the others are anyone's guess, laddie.

Whereas a 12-year old single malt whisky is purely and precisely that: one grand old whisky in all its majestic and undiluted glory.

distiller's art itself. The subtle aromas and flavours have never been quite fully explained, possibly because no one is sufficiently sober afterwards.

THE FACT THAT a proud single malt calls to

mind the misty glens, heather-blanketed hillsides, crystal streams teeming with trout, skirling pipes, etcetera, should also call to mind one other minuscule detail: *the price.*

Rest assured, with all their true canny, the Scots will endeavour to extract as much money from your pocket as they can in exchange for their best single malts. And who's to blame them?

The most noble array of single malt Scotch Whisky, this side of Skye.

However, there is a prevailing view that a single malt whisky is but another manifestation of the Scottish national trait: reluctance to part with things of value.

Like money.

Or whisky.

Sadly, many a novice Scotch drinker is convinced that a single malt whisky will not deliver his money's worth, whereas a bottle containing several malt whiskies will.

Ah, clever people the Scots. For nothing could be further from the truth.

THE TRUTH IS, a blend is merely a blend. Read our lips: A 12-year old blended whisky

HAVING GRASPED THAT inescapable fact, you may think the rest is easy. Not so, for the Scots are full of contradictions.

As if foreseeing the day when our Bar & Billiard Room would voraciously pry sizeable quantities of their precious single malt whiskies from their homeland, the Scots set about giving them virtually unpronounceable names.

Glenfiddich, Glenmorangie, Dalwhinnie, Auchentoshan, Bladnoch and Laphroaig. A fiendish deterrent, indeed, but one which can be simply overcome by the use of our single malt whisky guide and an index finger.

One final hurdle remains.

Unravelling the mysteries of classic single and rare malt whiskies is as daunting as the

OF COURSE, OUR Bar & Billiard Room offers many other aristocratic distractions.

A Krug, the Grande Cuvee predictably.

Or La Grande Dame 1985, secured at no little expense from the House of Veuve Clicquot.

Or an amber Belle Vue Gueuze from Belgium's master brewers.

Not forgetting the most fastidious array of fine armagnacs, cognacs, ports, coffees and Valrhona chocolates ever to be savoured over a lazy game of billiards.

SUCH IS THE Bar & Billiard Room. If not a singles bar, by every means a singular bar. And a haven which awaits you after work, after dinner or after the theatre, tonight and every night.

Full page business press in Singapore. A brand with a unique soul should be celebrated single-mindedly, if not single-maltedly.

FOR YEARS THE BAR AND BILLIARD ROOM WAS PATRONISED BY SOMERSET MAUGHAM.

AS WAS EVERYONE ELSE.

"Observing these people, I am no longer surprised there is a scarcity of domestic servants back in England."

SUCH COMMENTS did not endear him to Singapore's colonial elite.

Yet he strongly believed the world's best stories were to be found in the East.

Which consequently led to many of his stories starting the same way.

Or to be more precise, in the same place.

The Bar and Billiard Room.

At least two of his books, "A MOON AND SIXPENCE" and "OF HUMAN BONDAGE" were written in the hotel.

He was often found reclined in a leather armchair beneath a blue Havana haze spiralling up to lazy ceiling fans, absorbing the atmosphere, the alcohol and the lives of the expatriate planters.

Busily recording notes to be used, incriminatingly, later.

At other times, he'd be surrounded by an appreciative crowd. All laughing a little too loudly at his scything repartee.

But Maugham was also a great listener; patiently sitting and inquiring of your life as if you were the most interesting person he'd ever met.

Queues of adoring expatriate wives would divulge their personal stories to his attentive ear.

Like lambs to slaughter.

Not surprisingly, many of them were far from happy on finding their thinly-disguised lives, graphically mocked in the pages of his books.

There's no pleasing some people.

After all, he couldn't be expected to insult everyone in person.

"AMERICAN WOMEN EXPECT TO FIND IN THEIR HUSBANDS A PERFECTION THAT ENGLISH WOMEN ONLY HOPE TO FIND IN THEIR BUTLERS", he once penned.

When accused of rudeness, he retorted in a fittingly Maugham-esque manner: "THE RIGHT PEOPLE ARE RUDE, THEY CAN AFFORD TO BE."

Not that Maugham was completely misunderstood. Aleister Crowley once stated, "THOUGH MANY MAY RESENT THE CURIOUS TRICK HE HAS OF SAYING SPITEFUL THINGS ABOUT EVERYBODY, I HAVE ALWAYS FELT THAT LIKE MYSELF, HE MAKES SUCH REMARKS WITHOUT MALICE, FOR THE SAKE OF CLEVERNESS."

A fine testimonial which may not have been helped by Crowley's own notoriety, for being voted the wickedest man alive.

Whatever his faults, Maugham was undoubtedly a charming character who only added to the legend that is this graceful old hotel in the tropics.

The Raffles Bar and Billiard Room has long been synonymous with the famous and infamous.

And with its history come the finest cognacs, champagnes, single malt whiskies, vintage beers, connoisseur coffees and chocolates.

Along with some of the legendary conversation, to which many have been attracted and some subjected.

Poster campaign.

IT ONLY TAKES A COUPLE OF DRINKS TO BRING OUT THE COWARD IN YOU.

It was in March 1930 that Noel Coward and a friend quietly slipped into Singapore Harbour aboard an old Danish freighter from Siam. His friend was promptly rushed to the nearest hospital to spend a month recovering from dysentery.

NOEL, ON THE other hand, was rushed to the Raffles Hotel where he was to recover from a badly creased tuxedo.

Sitting on the verandah on his first night, the poor chap thought that he would die from the stifling humidity.

He should have been grateful.

After all, it was this weather that would eventually lead to him writing 'MAD DOGS AND ENGLISHMEN.'

Besides, the humidity eventually broke and was replaced by a light shower.

Coward, unused to the Singapore weather, thought it the most thorough-going rainstorm he'd ever seen.

The hotel's marble-floored verandah faced a brooding South China Sea and Coward was convinced that it was about to become part of the boiling, murky waters.

Proven wrong, he retired to the luxury of his suite, completely dry, but utterly miserable.

Fortunately, it didn't take him long to discover the few basic necessities that would make an Englishman's life bearable in Singapore.

The first being the Raffles Hotel's Bar and Billiard Room.

The second, the perfect gin sling.

The third, was some generous if not gullible sorts to finance the second.

(Apparently, a perfect gin sling can only be improved if paid for by someone other than the recipient.)

A couple of those and he was soon feeling himself again, offering some wonderful observations of the place and its expatriate inhabitants.

"SINGAPORE IS A FIRST RATE PLACE FOR SECOND RATE PEOPLE," he blithely proclaimed, to a far from appreciative audience.

The Bar and Billiard Room was a splendidly, civilised place, where white-jacketed patrons would casually commune under high ceilings and lazy fans, cosetted by attentive serving staff. And in keeping with etiquette, a strict dress-code was stringently adhered to.

Coward, taking no chances, stated, "I TAKE STOCK OF MYSELF IN THE MIRROR BEFORE GOING OUT; AN UNFORTUNATE TIE EXPOSES ONE TO DANGER."

His fortunes further improved when introduced to the Quaints, a local theatrical

group with a frighteningly varied, if somewhat dubious repertoire.

They would spend evenings collectively singing dance hall numbers around the Bar and Billiard Room's Piano. (Dance hall music, of all things.)

Spurred on by his brilliant performances at the piano, it wasn't long before Coward found himself on stage, "TAKING A PERFECTLY GOOD ROLE AND THROWING IT IN THE ALLEY."

Unfortunately, he also threw it into the waiting hands of critics.

The show closed after three days.

Well, at least it paid for his drinks.

The Bar and Billiard Room has long been synonymous with the famous and infamous, who would, and still do, wax lyrical over the finest cognacs, champagnes, single malt whiskies, vintage beers and, of course, Singapore Slings.

Because, in the right surroundings, with the right stimulation, there's a little Coward in all of us just waiting to be coaxed out.

ENTRY WAS DENIED TO THOSE NOT WEARING A JACKET, TIE OR A GOOD CHICKEN CURRY.

The compulsory white linen jacket and public school tie were largely successful in keeping out undesirables. The nouveau riche, Americans, chartered accountants and the like.

THERE WERE standards to maintain, after all. One couldn't allow patrons to dress for tropics just because they were in the tropics.

So it may come as a surprise to find a twenty-four stone, bearded giant wandering around the Bar and Billiard Room, barefooted in curry-stained pyjamas.

But Professor Peiter van Stein Callenfels was exceptional in more than just his attire.

The original model for Sir Arthur Conan Doyle's 'PROFESSOR CHALLENGER', Callenfels was a noted archaeologist and historian turned coffee planter. (The more cynical might consider that a natural progression.)

And like many of the region's planters, he would while away the hours nursing a few beers in the splendour of the Bar and Billiard Room.

Unlike many planters though, he would do so speaking fluently in four different languages.

For Raffles was a place where he could find what he considered the rarest of commodities.

Civilised conversation.

To Callenfels, this consisted of the fruits of his intellect bombastically thrust upon a preferably female audience.

After all, he did consider himself somewhat of a ladies man.

This could be attributed to his impressive physique, which spilled gloriously out of the gaps in his pyjamas and cascaded over the sides of his reinforced armchair.

Was it his fine head of hair and whiskers, which he proudly groomed only once a year?

Or perhaps it was his impeccable taste in curry, enshrined in a pastiche of stains down the front of his pyjamas.

Whatever it was, it cannot be denied that he did possess a certain charm.

And if one missed his stentorian boom, by some strange quirk of deafness, Callenfels could always be identified by the steady stream of serving staff briskly gliding between him and the bar, in an attempt to keep pace with his insatiable thirst.

Legend has it that he could consume up to thirty-five beers or ten bottles of gin in a sitting. And they soon learned not to insult him by serving less than a quart at a time.

(If only he'd been around during the thirties, his excessive consumption could have single-handedly seen the hotel through the recession.)

Not that his gargantuan appetite was limited to alcohol. He could voraciously devour his way through the entire Raffles Dining Room menu and had done so on many occasions.

It is even rumoured that Callenfels may have once eaten human flesh while living with cannibals in Sumatra.

Entirely possible, when you consider he ate everything else that wasn't fast enough to escape.

The Bar and Billiard Room has long been dedicated to the ageless pleasure of self indulgence.

The finest selection of champagnes, cognacs, single malt whiskies, vintage beers, connoisseur coffees and chocolates can all be secured in quantity (if need be).

Along with the legendary conversation that has long been associated with the place.

And while Raffles has attained lofty heights in hotel rankings across the world, it occasionally reminds us that aristocrats can also be fun-loving characters. A few years back, for example, our public relations company, MDK, perpetrated a classic April Fools' Day spoof. Raffles announced that an unpublished manuscript by Somerset Maugham, a regular guest in the old days, had been found at the hotel. Dozens of papers and TV channels picked up the story. When the hoax was revealed, the media enjoyed the fun and praised the creative initiative of the brand owner.

SOME FANTASIES

For every fairy tale that comes true, like the Raffles Hotel renaissance, life makes sure that we get our fair share of dreams that don't make it. Here are a few of them.

Through to the early 1980s, Tourism Singapore relied heavily on its duty-free shopping appeal, but a peek into the future told us that this magnet would steadily lose its power. New magnets had to be created and large, trendy theme parks were one popular direction to consider. In an effort to upstage the theme park experts in the late 1970s, our agency came up with what we saw as a brilliant idea: **100 hectares of a kind of "Instant Asia" experience**. (To give you some idea of scale, Los Angeles Disneyland is now about 55 hectares.) Each Southeast Asian country would have its own section to present its cultures in a lively, highly entertaining way, with constant changes in the shows and displays to keep everything fresh. And there'd be a central stadium for big shows by imported stars. In and around the theme park there'd be budget-priced hotels and bars and restaurants. A visit would easily occupy two to three days. Above all else, the site location was our *pièce de résistance* — an island just off Singapore's northeast coast called Pulau Ubin. This sparsely populated, largely jungle-clad island is a quick ferry ride from Changi Point, which is just ten minutes away from the international airport. We could transport overseas visitors from the airport to their Pulau Ubin hotel in 30 minutes, even quicker if some kind of bridge was built across the water. There were some kinks to iron out, but the concept seemed a winner to us. But it never left the drawing board. Someone had the sense to check the government's agenda for Pulau Ubin and their plan clearly did not include an invasion by hundreds of thousands of overseas visitors. Oh, well, on to the next idea...

Raffles of Singapore: The Movie. An Englishwoman called Agatha Christie wrote the novel *Death on the Nile*, and in later years this story was made into a highly successful movie. While it featured plenty of human drama, the film also captured a feeling and flavour about Egypt that greatly appealed to audiences, and it was credited with generating a huge surge of visitor traffic to the land of the Nile.

In another time in another continent, yet another English character founded Singapore. He was a man of many talents and led a rather spirited life, constantly fighting Dutchmen and his own East India Company, pushing women's rights and the abolition of slavery, designing the first road system of Singapore, creating the London Zoo, honing his brilliant botanical skills, and pursuing several fair damsels when it wasn't proper for him to do so. His name was Stamford Raffles.

The huge success of *Death on the Nile* as a tourist promotion instrument gave nectar to the idea of creating a movie around the life of Raffles, and just to make sure no one missed the key message, the working title was *Raffles of Singapore*. While set in the early 19th century, the plan was to show Singapore of today in the introduction and then go back in time to its beginnings; as well as displaying its rich historical texture, the movie would clearly position Singapore as the hub of the most exciting region on earth. Quite a tall order, but the professional screenplay writer we hired with funds generously provided by SIA had no problem with the brief. The idea went quite a way down the line. The BBC expressed interest in producing the movie and putting up half the production cost, with the proviso that they might decide to turn it into a 2-part TV movie special. As a costume drama set in the Regency period it was not a cheap production. As best we tried, we couldn't find anyone to fund the other 50% of the production. The script still sits in a drawer in the office, patiently waiting for some bold entrepreneur to bring it to life.

Talking about entrepreneurs, one of the best-known global entertainment brand owners in recent decades has been Bernie Ecclestone. His **Formula One Grand Prix** attracts an international following of some 250 million fans and the media coverage of this sport is judged by many as coming second only to soccer. Through the late 1980s, in its search for "wow" visitor events, Tourism Singapore was attracted to the concept of being the sole Southeast Asian venue on the Formula One Grand Prix circuit. The dialogue was extensive. Things warmed up, then suddenly seemed to cool down, and Singapore withdrew its interest. One rumour circulated that Ecclestone asked for too much money. Another linked the problem to cigarette sponsorships. Whatever the reason, I think it's a pity that Singapore let this one slip through its fingers. But I guess you have to be prepared to win some, lose some. Which brings me to a recent Tourism Singapore strategic shift that has put a new spin on things...

NEW ASIA

In the mid-1990s, Tourism Singapore brand owners reached a view that the nation's tourism identity in foreign markets needed to be more truly representative of what the product is today and how the product is expected to evolve over the next generation. The brand owner acknowledged that there are still some rustic pockets in Singapore, there are still some historical places, there are still centres where you can shop cheaply, and there are still nooks and crannies offering food in earthy, outdoor surroundings. However, these experiences are steadily fading away and to a large degree are being replaced by smart expressions of contemporary living — stylish buildings, voguish restaurants, slick shopping malls and fast-track people, a kind of New Economy social environment compatible with Singapore's commercial aspirations as a regional hub and as a cosmopolitan global city. So, in line with this trend, appropriate new advertising has been created with the umbrella theme, *New Asia Singapore.*

Looking ahead, Singapore will continue to become more high-tech and attract increasing numbers of business conferences and trade shows because of its efficiencies and space-age competencies. In years to come, however, I personally feel that the key reason why increasingly educated Asians and Western holiday tourists will come to Singapore will be to marvel at the beautiful greenery and how well the unique multiracial soul of Singapore still flourishes in a kingdom of skyscrapers and digital ingenuity. In my eyes Singapore is, and will always be, *the most surprising tropical island on earth.*

To close this chapter, a quick word about the team at the Singapore Tourism Board. Their prime focus, clearly, is to boost the number of holiday visitors and the convention/exhibition traffic to Singapore. As part of this agenda, they lead the charge on creating or reshaping events and venues to increasingly strengthen the appeal and quality of the Singapore tourism product. But the STB team also applies a lot of attention to other less glamorous but important things. For example, they bend over backwards to personally address every single tourist concern or complaint; and they act as a kind of policeman in the local tourism industry to help keep everything running smoothly for visitors. And while always maintaining a firm grip on domestic priorities, they also engage in extending their tourism expertise to other countries in Asia who seek their assistance. I don't think there are many NTOs on the world map who can match the depth and quality of service delivered by the STB team.

CHAPTER 6

ASIAN HOTELS:
A QUESTION OF
STAYING POWER

Can Asian hotel brands be a global force? "People service" is as natural to Asians as England losing in cricket to Australia so one could be forgiven for assuming that Asians are prominent global hotel chain owners. Strangely, for reasons I can't explain, they're not. A number of Asian-owned hotel brands have good networks in

Asia and the likes of Peninsula and Mandarin Oriental have several places in the West, but compared to the Hyatts, Hiltons and Sheratons, Asian hotel brands are not seriously on the global map.

Of all the Asian brands the one I fancied as having the best chance to take renowned Asian service across the world was Shangri-La. The brand is owned by one of Asia's most dynamic tycoons, Robert Kwok. It contributes only a small percentage of the total turnover in Kwok's empire, but is seen as his most visible brand. Shangri-La has enjoyed an enviable reputation in the industry; from the time the brand was born in Asia at the beginning of the 1970s, it set its sights on being the best quality hotel brand in the region and consumer surveys have consistently endorsed this vision.

In the early 1990s, my old associates Don Couldrey and Russell Jones took over the advertising for the brand and enhanced the memorable campaign, *Where else but the Shangri-La?* For several years after, the brand communications programme outshone its competitors in style and awareness. Shangri-La was consistently voted the best hotel brand in Asia and one of the best in the world. Shangri-La's future course was patently clear: it was destined to become a powerful global player, or so I thought.

Having your brand on cruise control does have its downsides; you sometimes relax too much. And that is what I think happened to Shangri-La. While key competitors gradually stepped on the gas, Shangri-La did not seem to take corrective action. It started to lose its shine. Its brand marketers were obviously distracted by other developments. The group created a new brand to meet more budget-conscious customer needs — Traders Hotel. Additionally, a cheaper, 3- to 4-star quality resort complex was built in Singapore and, for some odd reason, it carried the Shangri-La badge. As if these distractions were not enough, China was also thrown into the equation. Kwok has a big commitment to developments in China and the Shangri-La Hotel Group had to join in the fun (a bit like finding your way round Hampton Court Palace maze in a fog!).

Sadly, my dream of Shangri-La Hotels taking on the world is now possibly an idle fantasy. Indeed, it is now struggling, I sense, to stay round the top of the Asian premier league. The group has the

IF OUR OPENING OFFER KNOCKS YOU OFF YOUR FEET, THE BEACH WILL CUSHION YOUR FALL.

Honestly now, it's enough to make you weak at the knees.

Three days/two nights on the weekend for just $290 nett (per

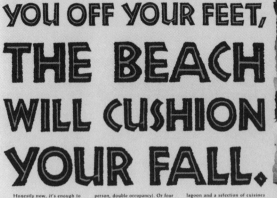

OPENS MARCH 2, 1993

person, double occupancy). Or four days/three nights during the week for a mere $293 nett (same again).

But it's not just how little it costs to get here. It's how much there is waiting for you when you do.

A lazy stretch of white sandy beach, enough water sports to fill a

lagoon and a selection of cuisines ranging from sumptuous Cantonese to delightful Pacific Rim delicacies.

You'll even find a Recreation Manager to help navigate your way through our considerable activities.

In fact, for far less than what you'd pay for a trip to Penang, Bali

or Phuket, you can relax in a corner of paradise just 15 minutes away.

And since we've included a lucky draw, you may find yourself walking away (or perhaps we should say walking back) with a return stay in one of our luxurious suites.

One thing's for certain. These

'Escapade' packages will only be available for a limited time.

So we suggest you ring Shelly on 371 1022 to reserve your place on the lighter side of Singapore.

Shangri-La's
Rasa Sentosa Resort
SINGAPORE

YOU'RE LOOKING AT THE TEMPTING PART. READ ON TO FIND THE BRIBERY.

Now that we've your attention, we'll come right to the point.

We're celebrating our opening with a rather remarkable offer.

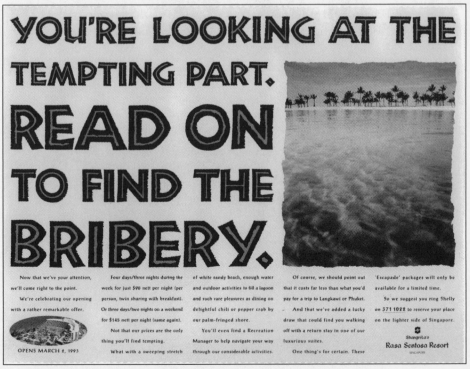

OPENS MARCH 2, 1993

Four days/three nights during the week for just $98 nett per night (per person, twin sharing with breakfast). Or three days/two nights on a weekend for $145 nett per night (same again).

Not that our prices are the only thing you'll find tempting.

What with a sweeping stretch

of white sandy beach, enough water and outdoor activities to fill a lagoon and such rare pleasures as dining on delightful chilli or pepper crab by our palm-fringed shore.

You'll even find a Recreation Manager to help navigate your way through our considerable activities.

Of course, we should point out that it costs far less than what you'd pay for a trip to Langkawi or Phuket.

And that we've added a lucky draw that could find you walking off with a return stay in one of our luxurious suites.

One thing's for certain. These

'Escapade' packages will only be available for a limited time.

So we suggest you ring Shelly on 371 1022 to reserve your place on the lighter side of Singapore.

Shangri-La's
Rasa Sentosa Resort
SINGAPORE

While I question the wisdom in using the Shangri-La brand name for the company's Sentosa resort in Singapore, I still enjoy the tonality of the advertising we created.

*Low-cost newspaper strip-size ads for the Shangri-La Hotel's
Sentosa location in Singapore.*

money to correct this branding challenge, but it will take more than money to get things right. It will need the skills of bright, focused, experienced brand builders. That is, if the group cares about the brand. *And maybe they do. Latest gossip is that the brand is opening up hotels in some Western capitals. Has the old flame been rekindled?*

THE RULES OF ENGAGEMENT

It's probably timely to take a short break from Asian brand stories and to regurgitate some of the fundamental nuts-and-bolts mindset hurdles that have to be faced in the mission of taking Asia to the world.

Asians are consuming knowledge faster than all other races, and their addiction to education is almost paranoid in its intensity. There is still, however, a deeply rooted "**trader mentality**" in Asia and no advanced Western education nor Western living experience can totally erase this inbuilt peculiarity; it's part of an Asian's DNA, so to speak. It's almost second nature to know where to buy the cheapest rice in town, or how much apartments cost in different suburbs, or the latest stockbroker discount fees. To some observers, the "trader mentality" is an invaluable asset as it provides one with the innate ability to get the best deal going. The critics, mostly Westerners, contend that this mentality hinders lateral thinking, stigmatises quality, and narrows judgement down to one thing — price.

Westerners sometimes forget that, above all else, the Asian businessman is pragmatic. In selling to Western buyers he will swiftly shift ground and be more value-centric than price-centric as and when the need arises. And as we've all witnessed, he's not coy about paying a premium for what *he* perceives to be a top-quality brand. (Mind you, I'd be inclined to remind him fairly regularly that quality communications work has its price.)

"**Stretching the envelope**" is another fashionable issue. The scenario is well known. Asians are culturally conservative, unimaginative, risk-averse businessmen, somehow lacking the entrepreneurial skills to win major marketing wars in the West against the awesome Western warriors! I mentioned this view earlier in this book and I'll say it again: let's move on from tired historical assessments. The 21st century Asian business-cum-brand owner, while remaining culturally less gregarious than his Western competitor, will be well educated, international, razor-sharp and confident. His entrepreneurial skills may be fuelled by the environment in which he lives, or by the organisation in which he works, or by his family and friends, or a combination of all these things. Then again, his entrepreneurial powers might well be the result of the right creative environment inside his head. Make no mistake about it, the young Asian entrepreneur will soon be ready to take on the world. This is Asia's century. And one final swipe at Western critics — it's a quiz question: How has SIA, owned and managed by Asians, succeeded so well for so long in the world's biggest industry, travel?

"Embracing global business practices." The late 1990s' regional economic problems exposed quite a load of dirty underwear in the banking systems of some Asian countries. A number of Asian conglomerates were heavily damaged and are still sorting through the rubble. But that's today. Asia is fully committed to globalisation as its best growth strategy. This commitment requires Asia to follow popular international business practices. Some Asian countries already do so; others are still getting there. One thing is certain: there's no turning back on the rules of engagement.

CHAPTER 7

A BRAND
DISTRACTED

Do Chinese businessmen believe in brands? The first thing they believe in is profits. And why not! The old traditional *towkays* value a "good name", which is more of a family association, but the concept of a brand having a life of its own is not that well understood by older businessmen. Which is understandable, as most of us in the Asian advertising industry have not done a good job in educating the marketplace on this topic.

However, one senior Chinese businessman I know proved to be the exception. His name was Wee Cho Yaw.

Mr. Wee first contacted me in 1974.

"Mr. Betty," he said in his Chinese-English accent, "I'd like you to handle my advertising needs," or words to this effect.

Mr. Wee, it turned out, was the son of the founder of the United Overseas Bank and became the agency's second client. UOB had bought into other local banks and upgraded its corporate identity.

Mr. Wee's brief was single-minded: to sell the brand. UOB's customer base was mainly Chinese-centric, and would continue to be so. However, Mr. Wee was in tune with the changing times and the nation's growth agenda. He could see that the English language and Western values would become increasingly influential in the years ahead. He understood from the start that the advertising should target new customers without alienating the existing older ones. He could see that his new customers would *have* to come from the younger end of the market; he understood the idea of making the brand more youthful, more international, to connect with emerging contemporary customers.

Thanks to the skills of an excellent graphic designer, we had a highly distinctive logo to play with, and we made this logo an icon for the brand. Mixing the strong trademark with a Western jingle and smart-looking (at that time) cinematography, the UOB advertising through the 1970s was the envy of the industry. And strategic brand building dominated the media schedule.

The brand owner also had a keen understanding of the value of taking a brand's personality across all communication vehicles. Our agency designed all the bank's incredible range of collaterals, right through to the bank's financial reports. And everything was in two languages, Chinese and English, which sometimes made life quite complex.

One time, for example, the bank management and our team were at a film studio reviewing a TV commercial when Mr. Wee suddenly switched topics and chided the agency on the quality of his bilingual Annual Report which had just been released. I thought he was unfair in his criticism and told him so. Before we knew it, our discussion turned into a heated argument. Mr. Wee then exited abruptly and I was left with an empty, sinking feeling. I had overstepped the mark with the bank boss. Had I humiliated him in front of his own management? It is absolutely unforgivable for anyone at our agency to be rude to our paymasters, let alone the agency's second oldest client and one of our most loyal supporters. With a nervous, heavy heart I contacted Mr. Wee the next day to apologise, only to find him disarmingly warm and forgiving — he very graciously put the incident down to my wild creative temperament.

As the bank grew, so did its service offering. New revenue opportunities created new divisions of focus, and each new division had its own unique set of business goals and its own set of customers. This expansive decentralisation programme brought with it empowerment, and empowerment at divisional level impacted on UOB's brand identity. The advertising often looked like it belonged to several different brands and the agency was also all at sea in this game. Controlling a brand's values in decentralised conditions is a sensitive issue that many growing companies face, and many have trouble handling it well.

I have no problem with the argument that different target audiences and different consumer feelings require different advertising solutions. What I do have a problem with is when the only thing that links all the different ads together is the company logo. Remember, please, that every single piece of advertising that carries a company's trademark or logo is brand advertising. And every worthy brand has a soul, a special personality. It is a fundamental responsibility for brand owners to leverage their personality in one form or another in *all* their advertising. It's all part of the brand-building exercise. It's part of consistently connecting in a certain way with your customer. It's part of putting yourself head and shoulders above the din of characterless advertising.

While the UOB brand communication programme has gone through some foggy weather in recent years, the bank's bottom line results have been good, which reflects the business skills of its top people. And raises an obvious view: that is, once the bank's brand communication strategy is sorted out, the bank's financial performance will go from good to "wow".

Building the UOB brand in 1979, not the kind of advertising expected from a local Singaporean bank in those days.

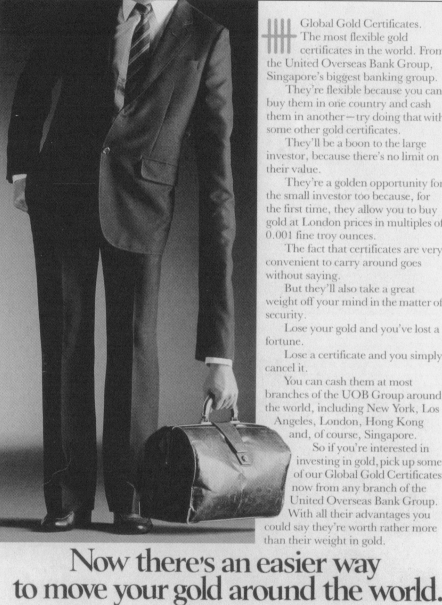

Global Gold Certificates. The most flexible gold certificates in the world. From the United Overseas Bank Group, Singapore's biggest banking group.

They're flexible because you can buy them in one country and cash them in another—try doing that with some other gold certificates.

They'll be a boon to the large investor, because there's no limit on their value.

They're a golden opportunity for the small investor too because, for the first time, they allow you to buy gold at London prices in multiples of 0.001 fine troy ounces.

The fact that certificates are very convenient to carry around goes without saying.

But they'll also take a great weight off your mind in the matter of security.

Lose your gold and you've lost a fortune.

Lose a certificate and you simply cancel it.

You can cash them at most branches of the UOB Group around the world, including New York, Los Angeles, London, Hong Kong and, of course, Singapore.

So if you're interested in investing in gold, pick up some of our Global Gold Certificates now from any branch of the United Overseas Bank Group. With all their advantages you could say they're worth rather more than their weight in gold.

Now there's an easier way to move your gold around the world.

US29/86

The brand's personality was taken across all communications.

Room to let. Rent free.

Whether you are an existing or new deposit account-holder with the United Overseas Bank (UOB) Group, we'll give you 50% off the normal rental rate for the first year if you open a new Safe Deposit Box with us. And that's just for openers. If, at the same time, you place with us a minimum S$5,000 12-month fixed deposit at the attractive interest rate

MINIMUM FIXED DEPOSIT AMOUNT FOR 12 MONTHS (S$)	SIZE OF RENT FREE SAFE DEPOSIT BOX
5,000	Extra Small, Small
7,500	Medium
10,000	Large
12,500	Extra Large

of 4.75% p.a., we'll give you a Safe Deposit Box absolutely rent free for a year. Of course, the higher the fixed deposit amount, the larger the box you'll get. Naturally, an offer this good can't last forever, so hurry into your nearest UOB Group branch or call us on 5392527, 5392530/31, 5392579, 5392650, 5392655 today. **UNITED OVERSEAS BANK GROUP**

Singapore's largest banking group : United Overseas Bank • Industrial & Commercial Bank • Chung Khiaw Bank • Far Eastern Bank • Lee Wah Bank

TO RELAX, SOME LISTEN TO THE SOUND OF THE SEA.

OTHERS SIMPLY OPEN AN ❶-ACCOUNT ⤀

For less stress and a peaceful life, open your ❶, the all-in-one money management account. Complete the application form opposite. Then sit back and relax.

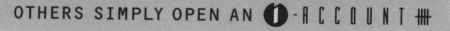

New customers had to come from a younger, more Western end of the market.

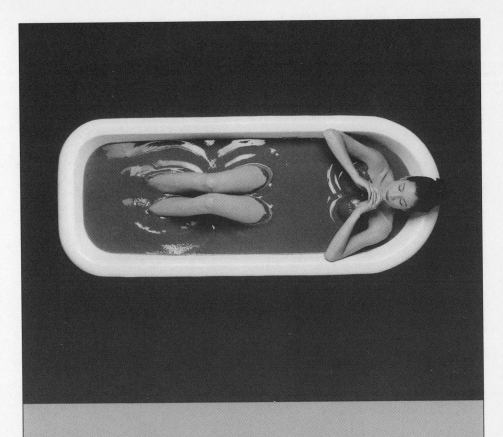

TO RELAX, SOME WALLOW IN WARM MUD.

OTHERS SIMPLY OPEN AN ❶-ACCOUNT ▥

For less stress and a peaceful life, open your ❶, the all-in-one money management account. Complete the application form opposite. Then sit back and relax.

CHAPTER 8

JOLLY JUNGLES: THE SARAWAK STORY

This is another case study of how to make a small budget work like a big one. The tourism authority of the East Malaysian state of Sarawak, Borneo had given us a brief for a global campaign. They wanted to reach the travel trade in Europe, Australia, Japan and on the West Coast of the United States, supported by consumer advertising where possible. A fairly standard brief, but ambitious insofar as the full year's global budget was only about $1 million.

The first thing we tackled was the creative strategy. That was the easy part, relatively speaking. The Sarawak Tourism brand is a rare and beautiful creature. Its rich history goes back seemingly forever, as does its mix of unique tribes and cultures. It has flora and fauna like nowhere else on earth. Waterfalls and giant caves, and mountains and jungles surround you wherever you go. Sarawak is a huge natural wonderland, one of the last great ecological adventure experiences on this planet.

To bring this remarkable brand promise to life, we initially experimented with colour illustrations that followed the style of the great French Post-Impressionist Henri Rousseau, who was famous for painting jungle scenes, and the results were exciting. But they didn't *quite* capture the essence of the brand, the adventurous spirit of the brand. So we drilled down further and finally hit the jackpot: the comic book illustration style that was popular in the early years of the 20th century, a period of great pioneering adventurers. Then, in keeping with that flavour, the advertisement headlines were crafted like book titles from *Biggles* schoolboy adventure stories, the text was given a distinct Victorian storytelling character, and supporting black-and-white illustrations looked like they'd been stolen from an early *National Geographic* encyclopaedia.

Having ironed out the creative for the media advertising, we then tackled the tourism logo design and the horde of literature that goes with the promotion of a tourism brand. The one distinct personality swept across the total stable of non-media publicity material. During the process it became patently obvious that the look and feel of the mainstream advertising should also be extended to postcards, T-shirts, posters and other stuff that visitors habitually gather at gift shops. In addressing that particular exercise, the idea of turning the delightfully disarming, indigenous orang-utan into a Sarawak icon (like the koala is to Australia) was put on the table. Thanks to poor salesmanship on my part that idea didn't get very far, which is a pity, because I still firmly believe it could be a long-term brand winner for Sarawak.

Getting the creative looking pretty good was only half the creative challenge. How best to employ the thin global publicity budget was the toughest issue. In line with what we judged to be fairly modest visitor targets, we finally convinced the brand owner to go the "concentration" route. In Western travel trade media, we concentrated bursts of advertising in just a few publications. To reach consumers we concentrated our focus just on Southeast Asia, and concentrated specifically on expatriates and younger-end, upmarket nationals. We then identified just *one* regionwide English language magazine to provide a decent reach of our target prospects, and negotiated a very special deal. *For every full page advertisement we ran, we received a full page of free editorial in a separate issue.* To top this off, we then did some rifle shooting by drilling down into club magazines, reaching heavy concentrations of expatriate members and playing the same barter game wherever we could.

Public relations rightly enjoyed a piece of the publicity budget. Our group's PR wing and manager of this total campaign crusade, MDK Consultants, applied the same "concentration" technique they used for the Raffles Hotel relaunch — enticing well-known syndicated columnists from around the world to experience the Sarawak adventure.

The campaign was a success. It boosted visitor arrivals; it was lauded by travel experts and won several top awards at global tourism conferences; it also scored extremely well at international creative award shows. But life can sometimes be very cruel. Just a year or so after the campaign launched, it became yet another victim of the huge Asian economic slump of the late 1990s. And to add more pain, a deadly, widely-publicised children's disease then swept across Sarawak and its darkness lingered on for many months. I am hopeful that in the not-too-distant future the brand owners will once again take this campaign back to the market. It thoroughly deserves a second innings, and more.

IT would be remiss of me to close this adventure story without a brief word about a bigger idea.

In the mid-1990s, I visited both of Malaysia's states in Borneo — Sarawak and Sabah — to try to sell them on the concept of promoting "Borneo" as their joint tourism brand. One state liked the idea; the other was ambivalent.

I've already given you a macro taste of Sarawak's tourism promise. Sabah offers yet another, quite different exotic canvas. While it boasts Southeast Asia's tallest mountain, the Sabah I love is its coastline — the sea, the sailing, fishing, arguably the world's best scuba diving experience, endless miles of palm-fringed beaches, freshly barbecued seafood and unbelievable sunsets. Clearly, both destinations can be enjoyed right now. What I'm talking about are the efficiencies and added power of marketing *both* experiences under *one* brand name — a brand name that in itself has unique equity. The massive island of Borneo is shared with Indonesia, but it's very feasible for the brand name Borneo to be perceived among consumers as the sole ownership of Sabah and Sarawak. All that's needed is the will.

Double-page spreads from the print campaign.

THE IBAN MAIDENS WERE TOTALLY MERCILESS. "NO PHOTOS,"
THEY LAUGHED, "UNLESS YOU DANCE THE NGAJAT!"

DRUM BEATS thudded out into the hot tropical night. Tribal gongs clanged. And the Iban girls, silver coins jingling on their tribal dresses, stepped forward with smiles of delight. For the honeymoon couple, there was now no possibility of escape. They were going to have to dance the *ngajat*.

But then no one comes to Sarawak just to sunbathe (even though the soft white sands, criss-crossed with turtle footprints, are ideal for this pastime). Instead, the wise traveller casts his fate into a boat and follows the call of the mighty Rajang River.

Over the years the river and its latticework of tributaries has borne countless generations of adventure-seekers – from traders and headhunters, to pirates and the odd novelist – deep into the ancient jungle. Through a botanic wonderland where proboscis monkeys squeal from the trees and lizards and frogs glide down from the skies. And where today you may stare into the eyes of an orang-utan, and be forever haunted by the feeling of how human he seems. Just as he, too, will be perplexed at how much like an orang-utan you are.

Warrior from the rainforest, as seen through 19th century eyes. Such romanticised images were typical of early western accounts of Sarawak.

get here in little over an hour. But the essential feeling of entering a different world is still the same. Especially at dusk when you break your journey upriver and sample the legendary hospitality of

In a timeless natural cycle, green turtles return every year to the shores of their birthplace in northern Borneo to lay eggs.

the longhouses – the ancestral homes of the tribes which are strung out along the river like beads on a string. Here you may find, hidden away in the cobwebbed corners, the accumulated baggage of Sarawak's fascinating past: ancient Chinese jars; an antique brass cannon; a faded picture of Queen Victoria; and, occasionally hanging from the rafters, a dusty chandelier of skulls.

The rule of the longhouse is simple and it hasn't changed since the days when Joseph Conrad and Somerset Maugham wrote their stories here by the flickering light of the fire-flies. Guests, it is felt, should always make a little contribution to the entertainment. So when the gongs strike up, push aside the remains of your chicken-in-bamboo supper, take one last sip from the heady *tuak* rice wine, and dance the *ngajat* for all you're worth.

Yes, a visit to this enchanted land on the northwestern edge of Borneo is proof that it is still possible to find adventure in this increasingly sanitised world. It no longer takes a week's sailing from Singapore by schooner, you can

Squirrels, lizards, frogs and even snakes are some of the normally earthbound animals in the rainforest that glide through the air on flaps of stretched skin.

For more information and a brochure about holidays in Sarawak, please contact the Sarawak Tourism Board in one of the following ways: tel: 60 82 423600 or fax: 60 82 416700 or visit our website at http://www.sarawak.gov.my/stb

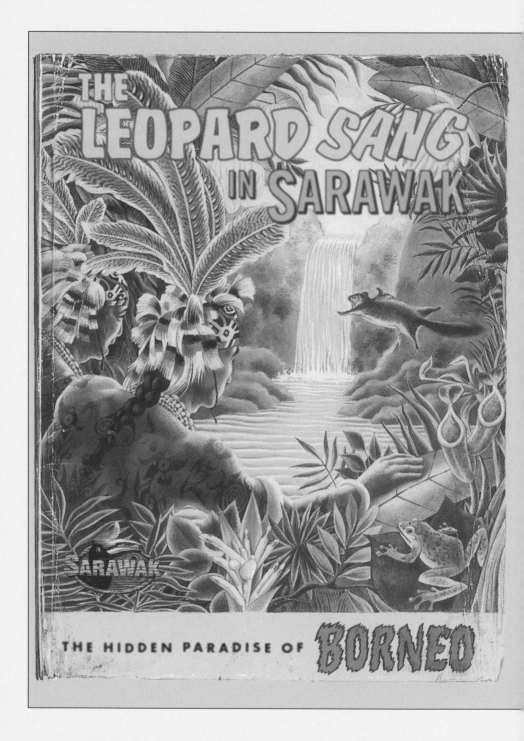

ARE THERE REALLY PLANTS OUT THERE IN THE RAINFOREST WHICH EAT ANIMALS?

THE IDEA had seemed just too far-fetched when Asun the guide first mentioned it to the young honeymoon couple. Then when he added that he would also be taking them to look for squirrels which flew and macaques which dived for crabs, they knew he had to be pulling their legs. (This was before he had even mentioned pigs sporting beards.)

But he was serious. Flying frogs and squirrels are actually some of the saner things you could encounter on a visit to Sarawak. Perched on the northwestern edge of Borneo just

The local name for proboscis monkey means 'dutchman' – a mischievous reference to the impressive noses of the early European visitors.

The stream of bats leaving the Deer Cave at dusk takes more than an hour to pass.

over an hour from Singapore, and covered with an expanse of primeval rainforest bigger than Austria, it's one of the last great lands of adventure left in this world.

Day begins here not with the common-place crowing of the cockerel, but the haunting sound of gibbons in the treetops, singing their hymn to the dawn. Among the foliage, you may see tiny deer the size of cats. Or hear, if you listen very carefully, the microscopic too-wit too-woo of an owl smaller than a butterfly. And nearby, find butterflies so big, that a Victorian naturalist – in one of his less sober moments – shot a specimen with his rifle.

The same Victorian naturalist complained that his sense of wonder almost died from overwork during

Assassins of the plant world, pitcher plants survive in poor quality soil by trapping unwary flies and slowly digesting

A Goliath among flowers, the Rafflesia is the world's largest flowering plant with a bloom that can measure up to a metre across.

his stay in Sarawak. You, too, may begin to doubt the evidence of your senses as you wander through caves bigger than cathedrals and trek across some of the oldest rainforest in the world. Or even encounter the famous carnivorous pitcher plants which trap flies in their saxophone shaped leaves and then digest them in a reservoir of corrosive fluid. Some varieties in Borneo grow so big that even drowned rats have been reported dissolving in the enzyme soup.

Day ends just as magically as it begins. Armies of fire-flies begin to flicker, phosphorescent mushrooms glow, and from the mouth of the great Deer Cave in Mulu National Park a river of bats emerges. Not just hundreds of bats. Nor even thousands. But a never-ending spiral of millions that will momentarily eclipse the Sarawak moon and consume three tons of insects before dawn.

Throughout the hot night they forage, over the dark canopy of the rainforest, over the gibbons sleeping in the trees, and over those strange pitcher plants with which they share the same taste in insects.

For more information and a brochure about holidays in Sarawak, please contact the Sarawak Tourism Board in one of the following ways: tel: 60 82 423600 or fax: 60 82 416700 or visit our website at http://www.sarawak.gov.my/stb

SAR 5

CHAPTER 9

AN AIRPORT BRAND THAT DIDN'T TAKE OFF

When Singapore moved its airport to Changi, it was an immediate success. Accolades poured in from around the world praising its smartness and efficiency. It was voted one of the world's best airports by travellers. A number of years later they decided to embark on Terminal 2. One of the world's greatest airports was going to be *twice* as impressive.

We had been involved already in some campaigns for this air hub. With the opening of the second terminal, my colleagues and I got very excited about the marketing opportunity this development opened up to us. The huge extension included a monorail service, a movie theatre, swimming pool, between-flight accommodation, and more entertainment, more restaurants, more bars and more shops — all sorts of things that few world airports could match at the time. We felt we were no longer selling a highly efficient airport facility; rather, we were selling a whole new, dynamic travel experience. And what better way to hammer home the message that Singapore Changi Airport was a lot more than an airport than to give it a totally different brand name.

We recommended *Airtropolis*. In our partisan eyes, the name had all kinds of pluses going for it. Just the thought of an airline's cockpit announcement, "We will shortly be arriving at the Singapore *Airtropolis*", sent an exhilarating shiver down our spine! We felt *Airtropolis* would dramatically lift Singapore's global image against its Hong Kong and Bangkok gateway rivals and provide more adrenaline for Singapore's positioning as a regional hub. We also saw this brand packaging as a more theatrical new icon for Tourism Singapore and a potential new national hero for Singaporeans.

AIRTROPOLIS

SINGAPORE CHANGI AIRPORT

We felt we were no longer selling a highly efficient airport facility; rather, we were selling a whole new, dynamic travel experience.

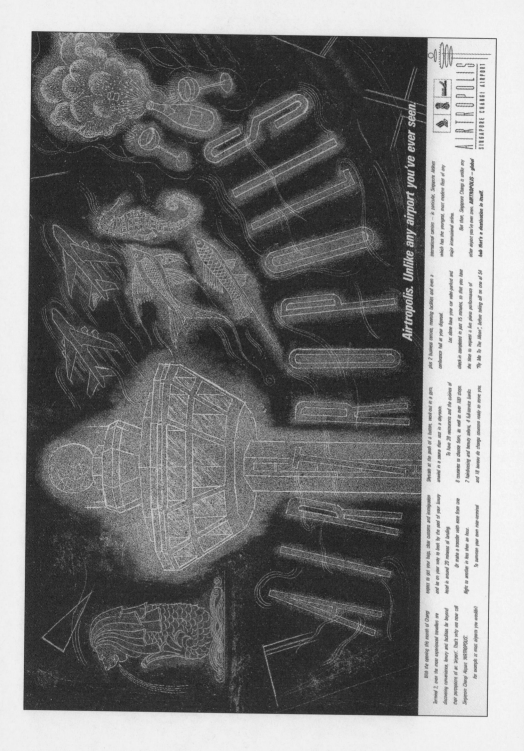

Airtropolis. Unlike any airport you've ever seen.

With the opening of this seventh of Changi Terminal 2, even the most experienced travellers are discovering convenience, luxury and facilities far beyond their perceptions of an airport. That's why we now call Singapore Changi Airport 'AIRTROPOLIS'.

For example: at most airports you wouldn't

expect to get your bags, clear customs and immigration and be on your way to back by the yard of your luxury hotel in around 20 minutes of landing.

Or make a transfer with ease from one flight to another in less than an hour.

To summon your own mini-terminal

Stretch at the push of a button, work-out in a gym, unwind in a sauna then eat in a skyroom.

To have 20 restaurants and the cuisines of 8 countries to choose from, as well as over 100 shops, 7 hairdressing and beauty salons, 4 full-service banks and 18 bureau de change counters ready to serve you,

plus 2 business centres, meeting facilities and even a conference hall at your disposal.

Let alone have your car valet-parked and check-in completed in just 15 minutes, so that you have the time to request a live piano performance of "Fly Me To The Moon", before taking off on one of 54

international carriers — in particular, Singapore Airlines which has the youngest, most modern fleet of any major international airline.

But then, Singapore Changi is unlike any other airport you've ever seen. AIRTROPOLIS — global hub that's a destination in itself.

AIRTROPOLIS
SINGAPORE CHANGI AIRPORT

The airport brand marketers embraced the idea. We developed space-age style advertising and launched the campaign. Then one day, out of the blue, we got a call to say they didn't want to use *Airtropolis* any more.

Singapore's international airport continues to enjoy an enviable reputation in the industry and is regularly voted the best airport in the world. The absence of *Airtropolis* has not affected its image or performance in the slightest, but I still think it was a big branding idea.

IN more recent times, many airports around the globe have grown into an animal that resembles a theme park more than a traffic station for air travellers. Which is great. I'd like to briefly mention one of them — the new Kuala Lumpur International Airport. Its construction concept follows the likes of the new Denver airport — you rail between the check-in/baggage complex and the aircraft loading/unloading complex. I personally think it is a wonderful airport and it beats the pants off the new Hong Kong airport and other Asian hubs, with Singapore being the sole exception.

As it is in life, of course, perception is always more powerful than reality and Kuala Lumpur airport's reputation is way below what it rightly should be. Somehow, consumers — locally, regionally and globally — don't hear or see much positive publicity about this brand. It took $2.5 billion and over three years to build Malaysia's grand new airport, but it may only take a *$2-million* advertising budget and one year to put it in the global hall of fame.

CHAPTER 10

THE
NEXT
WAVE

Can Asia produce a strong stable of global power brands? In this chapter, as in several other parts of this book, I'm consistently defining Asia as *all countries in Asia-Pacific, from India eastwards, excluding Japan.* (I see Japanese brands, like those of Western nations, as representing the mighty, heavily entrenched competition.)

The rules in this book also insist that an Asian global brand is one that is owned and managed from an Asia-Pacific base by Asian companies.

At present, Korea and Taiwan combined have a few decent global power brands, but with the exception of national airlines and tourism boards (which are disqualified in this review as their conventional charter already embraces global coverage), the buck stops just about there. But, for all sorts of positive reasons, I see this picture changing dramatically. I think the time is ripe for a lot more Asian brands to reach out and capture a healthy slice of global opportunities. This is Asia's century. So I'm setting some modest targets.

THE MISSION: TO HAVE AT LEAST 20 ASIAN POWER BRANDS IN THE WORLD'S TOP 50 BY THE YEAR 2020

It will not be a case of push and pull; it will be like riding on a tidal wave that grows in size and power as the years roll on.

Over the next two decades, non-Japan Asia's population will grow from 3 billion in 2000 to 3.5 billion in 2020 — *47% of the world's population!* Within this time frame, wars and revolutions and economic slumps aside, China is targeted by many experts to be the world's largest economy, with India not far behind Japan.

Over the next 20 years, powered by an explosion of wealth and education, a rapidly accelerated convergence of worldwide communications, and strong commitment by national governments to globalisation, 21st century Asians will become increasingly entrepreneurial, sophisticated and confident. They will embrace globalisation with the same vigour as Genghis Khan did eight hundred years ago, but this time round their methods of winning market share will no doubt meet slightly stiffer opposition.

As we all know, when you peel back the layers, marketing is still very much an esoteric exercise. It is knowing where the good opportunities exist, and having a sense about which ones will respond to imagination.

In global terms, the current Top 50 brand picture is on the next two pages.

It's also interesting to see, I think, what the brand picture looks like in Asia these days, as researched by *Reader's Digest*, which then follows.

Where do the best opportunities exist?

I applied a kind of "Assets" check to this question, and came up with this model (which, in hindsight, is simple common sense):

Each Asian country should first check its **Golden Assets**. This term refers to the natural commodities you have and usually export — for example, rice, wheat, fruit, tea, fish, cotton, timber, rubber, minerals, and so on. In Asia, most countries are blessed with Golden Assets. However, it's difficult to identify any Asian brand with serious global clout in this category. The opportunities are huge. It's time to correct this picture.

Another path to explore is what I call **Acquired Assets**. Here's where you springboard a branding opportunity on the back of an identity that enjoys strong credibility. For example, Australians are world famous for their sporting abilities, so an Australian sporting goods brand has a lot going for it even before it gets going. Asia's reputation for quality personal services and hospitality is a powerful asset on which to leverage an Asian hotel brand.

Then there's a third path. I call this the **Potential Assets** route. Or, to put it another way, you start with a clean sheet of paper. This focus tests your creative skills on all fronts imaginable. It's the toughest hill to tackle, but it can be the most rewarding. Mexico, for example, isn't exactly famous for its beer heritage, yet Corona is now a respected global brand. The Japan of today started its path to fame by painting Potential Assets scenarios some 50 years ago.

There's also a possibility of **combining some Acquired Assets with Potential Assets**. A hybrid example in Asia is the arts category. Looking ahead, the world's thirst for entertainment and for things of artistic, creative individuality will probably outpace supply. So the agenda can cover fine and performing arts, movie and book production. Why can't the Shanghai Theatre Circus become an ongoing global show as famous as Cirque du Soleil? What's to stop

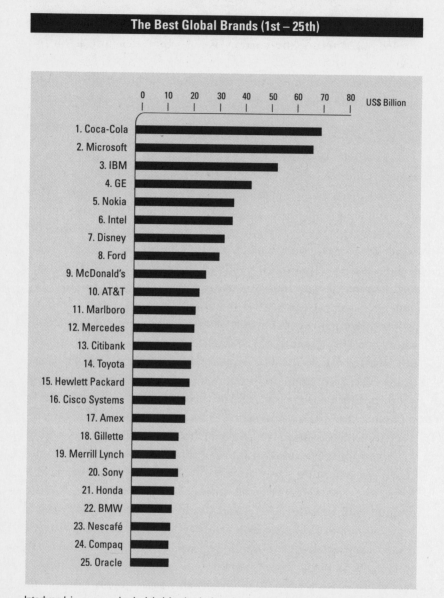

The Best Global Brands (1st – 25th)

US$ Billion (0, 10, 20, 30, 40, 50, 60, 70, 80)

1. Coca-Cola
2. Microsoft
3. IBM
4. GE
5. Nokia
6. Intel
7. Disney
8. Ford
9. McDonald's
10. AT&T
11. Marlboro
12. Mercedes
13. Citibank
14. Toyota
15. Hewlett Packard
16. Cisco Systems
17. Amex
18. Gillette
19. Merrill Lynch
20. Sony
21. Honda
22. BMW
23. Nescafé
24. Compaq
25. Oracle

Interbrand is a recognized global leader in brand valuation. Its valuations are based on an "economic use" approach, treating brands as financial assets with future earnings discounted to a present value. Three steps are involved – financial analysis to determine the proportion of total revenues accounted by the individual brand, market analysis to derive true brand earnings by deducting ownership cost of tangible assets and earnings from non-brand related intangible assets, and risk analysis to determine the degree to which anticipated future brand earnings should be discounted in computing a net present value of the brand.

The Best Global Brands (26th – 50th)

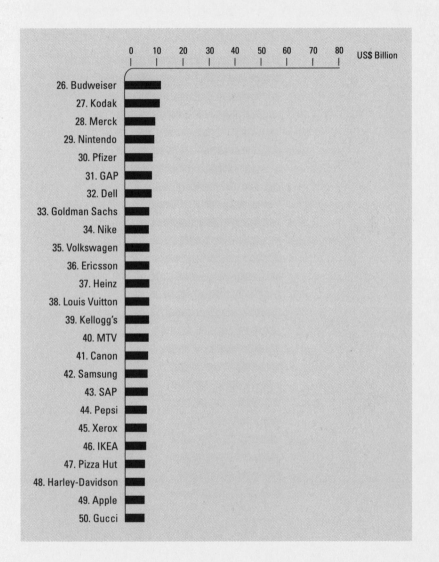

Source: "The Best Global Brands", *BusinessWeek,* 6 August 2001.
Data source: Interbrand, Citigroup, *BusinessWeek.*

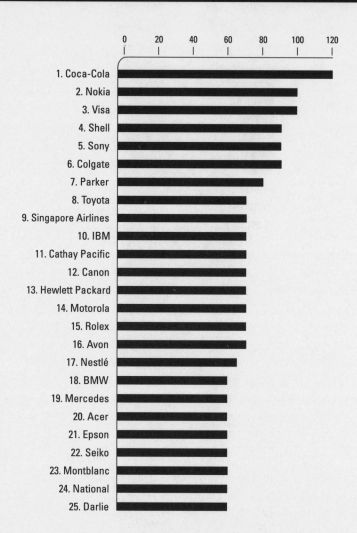

Top 25 Brands in Asia

1. Coca-Cola
2. Nokia
3. Visa
4. Shell
5. Sony
6. Colgate
7. Parker
8. Toyota
9. Singapore Airlines
10. IBM
11. Cathay Pacific
12. Canon
13. Hewlett Packard
14. Motorola
15. Rolex
16. Avon
17. Nestlé
18. BMW
19. Mercedes
20. Acer
21. Epson
22. Seiko
23. Montblanc
24. National
25. Darlie

Source: Reader's Digest Asia's SuperBrands Survey 2001 (conducted among *Reader's Digest* readers in Singapore, Malaysia, Thailand, Hong Kong, Taiwan and the Philippines). To arrive at the rankings above, each brand is given ten points each time it appears as a winner. The brand that appears in the most markets is then chosen as the Top Brand to be included in the chart. Each time one of these winning brands wins a platinum award, it earns an additional ten points.

the Bombay Universal Picture Company from becoming the biggest producer of Western-style dramas in the world?

Asia's success in global arts and entertainment will help fertilise the reception for Asian brands in the West. But it's advisable to do more. Several other Asian programmes need to be brought into play to leverage a bigger global respect and understanding for things Asian. It is desirable to spread the message about Asia's extraordinary history, which makes Western civilisation seem quite feudal. There's also a need to lift the bar on things like Asian fabric design, Asian cuisine, and even Asian success in popular sports. These energies, and more, are important supplements in the drive to successfully secure a handsome basket of Asian brands on the global stage.

Come with me now for a quick trip around parts of Asia for a commentary on several global power branding opportunities that I've identified. I've consciously selected an odd, diverse mix. There'll be no attempt to seriously drill down into brand strategies and creative ideas. I'll simply touch on a few existing brands, and also fantasise about creating strong global brands that currently do not exist, in the hope that one or two of the ideas will ignite a fire in the belly of Asian entrepreneurs. The mission, remember, is to have a minimum of 20 Asian brands in the World's Top 50 Brands league by the year 2020. Very recent world economic events will no doubt now put a different spin on some of the statistics in this chapter, but we're looking into the future as far as two decades or more, so I think the directional thrust of the mission remains unchanged.

Let's start Down Under…

AUSTRALIA: TIME TO STOP WALTZING

Australia has the 14th largest economy in the world. It is the world's biggest exporter of wool, cattle and beef, the second biggest exporter of dairy products and the third biggest exporter of fresh fruit, iron ore, bauxite, to name but a few. Less well known is

Australian inventiveness. The "black box" flight recorder, the rotary clothesline, the east-west engine and hundreds of breakthrough ideas in medical research, telecommunications and engineering were the products of Australian imagination. Australia's education system attracts thousands of foreign students. Australia's trophies in sport would sink the *Titanic*. Australian movie icons like *Crocodile Dundee* and *Priscilla Queen of the Desert* are loved around the world, as are Aussie music makers Olivia Newton-John, the Bee Gees and Kylie Minogue. The creativity that sparkles in the visual and performing arts and literature also fires the Australian marketing and advertising industry. Given all those resources and all that talent, why doesn't Australia have any global power brands beyond possibly Fosters?

Back in the 1960s, Australian author Donald Horne wrote *The Lucky Country*. His book chipped away at Australian apathy. Why were his countrymen, he argued, so content to live in their land of milk and honey without sweating too much, without looking ahead to a time when their luck might run out? Which of course it did, in the 1980s and 1990s. Few Australians genuinely understood Horne's message. More recently, a prominent American business consultancy set out to discover why Australia wasn't as prosperous as it should be. After surveying Australian businessmen, they reached the same conclusion as Donald Horne had done a generation before. There was a general contentment with an average, safe performance. The majority of business decision-makers continued to set their sights halfway up the ladder. The notion of being a tall poppy and pushing the envelope was too unsettling for them. But even Australia must change. Certainly Asian migration has stirred up some action and competition. And with better connections and a broader mindset, younger Australian businessmen in their 20s and 30s appear to be more energised, more committed to playing in the global league and not just the local Rugby League. I'm banking on them to establish a strong stable of Australian brands in the world's Top 50 table within the next two decades.

In this particular exercise, I've identified only one food product (Australia should rightly have at least three or four great global food brands). I've spread my examples across four diverse opportunities to illustrate the golden nuggets waiting to be mined in Australia.

Sports Brand

Australia Sport International is a government-backed company targeting to push export sales of sports-related products and services to $674 million by 2005. The Sports and Tourism Division of the Australian Department of Industry, Science and Resources is also growing the Australian sports and recreation industry around the world. At a conservative estimate, the Australian sport and recreation industry is valued at around $4 billion.

The global sporting goods market stands at $150 billion. Despite Australia's enduring credibility in golf and tennis, her exports are a drop in the ocean — with 25% of them going to New Zealand. Australia has some catching up to do.

Australia's sportswear track record looks more promising. Globally, sportswear notched up an astounding $25.7 billion in sales. Here again, Australia has credibility. Long before it was sold to foreign interests, Australia's Speedo was a cutting edge swimwear brand. In the 1990s, Australia's surfing prowess inspired surfboard and clothing brands like Billabong, Quicksilver, Hot Tuna and Rip Curl; for good measure add Mambo, the urban subversive label known around the world. These niche brands have been very successful. Billabong International, headquartered at Burleigh Heads, Queensland, racked up global revenue of $74 million in 1999–2000, a massive growth over 1998's $39.7 million. The Billabong brand appears on apparel for surfing and extreme sports like skateboarding and snowboarding. Its board shorts, swimwear, T-shirts, jackets, wallets and backpacks can be found in 60 countries including the USA, Japan and most of Europe. Billabong sponsors pro surfing competitions in Australia, South Africa and Spain. Founder Gordon Merchant still owns nearly 26% of the company which now employs 500-plus people.

Billabong, arguably a niche brand, has thrown down the gauntlet.

Where are the mainstream brands? Where's Australia's Nike? With global annual sportswear and sportsgoods turnover topping the GNP of many countries, Australia should target to have 15% of the global market by 2020.

How? Luck and timing play a big role in the success or failure of any marketing idea. In the sports goods industry, Australia will need a strong power base: guts and bucks. It's going up against the big guns, Nike, Adidas and Reebok. It's David versus Goliath. The first step is to accept that *one* David, concentrating all his energy, has a better shot than, say, ten little Davids. It would be far more efficient in the incredibly tough global arena to back one Australian horse only. From the start, the *one* brand should represent *all* leading sports goods lines and apparel. This one brand hero should be endorsed by every recognised Australian sporting idol across the world and championed by Australian celebrities at every chance. This *one* sports brand will become the proud and passionate global icon for every Australian and every world citizen who appreciates the tough, fun-loving Aussies. It requires some outrageous thinking to consolidate all the best sports goods makers into one dynamic marketing entity, one all-powerful icon. The very thought should bring tears to Kerry Packer's eyes as he donates the first $50 million to get the idea rolling.

As for the niche sports like surfing, horse riding, yachting, pleasure craft, I'd retain the existing individual brand names; they would not be part of the master "one-brand" plan.

The Boot

In 1887, British bootmaker James Oliver gave up his search for nuggets on the Ballarat goldfields and went back to making boots for miners and farmers. And the company he started, Oliver Footwear, is still there in the Victorian provincial city of Ballarat, and still in family hands. In fact, the fourth generation of Olivers has seen their boots travel a long way from the farm.

Oliver Footwear today is Australia's largest producer of industrial and safety footwear including combat boots and firefighters' boots. Their smelting industry boots can survive being dipped into hot metal at 960 degrees Celsius!

In the early 1990s, Oliver Footwear released The Boot range — and the big difference is they can now be worn as an inverted fashion statement. They look as smart with a suit as they do with jeans. They are exceptionally well crafted and incredibly comfortable to wear. As The Boot's appeal among young, well-heeled Western businessmen and women continues its upward curve, the time seems to be right to fine-tune its brand strategy, ensuring that it retains its somewhat macho, rugged, unpretentious niche character while seeking a huge revenue growth. Definitely its pricing should be premium-bent.

Global footwear sales are around $44 billion annually. There's a huge global opportunity to be exploited. Right now, Oliver Footwear turns out about 750,000 pairs of shoes and boots a year, yet exports only 20,000 pairs of boots a year.

I'm no betting man, but if The Boot does not achieve international fame and fortune, I'll donate the proceeds of this book to some home for retired book writers — *after* shooting the brand owners!

Aussie Beef

More predictably, beef is my next choice as a potential global power brand. "Throw another shrimp on the barbie!" has become a catchphrase when talking about things Australian. But in fact what is far more likely to find its way onto the grill is a thick slab of steak, because, by my reckoning, Australians eat more red meat on a per capita basis than almost any other nation on earth.

Not surprisingly, the red meat of choice is beef. Australia's benign climate and abundance of well-watered, wide open spaces make it a highly favourable environment in which to raise beef cattle. Cattle can be left to roam free year round in open grazing pastures with no need for the expense of providing them with protection against winter cold and little or no need for supplemental feed. The resultant product is grass-fed beef, quite unlike the richly marbled grain-fed beef which characterises the world's other great beef exporter, the USA. Australian beef, or "Aussie Beef" as it is branded in export markets, is a leaner, darker, arguably more healthy meat with a distinctive flavour and texture. In recent years, Australian meat producers have also begun producing grain-fed beef for markets such as Japan where this product can command a premium.

Australia's beef exports are substantial — about 20% of the world's total. Ironically, while Australia is the world's largest beef exporter, it's only the seventh largest beef producer, after the USA, the European Union, Brazil, China, Argentina and Russia, and a tad ahead of Mexico.

In 1999, Aussie beef exports totalled more than $1.5 billion, with a reported projected increase of 14% in volume terms from 2000 to 2001. Demand and prices have been rising sharply, with producers today enjoying the best prices in years. Everything looks positive and the government-backed Australian Meat and Livestock Corporation must take credit for a lot of this success. So what's the beef?

Very simply, I think the size of the export opportunity and Aussie Beef's export market share could be leveraged far more aggressively. Indeed, I believe Aussie Beef could become a global power brand if it is prepared to take risks and pioneer red meat consumption in emerging markets.

Priority to date has been given to Japan, and the payback from a large marketing investment is evident in the $0.7 billion worth of Aussie Beef sales to Japan in 1999. Which is great. And the growth in Japan must continue to be fostered. But I don't think so much of the marketing effort should be concentrated in Japan in the future. Closely-knit Japanese consortiums control Japanese distribution and the Australian dealers are now in the club. The Japanese have steadily taken over important abattoirs in Australia and have even bought into some of Australia's big cattle farms. In effect, they now essentially control the total production and processing chain of a good chunk of all Aussie Beef sold in Japan. Today, it is very much in their interests to enthusiastically promote the growth of Aussie Beef consumption in their home country. So let them lead the marketing charge rather than the Australian Meat and Livestock Corporation, while the Corporation takes more aggressive action against other global marketing opportunities.

Korea offers a big growth potential and the Australian meat lads are doing a fine job in developing that market. However, when things are moving along nicely, there's no better time to step on the gas and broaden the base — notably in China, Taiwan and Southeast Asia. The fact is almost half of all Aussie beef exports are going to Japan and Korea, while *less than 10%* go to Southeast Asia and Taiwan.

Of course, outside Japan and Korea most Asians are not renowned red meat eaters for historical and sometimes religious reasons. But the affluent "New Asians" of today and tomorrow are fast embracing new eating experiences as the explosive growth of Western fast food chains demonstrates. And while it is doubtful that all 2.75 billion non-Japanese, non-Korean Asians will try red meat, I'd settle for *just 10% of them* doing so within the next decade! The beef brand managers should take the lead by investing significant marketing funds in these emerging markets as part of, say, a 5-year plan to be the unquestioned number one quality beef brand in all worthy Asian countries by 2006. Indeed, "owning Asia" should be the key mission. The thrust into the mature red meat markets of Europe and the Americas of course needs a different strategy, but like good Australian wines the Aussie Beef brand should be present in all stores and restaurants as a great quality alternative to the local products.

How to get all this moving?

A savvy distribution strategy is essential. Product innovations are also integral to the scheme of things, and developments like organic beef have to be skilfully managed. The pricing strategy, however, is arguably the most sensitive issue to get right. Australian producers need to be incentivised and one obvious solution is better yields. Focus on boasting the Australian beef brand as the best quality meat on the market, worthy of the best premium price.

The toughest task is connecting with the end consumers; available publicity funds are limited, but getting to the consumer and building brand preference and loyalty is now top priority. It's time for the Australian Government to open up its coffers, as it did for tourism, and invest in taking the Aussie Beef quality story to the general public in key emerging markets on a determined scale. Target for Aussie Beef to dominate. Invest heavily in classic advertising and promotional support each year for the next five years for a great potential yield.

Naturally, you can bet your last dollar that your key competitor — the USA — will not sit idle as you try to eat into its market share. Nor will Argentina, until 1970 one of the world's biggest beef exporters, neglect to give Aussie Beef a run for its money; beef is still a critical component of that nation's economy. But I'm banking on Aussie Beef clearly becoming the number one beef brand among Asian consumers, and staying in front as a result of a consistently aggressive, entrepreneurial branding campaign. To *not* take the bull by its horns will only win the applause of Aussie Beef's competitors and, perhaps, a resigned sigh from author Donald Horne.

There is, of course, the constant health debate about consumption of red meat, with the opposition pushing negatives like the hardening of arteries and digestion problems. But if Dr. Peter D'Adamo has anything to do with it, beef should enjoy even bigger, healthier consumption. In his popular book, *Eat Right for Your Type*, Dr. D'Adamo argues that good health comes from eating the right food for your blood type. The majority of this planet's population has Group O type blood. And you've guessed it, Group O people should eat red meat regularly, says the good doctor.

Virtual Education

It makes eminent sense to me that Australia should spearhead the evolution of interactive learning. Australia has one of the best education systems in the world. It is the planet's third largest national provider of training and education in English to international students. Australian education is now a $2-billion-a-year business. In terms of earning foreign exchange, education ranks eighth after tourism, coal, transportation services, gold, petroleum, iron ore and aluminium — and ahead of wheat, beef and wool!

Telstra, Australia's leading information and communications

company, and Gilat, an Australian supplier of interactive learning systems, have joined forces to get commercialised virtual learning off the starting blocks in a big way. The cutting edge technology is buttoned down. Arguably though, the most critical component is content. And that is where Australian education institutions could well steal the march on their two biggest competitors, Britain and America.

Several Australian universities will open on-line campuses. One group of international institutions has already formed the Global University Alliance, offering Internet-based post-graduate programmes. Member universities can offer their programmes to a greater range of countries than ever, achieving economies of scale, greater collaboration in course development and lower costs for students. The Royal Melbourne Institute of Technology and the University of South Australia are GUA members along with universities in Canada, the Netherlands, the UK and the US. The GUA is located in Hong Kong, strategically serving North and South Asia. Another international grouping, Universitas 21, has 500,000 students enrolled, studying on-line at 18 universities in ten countries. Aussie members include the University of New South Wales and the University of Queensland. Some 44,000 academics are employed and the combined operating budget now exceeds $9 billion. Rupert Murdoch's News Corporation recently became a joint-venture partner. Meanwhile, the University of South Queensland offers 40 fully accredited courses to 20,000 students, only a quarter of whom physically attend lectures on campus.

With the Australian Government strongly supporting the vision of making Australia a global centre for virtual education, everyone is driving in the same direction. But, let's take stock for a nanosecond. Is everyone focused on the same objective?

Now is the time to establish *one* strategy that will take Australia's offerings to the world. What is required is an icon, a corporate brand, to crusade the global position. This one, single brand would represent *all* Australian virtual education programmes — whether 20 different Australian educational institutions offer them, or 120 do. The Australian Government and all the participating educational institutions would fund it. No, having one brand does not mean there will be some form of central control, just common agreement and application of some branding guidelines. All participating individual institutions can push their own brand wheelbarrows as well, if they so desire.

The advantage of having one umbrella brand will be the communications potency of its voice. Rather than scores of different Australian institutions scrambling to be recognised and respected, Australia will have one icon, one holistic statement that flies the flag in cyberspace. It would be like Star Alliance is in the airline world, a true global power brand.

CHINA: THE AWAKENED GIANT

Marketing and advertising are acknowledged tools of capitalist development, so China has been out of this game for quite some time.

History credits the Chinese with giving the world printing and gunpowder, ironically according to some reports in the same year — 1040 — yet remarkably Johann Gutenberg (1436) and Guy Fawkes (1605) are the names associated with what historically are Chinese creations. There is no universally acclaimed Chinese-branded printing equipment, even though Pi Sheng invented printing from movable type — in his case, individual characters were carved in fine clay and hardened by slow baking — long before Gutenberg arrived on the scene and had his name perpetuated in the Gutenberg press. Likewise, Tseng Kung-Liang cooked up his gunpowder formula so the Chinese could launch rockets and firecrackers to amuse their emperors, but today the world celebrates Guy Fawkes Day, Guy Fawkes Night and Guy Fawkes Carnival with extravagant fireworks to perpetuate the memory of the Gunpowder Plot and the sharpening conflict between the Bishop of Rome and the English Monarch.

"Made in China" has been essentially the sole recognised trademark of everything coming out of China. The absence of private Chinese brands is not surprising. China has, since ancient

times, been insular — why else build the monumental Great Wall?
— keeping its achievements and products (and, one suspects, its
women) within the gates, and the barbarians outside. There is an
even more compelling reason for the absence of branding as we
know it today. For example, wonderful Chinese porcelain, the
delight of modern collectors, has no brand names. Pieces are
known by dynastic patronage: Song, Ming, Qing. This is equally
true of exquisite Chinese furniture, paintings, artefacts and other
marvellous Chinese collectibles (some of them purloined by
colonial overlords) which such houses as Christie's and Sotheby's
celebrate in multimillion dollar auctions.

There is also the question of quality of Chinese products. The
mindset and excesses of Mao's unsuccessful attempt to make China
the largest producer of steel in the world by setting up backyard
furnaces still endure on Chinese factory floors. Where production
volumes and not quality are the clarion call, thousands of
companies turn out billions of dollars worth of shoddy goods year
after year. By most estimates, $300 billion "worth" of junk Chinese
goods are sitting in warehouses around the country. This represents
about one-third of China's gross domestic product.

If emperors and their dynasties effectively preempted craft and
skill in ancient times to add to the glory of their regimes (and snuff
out private brand building), Mao's creation of a command society
killed off innovation, risk-taking and private enterprise which,
together with corruption, had thrived in Chiang Kai-shek's time. It
took three decades and Mao's death before China introduced free
market reforms in 1979 under Deng Xiaoping, changing the shape
and course of China's $990 billion economy. Since then, the
Chinese economy has stood out among East Asian economies,
delivering high growth and declining inflation. The tortuous
process of dismantling state-owned enterprises, which began with
Deng's reforms, is continuing while private enterprise is flowering.
There is no turning back. China is firmly focused on sustaining
growth and the momentum of reform, and will integrate further
with the world economy as a result of its WTO membership. The
dragon is now strengthening its powerhouse muscles and once it
gets really motoring, the world will shake.

There are, as expected, some major problems that need to be ironed out. China's state-owned sector desperately needs restructuring. In 1999, a report in the *China Daily* disclosed that China's government industries had $60 billion worth of idle equipment sitting in state factories, accounting for around 8% of the assets of state enterprises. China's banks need help, too, weighed down as they are by bad loans, mostly owed by state enterprises. For a successful reform of these sectors, China needs to sustain sufficiently rapid growth to cap the social costs of restructuring, particularly large increases in unemployment, and to stem the huge seepage of funds from state coffers through the machinations of corrupt cadres and party chiefs.

The light at the end of the long tunnel is the private sector. For the purpose of our branding study, this is where we should be looking for individual China-created products and services that will someday soon become universally powerful. There is already a high level of energy and dynamism in China's private sector, which today contributes almost as much to the GDP as the lumbering state enterprises that have been the bulwark of the Communist Party's economic power since 1949.

The International Finance Corporation, the private sector arm of the World Bank, claims that private businesses in China generated 33% of China's GDP in 1998, compared with 37% from the state sector. The remaining GDP contribution came from agricultural businesses and companies with a mix of owners dominated by state interests. The London *Financial Times*, in a recent report (11 May 2000) said the IFC's findings may help to reshape the classification of China's economy which is officially called a "socialist market economy" but which is, "in many ways, scarcely less capitalist than some in the West".

Significantly, in 1999 the Chinese constitution was amended to elevate private enterprise to a place alongside the state sector in China's economic ideology. And it is in China's inexorable drift towards capitalism that we will find, as we scan the distant horizon of Chinese products and services, the signs of great global brands to come.

But first, a brief word on the existing "Made in China" generic branding. Clearly there's no big problem continuing it, but it's time to seriously leverage ownership through distinctive "private" branding in key categories. Some years back, for example, a New Zealander developed a special fruit in his country and gave it the brand name Kiwifruit. This fruit and the brand name grew in popularity around the world and the future looked fabulous for the New Zealand growers-cum-owners. In fact, Kiwifruit became *so* popular that it was eventually planted and grown in other parts of the world under the same brand name — Kiwifruit. A great global success story, but not for the New Zealand inventors. You see, they somehow didn't get round to registering the name Kiwifruit outside New Zealand. The fruit grown and marketed in other continents under Kiwifruit was owned by global competitors. And it wasn't long before those competitors, due to lower costs and closer location to the big USA and European markets, cut the knees off Kiwifruit exports from New Zealand. In the case of China, you have Golden Assets such as Chinese teas and traditional Chinese medicines that are being clearly exploited globally by Western brand owners and it's time for China-based, China-owned companies to claim commercial brand ownership of these great assets. But more about this a bit later.

In this overview, I've identified just seven potential global power brands and most of them could join the World's Top 50 Brands league within the next 20 years, if not sooner.

Qingdao Haier

For our first sighting, let's look at an enterprise with a vaguely Germanic name: the Qingdao Haier Group, China's leading manufacturer of household electrical appliances — washing machines, airconditioners, ovens, toasters, cookers, refrigerators, and so on. Haier is a strong Acquired Asset in China.

Founded in 1984, it was originally known rather unfashionably as the Qingdao Refrigerator Factory. The group in fact turns out some 9,000 kinds of products, many of which have passed stringent technological tests and won ISO 9001 certification in 20 countries, enabling the group to market its products internationally. It employs 20,000 workers in China, including a significant number of foreign experts.

In a remarkable twist, Haier — which exports shiploads of refrigerators to the United States annually (the original technology was sourced from Liebherr of Germany in 1984) and saw its 1999 exports rise close to 25% year-on-year — now has a $30-million production facility in South Carolina. Why? Haier Group strategists say manufacturing in the United States, despite higher costs, will boost the brand's acceptance globally and allow it to use a "Made in America" label. It is interesting to note that one of Wal-Mart's top-selling refrigerator brands is Magic Chef. No prizes for guessing who manufactures it. Haier's president Zhang Ruimin says, "When Americans think about Haier, we want them to think it is an American company."

Haier plans to absorb the higher US production costs without penalising American customers who appreciate Haier's competitive price advantage over rival, mostly US, Japanese and Korean, brands. (It's that neat little mechanism of subsidising your overseas prices by dunning your domestic consumers, which the Japanese have elevated to an art form.)

Haier executives claim that the German Government encourages people to buy Haier's energy-saving, freon-free refrigerators by offering them a 50 Deutschemark subsidy for buying an environmentally-friendly product. Haier is also big in France, Japan and Australia. It claims that 90% of all washing machines imported by Japan from China carry the Haier badge. It is reported that exports of technology and products in the year 2000 exceeded $280 million and will hit $1 billion by 2005. Meanwhile the group's annual gross turnover is currently close to $5 billion.

Haier's global strategy is two-pronged:

1. It is establishing manufacturing plants overseas.

2. It is co-venturing manufacturing in certain countries by licensing its proprietary technology and creating joint ventures. The countries initially involved are Pakistan, India and Yugoslavia.

Interestingly, in the technology transfer area, Haier had set up Hotline-Haier Appliances Ltd, a joint venture with the Delhi-based Hotline Group holding 70% equity. The company acquired 32 acres for a manufacturing facility. The plan was to roll out 65 products — microwave ovens, vacuum cleaners, refrigerators, deep freezers and airconditioners among others — priced 10% below competing products from current market leaders in India, Samsung and LG. After a year, the partnership was aborted in September 2000, with Hotline citing investment and pricing issues as the cause.

Elsewhere, notably in Malaysia, Haier has built a manufacturing plant in Puchong, Selangor, which currently assembles washing machines with kits shipped from Haier's China plants. That, too, is a JV, with local partner Basswinn Sdn Bhd, Haier's sole agent in Malaysia.

Haier has in recent times won plenty of plaudits for product quality and innovative management. In terms of revenue growth among the world's fastest developing electrical appliance enterprises, Haier was ranked first in 1995 and 1996. On 30 November 1998, the London *Financial Times* ranked Haier seventh in its list of outstanding Asian transnational companies after Toyota, Sony, Kao, Honda, Canon and Fuji.

Haier is patently geared for global stardom and I've set it to be among the top three home appliance brands in the world within the next decade. That is, so long as it's prepared to step onto the world communications stage and connect frequently with the global consumer, not as a US brand, not as an Asian brand, but as a proud international brand — from China.

Konka Group

Haier is not alone in seeking to build a global power brand. An *Asian Wall Street Journal* report (24 April 2000) names such companies as Konka, Huawei and Legend as doing some energetic brand building. The *AWSJ* quotes the Konka Group as saying, "We are trying to break the stereotype ... that China makes lousy goods." In 1999, Konka rolled out four and a half million colour television sets and won a design award in the United States, but the "Made in China" label is still a sticking point. Observes one company spokesman, "Lots of merchandisers have asked us to take off the 'Made in China' label or switch to a Japanese brand, but we won't do it. People are going to change. They will understand 'Made in China' doesn't mean bad quality any more."

The same *AWSJ* report notes: "China's success in the global economy will depend to some degree on the ability of its companies to build popular brands. Japan did it in the 1960s and 1970s. South Korea did it in the 1980s. Now, Chinese businessmen who have spent years making products and putting other firms' names on them, say it is their turn..."

Chinese businessmen are not alone in this uphill struggle. The Chinese Government is providing plenty of help — subsidies for research and easy access to Chinese capital markets for companies creating quality products are some of the incentives. There is also solid support for the home players against overseas competition, through import restrictions, higher tariffs and bureaucratic nit-picking. Predictably, this active intervention by the Chinese Government has drawn criticism from the United States, China's biggest customer, whose trade deficit with China had escalated to nearly $70 billion at the end of 1999. Small wonder then that Chinese brands have registered significant success in fighting competition on their home turf. As the *AWSJ* reports, "Six years ago foreign brands dominated the Chinese television market, grabbing 70% of the sales. Now, led by Konka, Chinese firms account for 80%."

This scenario is being replicated in other areas such as computers...

Legend

Just four or so years ago, some 80% of the computers sold in China were foreign brands. Today, Beijing-based Legend Holdings and two other domestic computer makers have cornered over 50% of the market, while companies such as IBM, Hewlett Packard, Compaq and Dell have collectively been reduced to 15%.

This company is my pick to be a global brand leader within the next decade. Excluding Japan, Legend already ranks as the largest PC seller in Asia-Pacific and is growing stronger each year in the servers market. Importantly, Legend aims to become an Internet service powerhouse. It recently restructured into two divisions, Legend Digital and Legend Computer Systems, and has embarked on a huge growth mission. Legend is already in the personal digital assistance or handheld PC market. Partnering Motorola to produce "Palm Net", Legend is also actively developing other Internet-related products and services.

The size of the global market for PCs and accessories is mind-boggling, despite some hiccups. Some predictions put the figure at $800 billion by 2020. I see no reason why Legend (wonderful name, isn't it?) should not achieve 10% of this market 20 years down the road, so long as it follows the capitalist rules of marketing — a key one being brand connection and bonding with customers. The communication investment should be embraced vigorously, starting now, with initial focus on Asia-Pacific. One competitor, IBM, invests 0.6% of its revenue on advertising, Compaq 0.8% and Acer 0.3%. Legend has some catching up to do in terms of brand awareness and the quicker it does this, starting in Asia-Pacific, the faster it will realise the lofty target I've set for it. I also venture the view that the "catch up" advertising move will prove more economical in the long run; what you spend today to penetrate a marketplace will cost you at least 5% more next year, and so on. You improve market share much quicker, and you fight inflation more effectively.

The brand communications act for Legend on the global stage will be competing with some of the smartest, most famous brands known to man. Which makes the challenge immensely exciting. The name "Legend" has a ring about it that presents an opportunity for breakthrough creative. It must clearly be global in presence, with a proud Chinese pedigree.

Tsingtao Beer

As Japan did post-war, followed by Korea in the 1970s, Chinese enterprises in the period of economic reforms have relied on imported technology and getting manufacturing skills through transfers of manufacturing arrangements. There are, however, a few exceptions, a prominent one being Tsingtao Beer.

Founded by German settlers in 1903, Tsingtao embarked on an aggressive domestic marketing and export drive in the wake of Deng's economic reforms. Today, Tsingtao is sold in over 40 countries. Tsingtao, China's biggest brewing group, owns numerous breweries in Heilongjiang, Jiangsu, Shandong and Shanxi provinces with annual production of about 20 million hectolitres. The company is also involved in a joint venture with Japan's Asahi Breweries. Tsingtao accounts for 90% of China's beer exports and is regarded as a premium brand in the high end of the domestic market. Its top-selling brands are Tsingtao Beer and Gold Label Tsingtao.

While open to challenge, I'm told that China is the world's second largest beer brewer after the United States. Apart from Tsingtao, there are scores of other breweries in China. Beijing's Yanjing Beer Group Co. and the Guangdong Zhujiang Beer Co. Ltd. are challenging Tsingtao's primacy. With total Chinese beer production today *47 times more* than in 1979, Chinese tipplers are challenging the Germans and other Westerners for the title of the world's biggest swillers of beer. Worldwide per capita consumption is something like 25 litres, while in China it is 16 litres. But a US trade publication, *Southern Draft Brew News,* is forecasting that the Chinese will overtake the world in beer consumption in a nifty four years.

The Chinese passion for beer has recently spawned a number of new varieties, notably light beer, white beer, black beer and even a non-alcoholic brew called "Fitness Beer".

The world beer market has taken a hit from some other alcohol categories but it will conceivably grow a further 50% by 2020, assuming a conservative annual growth of 2%. In 1999–2000 fiscal, Anheuser-Busch had around 9.2% of the world beer market; Heineken 5.7% and Carlsberg 3.1%. Outside of China, Tsingtao's share of the world market is 1%. It has nowhere to go but up, and should target for a minimum 5% of the global market — excluding China — within the next decade. Predictably, beer brands around the world have their loyal, bonded customers, but up to 50% of all beer drinkers can be persuaded to switch loyalties, particularly at the younger end of the equation. National — even parochial — pedigrees have played a big role in building beer brand equities, but as the world is shrinking in so many forms, so too is the beer drinker becoming less insular and more adventurous. (How else did Mexican beer get so popular?) This trend will continue.

Tsingtao should launch an aggressive 10-year plan to become one of the top three beer brands in the world. Aside from having the brewing capacity (joint ventures included) strategically positioned, it's totally a marketing exercise and an exciting one for brand builders who revel in all the emotional arguments. Tsingtao's pedigree is excellent, and its name instantly stamps its place of origin. Packaging, pricing and new variants can play important roles, but the key thing to pin down is the brand's soul — a fun challenge that sorts the wheat from the chaff, so to speak.

Tong Ren Tang

Let's move on to another huge growth opportunity — traditional medicine — one of China's greatest Golden Assets. Some 6,000 years ago, Chinese medicine men dug deep into Nature to find relief and cure for man's ailments. The grand daddy of them all was Shennong, China's celebrated herbal medicine master who lived and practised his discipline at that time. Successive generations of pharmacists have given today's practitioners of traditional Chinese medicine (TCM) a spread of some 8,000 natural medicinal products. While TCM encompasses a range of techniques and materials, those most commonly known are herbal products, acupuncture and massage. The resurgence of TCM has also spawned interest in other Asian countries, which are now seeking to create TCM products using modern pharmaceutical research and production techniques. Interestingly, the School of Health, Biological and Environmental Sciences of Middlesex University in England recently began offering a degree course in traditional medicine.

Despite the huge growth in TCM, there is a distinct absence of globally-known TCM brands from China. But this will change. One company I've identified, China Beijing Tong Ren Tang Holdings

Corporation Import and Export Co., has been in business for more than 330 years. The acknowledged leader in the TCM industry, Tong Ren Tang — to call them by their widely-used shorter name — is gearing up to penetrate the international market. "We will strengthen our position in Southeast Asia, and explore new markets in Europe, the United States, Latin America and the Middle East over the next eight to ten years," says the firm's general manager.

Tong Ren Tang is currently refining their production techniques and packaging, and says products will achieve international standards and satisfy universally-accepted procedures. The process is evolving rapidly at Tong Ren Tang which in 1999 won licensing for four of their products in the United States — a climacteric health product, a ginseng-peony extract, an isatis root standardised extract (isatis, in case you're wondering, is a herb of the mustard family), and a pancreas health product. And they're just the start. Recently, Tong Ren Tang announced they had developed three new export-oriented products: a stomach-soothing tablet for children, an active pearl powder treatment and a guttate pill for improving cardiac and cerebral vascular conditions.

Tong Ren Tang is clearly on the right path to becoming a great global power brand. They have the best credentials in the industry. They just need the services of a smart strategic planning and marketing team to package the brand as the premium TCM in the industry.

Chinese Tea

Another Golden Asset opportunity — Chinese tea. China is the home of tea, where tea shrubs were recorded as far back in time as five to six thousand years. China started exporting tea more than a thousand years ago and today produces essentially six types — green, red, greenish black, yellow, white and black, plus a variety of herbal teas. In fact, thirsty generations of Westerners have even co-opted the Chinese word for tea, *chá*.

Second only to India in tea production, China does not own one single well-known brand in the world market. And the world market is fairly healthy — I calculate the current annual production to exceed 2.9 million metric tons, and to grow about 10% every year. Western companies, notably Unilever (through its Lipton brand), buy a lot of Chinese tea, and in recent times have been buying China's local brands, too; Unilever acquired the most famous brand, Jing Hua.

I couldn't find any Chinese flagship company in tea production and trade, so here's a golden opportunity for an entrepreneur to build a Chinese tea global power brand from scratch — with, of course, the incredible heritage to underpin the communications strategy. As well as marketing conventional teas, the brand should obviously explore new taste experiences and, like a fine wine producer, take exclusive blends to the world market from "privately-owned" tea plantations. Traditional Chinese medicinal herbs should also be more vigorously addressed from the standpoint of producing exclusive "health care" teas — the trendy "life sciences" field offers wonderful potential for tea brands.

Whether you think of tea as a hot or cold beverage to quench one's thirst, to refresh, to relax, to stimulate, to help relieve pain, to help prevent sickness, to help strengthen your body, to help lengthen your life, the scope of its benefits is pretty well unlimited. China's first truly global tea brand should be immensely successful, not only through its superior credentials, but also through its superior imagination.

Sports Brand

Finally, a jump to sportswear and a Chinese sports brand.

The annual global sporting goods market is worth about $150 billion; global sportswear turnover is worth $25.7 billion. With just about everybody doing more walking, more gyming, hitting more balls and generally wanting to be fitter, healthy growth is a given. Then you have all those folks who now think it smart to wear sports shoes and T-shirts to social evenings, and the bonuses keep on mounting! It's a tough business, but a good business to be in. Nike's net profit for 2000 was $579 million.

My target is for China to have the world's top brand in this category within the next 20 years.

At present there's *no* widely recognised Chinese company or brand making sportswear under its own brand name. So to all intents and purposes we can start with a clean slate. Which is fine. It's now just a matter of shaping a brand strategy, doing a business plan, involving some global entrepreneur in this field, and finding the funding.

Clearly there are several assumptions in proposing this development. One is that China's extensive experience in providing the raw materials and producing sportswear products for some of the great global brands of today will be transferred to the new brand. Another is that the substantial earnings derived from China's massive domestic market for sportswear in the future will sustain the strong global marketing thrust.

Assuming, too, that China emerges as a global sporting powerhouse over the next two decades, with world champions in most popular sports, this success will reinforce the credibility of the Chinese brand in the global playing field.

Endorsement is king in sportswear marketing, and always has been, so as well as giant Chinese champions the brand owners should not be bashful about getting great Western names to endorse their Chinese brand. It only takes money. Your pedigree is China, but your attitude is full-on international. This attitude should be reflected in the contemporary global styling of your personality and the endless stream of cutting edge products you bring to market. Within 20 years from now, at least one Chinese brand could be a $20-billion annual business.

THERE is a kicker to the branding China equation we must not overlook. China's membership in the World Trade Organisation will inevitably change some of the fundamental parameters of production, pricing and marketing both within China and outside for Chinese enterprises.

Predatory Pricing

When Japan mounted its challenge in the American and European marketplaces in the 1960s, predatory pricing rather than product uniqueness was the key to success. The Japanese subsidised prices on their export products by charging much higher prices to their domestic consumers; this cushioned the lower, often non-existent margins on their export sales. The Japanese also exploited the advantages of a cheap yen, given that General MacArthur had fixed the yen to dollar parity at 360 : 1. The Americans and Europeans grumbled, but neither UNCTAD nor bilateral trade agreements had enough teeth to neutralise "dumping" and the bun fight to change the yen–dollar parity took a decade to resolve. Finally, both the Japanese Ministry of Trade and Industry and Japanese banks helped to underwrite the exports drive of the *zaibatsu* in what turned out to be a remarkably effective, cosy and complementary relationship between the government, institutional money and the captains of industry. The Japanese had American and European industrialists and manufacturers on the ropes. By the time regulatory safeguards on imports were put in place, and the yen went off the dollar peg in the early part of the 1970s, the Japanese had already taken control of the commanding heights of several key economic sectors in the US and Europe — steel, automobiles, electrical and electronic consumer appliances, shipbuilding, motorcycles, pneumatic tyres, glass and a slew of high-ticket items.

Today, despite a more expensive yen, Japan remains competitive because it bought enough time in the early post-war years to refine its product technology, unleash a raft of technological innovations, and introduce the world to unique production techniques and values.

China and other Asian competitors, which are still largely anchored to old economy products and technology, have no such advantage. Product quality, innovation, new technologies and savvy marketing are what it will take to build viable beachheads in export markets. How China will respond to this challenge will not only influence the pace at which China's global power brand contenders penetrate international markets, but also the very substance and shape of the Chinese economy.

REINVENTING INDIA

In the 40 years after independence from the British Raj, a bloated Indian bureaucracy controlled and managed the economy, effectively killing off entrepreneurship. Nowadays India is liberalising fast, deregulating on several critical fronts — power, telecommunications, banking, equities markets, heavy engineering and foreign ownership and investment. Central government control has significantly loosened. War has been declared on corruption. The bureaucrats' mindset is being slowly but surely altered to fall in line with the nation's new economic aspirations.

Even the great industrial dynasties have been served notice. Back in October 1996, *The Economist* reported that among the 250 biggest private sector companies, family businesses accounted for about 70% of India's total sales and net profits. We're talking Big Families — the Tatas, Birlas, Singhanias and Thapars — that have carved up big industries. In vehicles, the Tatas make lorries, the Birlas make Ambassador cars, the Bajaj family makes two-wheelers and the Mahindras make jeeps. According to *The Economist* the most famous family, the Tatas, ran some 70 companies making everything from tea to watches in which the parent company's stake was rarely above 15%. By liberalising the economy, the government exposed local businesses to market forces for the first time since Indian independence in 1947. One outcome was to force the conglomerates to sort out their run-down businesses or sell them. Another was that foreign corporations could buy out their Indian joint-venture partners and impose their own standards on the business. While many Indian businessmen are in two minds about the changes, the younger, Western-educated members of the leading families saw the benefits of concentrating on "core competencies". More transparent corporate affairs are in the offing which no doubt pleases the foreign merchant banks keen to generate new corporate finance.

India has already flexed its muscles in global brand building. India's Tata Group bought the venerable old British tea brand, Tetley. Tata paid £271 million for the Tetley Group, maker of the world's second biggest brand of teabags, beating Sara Lee Corp. to the post in the process. Tetley sells more than 2.5 billion teabags a year, second only to the Anglo-Dutch group Unilever that owns Lipton and PG. Tetley has brand leadership in the UK and Canada, and is the fastest growing brand in France. Tata Tea is the largest integrated tea company in the world with additional interests in coffee and spices. Tata produces more than 60 million kilograms of tea from its gardens in Assam, West Bengal, Kerala and Tamil Nadu. The deal was the largest overseas acquisition ever undertaken by an Indian company. Tata has about 23% of India's tea market, 24% of America's instant tea market and now with Tetley on board it can compete more equitably with the marketing behemoth Unilever.

Aside from tea, I've set India to have seven global power brands by 2020.

Textiles

There's a ton of credibility and stature about fabrics from India, but little or nothing is known about their makers. At least two Indian textile manufacturers should take up the global power branding challenge.

How to go about doing this? Some fundamental tips.

I'd take a leaf out of the book of the French fashion houses and follow their methods in driving brand identity. Have physical presence through your own smart boutique stores in five or six big global fashion cities. Introduce new "international" designs each year and be prepared to be occasionally outrageous.

Endear yourself to the global fashion media editors to ensure consistently sympathetic editorial. Collaborate regularly on promotions with other compatible Indian brands.

While Indian in heritage, you're international in your vision. Your advertising should be deceptively simple and elegant. It's important to do something quite startling once in a while — otherwise you will perish. Remember, too, that consistency of presence and personality through the years is fundamental to a successful branding programme.

Taj Hotels

The biggest hotel chain in the world, Holiday Inn, has annual sales turnover of around $6 billion. Swanky, upmarket Four Seasons Hotels, with a 26-country chain, had annual revenue of $2.8 billion in 1999, a 250% gain over the year before. The global travel industry devoured *$455 billion* of customer receipts in 1999, up 3.1% over 1998. From 1950 to 1999, international tourist arrivals had grown at an average annual rate of 7%. There is definitely room for one more global hotel player.

Asian standards of quality personal service are renowned globally; they are the perfect Acquired Assets of any Asian hotelier. An Indian hotelier can certainly leverage them. In fact, an Indian hotelier has two *additional* Acquired Assets around which to build a strong 5-star global hotel brand. First, the sheer scale of luxury and spectacle reminiscent of the old maharajahs; who knew more about treating themselves and their guests to every conceivable luxury? And when it comes to marketing exotic resorts, romantic getaways and honeymoons, only the Indians can call upon a second exclusive property: *Tantra*. After all, the Indians conceived the *Kama Sutra* and *Ananga Ranga*.

Owned by the dynamic Tata group, Taj Hotels can become one of the top three global hotel brands within the next 20 years. Currently, there are Taj Hotels in ten countries.

The flagship hotel in Bombay is one of India's noblest old colonial structures. It overlooks the ceremonial Gateway to India on the Bombay foreshore where British royalty first set foot on the subcontinent. Legend tells us that the architect committed suicide when he realised his hotel had been built back to front. In the heyday of the Raj, maharajahs rode their stallions up and down the grand staircases. With such fables attached to its name, the Taj brand has a priceless pedigree to offer world travellers.

Some initial brand-building thoughts:

1. Focus on the high-ticket customer base like Four Seasons and Grand Hyatt. Target to institutionalise every Taj Hotel around the world as the theatre for all things beautifully Indian — through its décor and definitive

Indian restaurant, and by positioning it as the prime location for Indian performing and visual art shows, exhibitions of Indian antiques, and launches of new Indian textile designs.

2. In the initial years of global network expansion, highly skilled public relations and promotions should lead the brand-building charge supported by eclectic-style advertising in narrow vertical media like *The Economist*. Until such time as the network is established in 30 key destinations, the global communications budget could be contained at a modest level; even in the maturing period of global brand building this budget would probably not need to exceed 4–5% of revenue.

3. A beautifully-crafted website would celebrate the uniqueness of Taj Hotels and provide special pages of exclusive Indian recipes from the kitchens of the Taj along with special access to Indian tourism travel planners. To underscore the brand's pedigree, the site could host regular Indian art auctions.

4. The Taj customer database would treat every guest as royalty even months after they have checked out. Bonding would occur through highly intelligent connections at least four times a year.

To the world at large, Taj should evolve into an icon of all that is gracious and beautiful in India. And India's national tourism authority, no doubt, will eagerly underwrite a big slice of Taj's ad spend.

Electronics

I'm talking here about lifestyle electronic products — those entertainment gadgets like TVs, VCRs, CD players, DVD players, and video cameras. As we all know so well, the Japanese govern this territory in every corner of the earth and spend huge sums on research and development, on brand communications, on distribution, and everything else you can imagine, just to stay ruthlessly ahead. Because it's a game of constant, rapid change, the competitive environment is boiling hot. But the stakes are equally incredible. In 1998, this industry's global turnover exceeded $400 billion. So I figure it's time for India to step seriously into this playing field. Why?

The huge goldmine is certainly the carrot, but equally as important, I think that India has got the great people — the mad, creative minds — to quickly match and successfully outpace the Japanese at their own game. This is essentially a start-from-scratch exercise for India, but the technological expertise that's growing at the rate of knots in the IT industry can be refocused (well, some of it) to harness the drive for India to have a great global electronics lifestyle brand within the next two decades — perhaps even earlier.

Following the Second World War, Japan developed from a regional, cheap end maker of suspect brands into a dynamic global brand leader in many product categories, in the space of 25 years — a remarkable achievement. Through its breathtaking efforts in the IT industry, India will emerge on the world stage as the smartest IT act in the business within the next few years. Developments in categories such as consumer electronics have the potential to enjoy similar favour and acclaim amid the hype of it all.

Information Technology

India is on the threshold of becoming the world's number one IT player. It is no lofty boast; India is creating leading edge proprietary technologies in computer chip design, Web-based services, telecoms and 3-D software. Indian universities churn out 120,000 engineering graduates a year. Another 780,000 engineers graduate every year from India's polytechnics and specialised computer training institutes. (There are 3,000 such institutes up and running now; on average, an additional 1,000 new institutes have opened *every month.*) Thousands of Indian high-tech graduates who have already made it to the top in the United States are returning to India to spearhead the launch of a slew of IT-based companies. In turn, these companies enhance India's reputation for high quality. How high? Of only 21 companies worldwide that hold the Carnegie

Mellon Software Engineering Institute's highest ranking for excellence, 12 are from India.

BusinessWeek threw more light on the matter on 21 February 2000: "Despite world-class skills and education, India's army of engineers has mostly been used as cheap contract labour, performing the tedious task of writing reams of software code for foreign giants from General Electric to American Express. Many thousands of others migrated to the US, staffing the labs that produced cutting edge products for companies such as Intel, Sun Microsystems and Cisco." One such Indian expatriate was Tushar A. Dave, founder of Armedia Inc. A physicist and computer engineer, Dave had a successful career at Intel developing microprocessors. He returned to India and started a semiconductor design company in Bangalore, India's Silicon Valley. The breakthrough came in 1998 when Armedia designed a chip that instantly decoded the vast flood of digital video in highly compressed television signals. The chip made it possible to view high definition programmes either on new digital TVs or on existing sets. Armedia caught the attention of US chipmaker Broadcom; it had the know-how to compress video images for digital broadcast signals over satellite and cable, but not the technology to *de*compress it for TV viewing. In 1999, Broadcom bought Armedia for $67 million. As Broadcom CEO Henry T. Nicholas III said, "It has been a seamless transition. It helped us build the world's most highly integrated HDTV chip..."

Software products accounted for about $6 billion in exports in 2000, one-quarter of the growth in India's $400 billion economy which is slated to achieve 5–7% expansion. McKinsey & Co and India's National Association of Software & Service Companies (Nassacom) have forecast that by 2008, India's IT exports could hit $50 billion, while domestic IT revenues would touch $40 billion. That would translate into 2.2 million new jobs in India and push India's annual growth into the 7–8% range. Indian IT entrepreneurs, it seems, may well have the means to drag India out of its historic poverty.

So far, so good. India now has to firmly secure two branding positions to rise from playing the flute to orchestra leader. The first task: India needs to brand herself. On the surface, for reasons widely known, this does not seem a tough assignment. But it is naïve to take things easy in an industry that moves and shakes so quickly, so a special brand-strengthening insurance programme is recommended. *India Advantage*, for example, communicates a high-ground brand attitude that challenges the international IT leadership of the US. *India Advantage* is, say, the national branding device on every software product leaving India. A self-funding global public relations campaign, operated by Nassacom, would replace ad hoc news announcements; each new Indian IT breakthrough would be a superbly orchestrated event for the world media. The PR programme would pay for itself by making India the venue-of-choice for IT conferences. Nassacom, conference organisers and hoteliers would pool their resources to ensure maximum returns in both awareness and profit. India would become the Cannes of the IT world; a glittering annual IT awards festival recognising the best new global developments and personalities would seal India's position on the world IT calendar. The *India Advantage* website would be unbelievably spectacular. India would grow its own IT stars, the Indian "Bill Gateses", who would become the next generation of household names.

The second branding agenda: target for *at least* four global brands to emerge with the *India Advantage* within the decade. The imperative is for IBM, Intel, Digital and Microsoft to make way for Indian brands like BPL, Wipro, Infosys, Sankhya and NIIT.

India's largest cellphone operator **BPL**, with annual sales of $1 billion, develops analog chips for cellphone voicemail systems marketed under Japanese brands like Panasonic. BPL also designs sophisticated switching products for the air traffic control systems sold by America's Harris Corp. Rajeev Chandrasekhar, who developed microprocessors at Intel and worked on the team that produced the Pentium chip, heads BPL. It was the first Indian company to introduce e-mail access through the cellphone and aspires to be India's top player in the wireless Internet.

Meanwhile, one of India's biggest software service companies *Wipro Technologies* plans to move its headquarters from Bangalore to Santa Clara, California to capture even more top-end US business. Wipro makes microbrowsers for Japanese mobile Internet products, manages e-commerce sites and designs Web security systems. CEO Vivek Paul has 6,500 engineers on his payroll. Wipro's business has grown by an annual 59% since 1995. Revenue for 1999 topped $220 million. Paul believes he has to seize the initiative and plug into American opportunities on American soil.

Another contender for an IT global brand is Bangalore-based **Infosys**. Led by CEO N. R. Narayana Murthy, Infosys has carved its reputation developing software for foreign companies and e-commerce websites for such clients as CBS Sportsline.

Meaning "knowledge" in Sanskrit, **Sankhya Infotech** is one of only three companies in the world to develop a complete package of 3-D animation for aircraft simulators. Amazingly, the company started only a couple or so years ago and now does one-third of its work for Airbus Industries. Its speciality is compressing aviation training programmes into modules of 64 megabytes or less so they can be sent over the Net. Another project will see Sankhya develop simulation software packages catering for different languages and accents. A joint venture with Israel's Magic Software produces virtual reality software. Founders N. Srinivas and N. Sridhar took their company public in 2000.

The global race also includes an education brand: **NIIT**, India's computer education institute. NIIT already has operations in China and teaches engineers in a variety of languages. Why not make NIIT the premier global IT training institute? Indeed, why not!

INDONESIA: TO BE OR NOT TO BE

If you're looking for something bigger than Texas, try Indonesia. Its total land area is almost *three* times bigger than the Lone Star State — 1,826,400 square kilometres, and home to over 200 million people. The natural resource base includes petroleum, tin, nickel, timber, bauxite, coal, gold and silver. Indonesia is the world's largest exporter of liquefied natural gas. Its fertile soils grow a dazzling array of cash crops. It's a tourist paradise. It *should* have been an economic dynamo.

When Indonesia declared its independence from the Dutch in 1945, there was little to celebrate. For one thing, the colonial power refused to acknowledge its independence until 1949. Indonesia's 17,000 islands, of which only 6,000 are inhabited, had been ravaged by war, undermined by ethnic and religious divisions, and were virtually ungovernable. The Dutch had very little cash to leave behind in the national kitty, even if they had wished to; their own country was still recovering from the Nazi Occupation.

Sukarno, Indonesia's first president, was a charismatic national hero who approached his country's problems with a mixture of genius and less commendable virtues. To his credit, he made a nation of the disparate tribes using a new, officially constructed language, Bahasa Indonesia, that was a modified, simpler form of Malay. He created a powerful military machine. His army, navy and air force had the Russians, Americans, Europeans and eventually the Communist Chinese supplying his weaponry. Almost to the end he was able to count on the armed forces to keep him in power.

Sukarno was a great builder of monuments, both ideological and bricks and mortar. The latter variety endures to this date, reminders of the man's folly. He staged the first Afro-Asian heads of state congress at Bandung and emerged as a potential new global statesman. But as his domestic situation sank further into chaos he needed a distraction. Aided by the ambitious leader of Indonesia's pro-Beijing communist party, the PKI (Partai Kommunis Indonesia), he dusted off a dream: a Malay empire that would encompass Malaysia, Singapore, the Philippines and the Muslim region of southern Thailand. The dream would be secured by armed confrontation — *Konfrontasi*. Bombs went off in Singapore. Armed saboteurs struck Malaysia. The Indonesian army infiltrated North Borneo. But by 1965, Sukarno was little more than a communist puppet. Impatient to take over, the PKI staged a coup. All the top generals were massacred and their bodies hurled into the oddly named Crocodile Well by female members of the PKI. In the uproar that followed, countless numbers of innocent Indonesian Chinese were butchered; by some accounts, over a million died. One general, dismissed as being of "no account", had survived. His name was Suharto.

After three decades of Suharto and crony capitalism, however, Indonesia's future is as bleak as ever. The banking system is still sad. Corruption is deeply rooted. Foreign investors play a wait-and-see game. Serious economic transformation is in abeyance.

Almost 75% of Indonesian businesses are in technical bankruptcy. Not surprisingly, when *Asiaweek* ranked the top one thousand Asian enterprises in 2000, only four Indonesian corporations made the cut, and some at the lower end of the table. They were the state-owned oil company Pertamina (48th), Indah Kiat Pulp & Paper (883rd), car assembler Astra International, now majority-owned by Singapore's Cycle & Carriage (615th), and power generation company Per. Listrik Negara (582nd).

The less cynical might be tempted to discover hope, not at the commanding heights of the Indonesian economy, but in the more traditional areas. Despite all the doom and gloom, I'm optimistic about Indonesia's long-term future, and in this exercise I've identified five strong global brand opportunities.

Indonesian Coffee

While the widely-used American idiom for a cup of coffee is "Java", the contents are more likely to come from Colombia or Brazil. However, Indonesia is the world's third largest coffee producer, harvesting from 430,000 to 450,000 tons annually — but a marginal exporter. Only 20% of this total production is actually exported. Ninety percent of the harvest is the commonly used *Robusta*, grown primarily in South Sumatra, Lampung and Bengkulu, while the other 10% is the premium *Arabica* variety cultivated in Aceh, North Tapanuli, North Sumatra, South Sulawesi and East and Central Java. World coffee consumption is growing; the International Coffee Organisation says it will climb by 35% over the next 50 years.

The ball is in Indonesia's court to build a global brand for Indonesian coffee. Some suggested first steps:

1. Set up a joint venture between the government and private enterprise. Call it the Indonesian Coffee Brand, for example. Operate it like a high-powered commercial entity, encouraging coffee growers to process

domestically through a centre rather than merely exporting coffee beans.

2. Establish an experienced marketing team. Lean on foreign expertise to start with. Map out a global brand strategy.

3. Give processed Indonesian coffee a brand name. I personally like *Bali*. This celebrated name lights up all sorts of positive creative opportunities. Furthermore, Bali coffee already exists, but in a small way. It's a strong, distinctive taste.

4. Channel new domestic and foreign investment into plantations to keep production and quality up. Overlay new processing and packaging technology. Bring new acreage under coffee cultivation.

5. Refine plantation-to-market penetration. Indonesian coffee growers are currently operating on a wing and a prayer when they seek to sell their crops.

The bottom line is that Indonesia produces fine coffee. Its *Arabica* variety offers a potential premium product invaluable in any branding exercise. Properly branded, Indonesian coffee will find a highly profitable expanding global market. Within the next 10 to 15 years, *Bali* coffee could well be one of the world's top-selling coffee brands.

Instant Noodles

After China, Indonesia is the world's second largest manufacturer of the unpretentious instant noodle. The dominant producer is PT Indofood Sukses Makmur, a company listed on the Jakarta Stock Exchange. Hold your breath. The world apparently consumes some 44 billion packs of instant noodles a year — with Indofood producing 14 billion of them!

The company's domestic market share is 90% with three instant noodle brands — Indomie, Supermi and Sarimi. It sold a staggering 2.4 billion packs in the first three months of 2001 as recession-hit Indonesians switched from rice to noodles. It exports the rest of its production to 45 countries.

Apart from noodles, its other products are vegetable oil, wheat flour, baby foods, snack foods and food seasonings. Indofood is a major player in edible oils trading and distribution.

After a troubled period following the collapse of the Salim empire (Bank Central Asia et al), Indofood returned to profit. In fact it reported a net profit of $67 million for 2000 on total sales of $1.5 billion for all products. But it still has a huge foreign debt overhang: *$700 million.*

On the positive side, global consumption of instant noodles is expected to reach 100 billion packs by 2010 — more than doubling the market. Clearly, for Indofood to sustain its share of the expanding pie, it will need to substantially increase production at its 121 manufacturing plants and push its exports harder. (The company needs to expand exports in order to increase forex earnings so it can retire its foreign debt.) With 90% of the domestic market already in its pocket, real growth must come from penetrating overseas markets where it faces stiff competition from export rivals in Japan, China, Taiwan, Malaysia, Korea, Singapore and Thailand.

The opportunity for Indofood to make one of its brands — say, Indomie — a global household name leaves one slightly breathless, and this possibility is just five to ten years away! It's certainly going to be a tough journey with slick Western marketers and hordes of marauding Asian brands also determined to lift their market share, but if Indofood drives Indomie and maintains the focus and grit that have carried it to where it is today, I think Indomie will be one of Indonesia's proudest global brands.

Furniture

Indonesia has been a skilled producer of fine furniture for centuries. With 67% of the nation's land area blanketed by forests and woodlands, Indonesia has an abundant supply of timber and rattan. But today Indonesia is still a fairly modest exporter. In 2000, export sales were reported at $1.4 billion. Buyers from all corners of the world purchase direct from Indonesian factories. The Indonesian trademark is highly respected, but the time has come to leverage more power and yield with a highly distinctive brand label.

The industry enjoys substantial supply of quality raw materials, a large pool of skilled, low-cost workers, and the ability to create reproductions of old Balinese, Javanese and Dutch period furniture. But growth is inhibited by a failure to introduce modern technology and equipment, inadequate funding, poor marketing and no recognisable brands.

If the brand issue is addressed intelligently and other fundamentals put right, I would assess, being the brilliant optimist that I am, that a steady $3-billion export market can be achieved within five years. Some basic starting points:

1. Focus planning, investment and technological innovation on Jepara and Yogyakarta, the two areas in Central Java which are dominant producers for the export market. Both areas are famous for woodcarving, furniture and handicrafts. The furniture produced is classified in three categories: *priyayi*, noble designs; *pesisir*, designs from coastal areas; and *pedalaman*, designs from inland areas. The three categories provide a stunning portfolio of products reflecting the grand royal traditions, classical Dutch and Indonesian styles, and those with strong Chinese, Indian and Arabic influences.

2. Much like the Western wine industry model, consolidate the region's capabilities and establish an experienced marketing-centric unit to drive global brand growth. Initially, apply branding solely to the top-quality furniture — it must be positioned as the best in the industry. *Jepara* seems like an excellent brand name.

3. Participate in international furniture exhibitions and fairs. Display the brand on a www.jepara.com website. Vertical marketing is needed along with classic advertising and PR activity.

4. Open new markets in the Middle East, Russia and Australia.

5. Exploit Indonesia's ability to offer genuine wooden furniture as opposed to laminates and chipboard products.

6. Set up wood-processing factories to ensure kiln drying and treating. Invest to guarantee future technological leadership and product quality.

Looking further down the road, I would envision several Indonesian furniture global power brands, but I'd be inclined to start with *Jepara*.

Batik

One of Indonesia's traditional colourful textiles, batik is made of either cotton or silk, or a mix of the two. There are two types: *Batik Tulis*, which is hand-drawn, and *Batik Cap*, stamped. Batik is a highly creative art form, strongly ingrained in Indonesian and Malay culture. It is still a cottage industry and labour-intensive. Manufacturing involves various stages — waxing, dyeing, drying and boiling lengths of cloths embellished with intricate Javanese designs drawn from culture, nature and religion. Indonesians use batik to make formal and traditional clothes, bed and table linen, napkins, scarves, neckties, curtains and tapestry. Three Javanese cities are famous for batik: Yogyakarta, Solo and Pekalongan.

Already some batik makers have begun to develop products for the export market, proving that a global batik brand is a realistic target. Established in 1972, *PT Ardiyanto Wijayakusuma Batik* employs 700 workers. The company is named after the founder, also a designer. Its products are first rate and have been shown off in museums, galleries and exhibitions in many parts of the world since 1973. *PT Batik Keris* started as a family business in the 1920s. Today it operates 50 company-managed sales outlets in Indonesia and exports to Europe, the US and other Asian countries. It also manufactures gold, bronze, ceramic and wood handicrafts. *Iwan Tirta* has pioneered batik for fashion wear and home furnishings.

In business since 1971, the company is named after the founder. His home furnishing lines have won Iwan Tirta splendid coverage in the *Architectural Digest, Maison et Jardin, Vogue Living* and the *New York Times.*

As its furniture has done, so Indonesian-made batik has earned a good global reputation. It has a niche brand presence in selected Western boutiques. But the buck stops there. Indonesia's textile exports were $7.3 billion in 2000; garment exports were around $3.8 billion. Given that the world textile and garment market is estimated to be worth $350 billion annually, Indonesia is a minnow.

An Asian precedent exists to inspire Indonesians: the international fame and fortune of Thai silk. The challenge is to do for batik what Jim Thompson did for Thai silk. Subject to some probable upfront corporate restructuring, the export market potential for Indonesian batik that is championed by an enterprising brand could be *ten times* its current achievements. And that's being conservative. A savvy international venture capitalist and an equally smart Indonesian organisation could get together and attack this great global brand opportunity.

It is a 5- to 10-year plan. The brand must travel first class all the way; nothing must rival its designs, its innovative styles and the quality of its fabric and finish. Focus should be on women's fashion. A personality should be identified to champion the brand. This charismatic personality, male or female, should be a leading Indonesian partner in the company, and extremely creative. The brand should be centred on an Indonesian showroom and factory complex that would become a famous tourist destination in its own right. Something of its character would be present in the brand's own boutiques in fashion cities around the world. As the favourite global batik brand within ten years, an annual $15 billion business is in the offing.

Motorcycles

As was the case in most Third World countries, the headlong rush to develop a genuine, full-blown automobile industry has been largely unsuccessful. Astra, the largest of the Indonesian outfits and basically an assembler of Japanese knockdown kits, knows how tough the business is. Astra was felled by massive foreign debt in the wake of the Asian financial crisis. Now majority-owned by Singapore's shrewd and resourceful Cycle & Carriage following a massive restructuring, it has returned to being primarily an auto assembler. But for Indonesia and other emerging nations, the better bet for acquiring technology and creating a new brand could be motorcycles. Limited consumer purchasing power, congested roads and high automobile licence fees make motorcycles a sensible mode of transportation for the masses, especially in Asia's poorer and crowded cities. And for Indonesia, a precedent exists.

Long before it became a recognised auto-manufacturing nation, India went to school on turning out motorcycles and scooters. India was so successful that Indian manufacturers bought out such venerable Italian makers as Vespa and Lambretta. Today, advertisements in regional and international magazines proclaim the virtues of Bajaj two- and three-wheelers, close relatives of the Vespa. Bajaj is now in fact the world's largest scooter producer.

Indonesia can go the same route. There is a vast domestic market to sustain a transfer of technology and manufacturing, eventually creating an Indonesian power brand. There is no shortage of potential joint-venture partners; Honda, Kawasaki, Suzuki, Yamaha, Bajaj and new upcoming Chinese, Taiwanese and South Korean brands.

The sums look good, even though market size statistics are currently skewed. Figures for 1999 show domestic sales running at 581,000 units, but increasing to 719,000 units by the end of year 2000. The currency crisis and political upheaval are blamed, but it could also be a case of creative sales reporting as the government tinkers with its import policy on CKDs (Completely Knocked Down) vis-à-vis CBUs (Completely Built Up) bikes. Now, a more coherent policy is being looked at, one that would reward assemblers who seriously work towards creating Made in Indonesia motorcycles to initially satisfy domestic demand and eventually pursue the export market.

Several things have to be sorted out before Indonesia can

seriously address the global marketing of motorcycles. But that day will surely come in the not-so-distant future. Motorcycle sales in China for 1999 were anywhere from 8 to 10.5 million units. With sales of 2 million rising to 3.5 million by 2003, India is the world's second largest motorcycle market. In 2000, the Japanese bought 840,000 new motorbikes, the Taiwanese 759,000; the Vietnamese snapped up 500,000, the Thais 788,000. Malaysians climbed onto 260,000 new motorcycles and by end-2000, an estimated 150,000 will have been sold in the Philippines. Further afield, North America accounted for 500,000 new bikes in 1999, and Europe another 1.15 million!

Over 20 million motorcycles are sold worldwide every year. While about half are produced in China, the huge market universe is a compelling reason for Indonesia to seriously get into the global market with its very own brand. I look forward to Indonesia taking a 15% world market share, producing about three and a half million units a year. Well worth the ride, one would think.

MALAYSIA: RIGHT ON TARGET

Malaysia needs no encouragement to lift its game in global brand building. Come 2030, Malaysia plans to have a population base exceeding 30 million, up from the present 21 million. Rich in agricultural and mineral resources, Malaysia has set its sights on being a formidable manufacturing centre and Southeast Asia's Silicon Valley. The capital, Kuala Lumpur, is now the proud owner of the world's tallest twin towers; Port Klang, Malaysia's seaport, is chipping away at Singapore's trading port supremacy; a brand new airport rivals Changi and Hong Kong in terms of architecture and scale. Malaysia even upstaged her neighbours by building the first Formula One Grand Prix racing track in the region and is now on the world circuit.

Malaysia's resources are enviable Golden Assets, and contrary to many experts' opinions, I feel Malaysia has the right resolve to carve out some great global power brands in the next 20 years.

Proton

At first, Malaysia's vision of a national car was greeted with scepticism. But no one is laughing any more. Proton is the pride and joy of the government. "Proton", an acronym for its manufacturer Perusahaan Otomobil Nasional, is made with Mitsubishi involvement. Malaysia currently produces about 200,000 Protons a year from plants that have an installed capacity of 240,000 units. Its two main export markets are currently the UK and Australia, with smaller exports to Singapore and Sri Lanka.

Proton has achieved measurable success, but tough challenges lie ahead. The brand is heavily reliant on domestic sales, so when the new ASEAN tariff regulations on foreign automobile brands are lifted in 2005, Proton will no doubt feel some pressure. The inroads made into Australia and the UK could also come under pressure, with those markets introducing new, tighter emission standards.

Car manufacturing is no business for the faint-hearted and the Malaysians know this. Their investment is huge and extremely vulnerable to swings in the economy. Competitors are gigantic and ruthless. If the product offering is not up to speed, customers are quick to switch loyalties. The Proton brand owners know the game and despite the dark clouds ahead, their resolve should not wane. However, I feel they do need to be substantially more aggressive. They should address the folly of limited international market penetration. They should set their sights on becoming a bigger, much bigger global brand. It is an awesome ambition, considering the scale of the competition. But the people who drive Malaysia have lofty ambitions for their nation and Proton could become an honoured icon of Malaysia's global commercial aspirations.

The real fun starts with the development of a global brand strategy. I'm sure the brand owners have one, but perhaps it needs some fine-tuning in line with my more aggressive global vision for Proton.

Let me share one scenario with you. Looking at the global automobile industry through to, say, 2020, it is patently obvious that Proton will play a "challenger" role in the scheme of things, which establishes a great mindset for everything it does. Proton will always aggressively *attack* opportunities, rather than *defend* positions; it will be more youthful, more lateral, more individualistic in its rational and emotional brand promise, and its global advertising will clearly signal this personality.

The principles of this strategic direction are fairly easy to understand, but can be the most difficult to put into practice. Nonetheless, if you get it right, it's a great platform because youthful spirits in both mature and maturing markets across the world are consistently similar in their feelings and taste. (If you need further proof, the success of the Mini and the VW Beetle should inspire you.)

Proton is not currently this type of character, but with the support of skilled brand builders it probably could be in five short years or so. Then again, there are numerous other strategies to consider. Getting it right is well worth the effort.

Eu Yan Sang

Now let's swing from personal transportation to something even more personal — your health and your physical looks. Just about every piece of lifestyle reading matter in the world today covers these topics and the level of interest and volume of business in this category is ballooning, and will continue to do so.

At the forefront of this upsurge is China's ancient and proven pharmacopoeia, or what is commonly called traditional Chinese medicine. In my macro reading of some great global branding opportunities for China, I identified TCM as a Golden Asset ready for explosive brand growth. A predictable thing to say for the original home of this product, but now I'm proposing another global TCM brand prospect — this time from tropical Malaysia.

While it might seem an odd choice at first glance, it's easier to chew once you understand that the Chinese have embraced Malaysia for more than 125 years and the Malaysian climate is compatible for growing Chinese herbs. The TCM brand name I've identified, Eu Yan Sang, was established in Malaysia in 1879 and has impeccable credentials.

Originally, Eu Yan Sang started out producing herbal remedies to help heal coolies in the tin mines of Perak whose only other remedy was to take opium. Presently, the brand has its own retail outlets in Malaysia, Singapore and Hong Kong, and is marketed mainly in Asia with limited penetration in Western markets. The Eu family has owned and operated the company since the firm's birth and the fourth generation team is now in command. Eu Yan Sang went public on the Singapore Stock Exchange in 2000 as part of a plan to flex its global muscles.

I think the foundations are now in place for Eu Yan Sang to take off around the world and for the brand to be potentially one of the most powerful global names in its field within the next decade. I conservatively predict that the traditional Chinese medicine industry will gross $100 billion annually by 2010. The stakes are high, so the competition from the mighty American and European giants who are penetrating the TCM market will predictably be relentless. But Eu Yan Sang has something the Westerners can't come close to — its long-established pedigree. And Eu Yan Sang must obviously flog this big difference. Of course the war will also be against a few brands with similarly classic credentials, so Eu Yan Sang must be prepared to build brand awareness and loyalty by investing a good percentage of its revenue on advertising.

Getting this right will make Eu Yan Sang a global household name. And bring fame and fortune to its birthplace, Malaysia.

Boh Tea

In many ways, tea is a strange eruption on Malaysia's agricultural landscape. Malaysia has always been seen as a major rubber producer, with palm oil a more recent addition. Tea has been grown in Malaysia from around 1930, almost as an afterthought by the British who ruled Malaysia and perhaps more importantly gave the world the culture of tea drinking.

Malaysia's topography and climate do not offer the ideal conditions for developing the type of tea plantations that have given China, India and Sri Lanka such dominance among tea producers in a global production output currently estimated at around 2.9

million metric tons annually. The Cameron Highlands in Malaysia have the elevation — 1,520 metres above sea level — and the climate needed to grow tea and that is where the activity is focused today. The frontrunner is Boh Plantations Sdn. Bhd., an enterprise owned by the Russell family and Permodalan Nasional Berhad.

By global standards Boh is a small producer — four million kilograms annually. It has four estates totalling 1,300 hectares in Malaysia: Boh Estate, Sungei Palas Estate and Fairlie Estate, all in the Camerons, and Bukit Cheeding Estate in Banting, Selangor. The Bukit Cheeding Estate, incidentally, is in the lowlands, producing a rougher, stronger variety that is generally used for blending with higher-grown varieties and concocting the local favourite *teh tarik*.

While Boh in its present form will achieve neither mass reach nor recognition in the global marketplace, it has the fundamentals for doing so in the top-quality end of the market.

Boh is a dynamic company and growing fast relative to its size. 1990's production grew by 5.5% and unlike the big MNCs where tea brands are merely just one of many categories in their stable of products, the Boh company focuses on just one thing — tea. Boh Plantations have two flagship products, Boh and Boh Cameronian, both with very high visibility in Malaysia and, to a lesser extent, Singapore. Boh Plantations produce a variety of other brews, among them three types of loose tea, tea bags and tea dust. It also has proprietary interests in a range of Black Tea, Garden Tea, Sri Songket Tea, Three-in-One Tea, Iced Teas, Fruit and Herbal Infusions Tea, and speciality tea and fine tea dusts for use in the local coffee shops.

The potential for increasing brand value and widening market share overseas is with Boh Cameronian and Boh. Exports of the two brands are currently running at 10% of production volume and mainly reach buyers in Singapore, the US, Japan, Brunei, Denmark, Hong Kong, Australia and Taiwan. Boh Plantations recently launched a range of iced teas for the international market that have been exceptionally well received in Australia and Taiwan. But clearly, a whole lot more effort is needed to lift Boh onto the world stage.

Frankly, I'd consider two routes. Keep Southeast Asia essentially as it is in terms of broad-based product range, pricing and appeal, and address the rest of the world as the best quality tea brand in the business, keeping yields at the high end.

The global expansion route plainly needs a healthy dose of funding to boost R&D (identifying product differentials and introducing fantastic innovations), as well as to lift production capabilities and build the brand identity. Given that Boh has adequate financial support, I like its chances of becoming the Mercedes-Benz of world teas. The company thinks and breathes tea, and nothing else, which gives it great focus. The concept of "private blend" brands is gathering favour and loyalty among discerning consumers. The family that created the brand 70 years or so ago still manages the brand — obviously there's something very special, very rare about that. It's all worthy "added value" material. And Boh should definitely aim to continually elevate the value of tea.

If all goes well, Boh's 100th anniversary gift to its favoured clientele could well be vintage Boh Tea from the highlands of southern Tibet, discreetly presented in a Dom Perignon-shaped bottle, naturally.

THE PHILIPPINES: IT WILL RISE AGAIN

The Philippines is a volcanic archipelago of 7,000 islands, most of them uninhabited; in fact, the 11 largest islands account for more than 94% of the country's total land area. Luzon in the north has the highest population and is usually referred to as the Tagalog-speaking region. The other main islands are the Visayas, including Negros, Cebu, Leyte (Mrs. Imelda Marcos' bailiwick), Samar and Panay in the centre, and Mindanao and the Sulu Archipelago in the south.

The population of the Philippines is in excess of 80 million and rising. Filipinos breed prolifically, a fact worth noting when we get around to evaluating the branding of migrant labour. High population growth is due largely to the dominant influence of the

Roman Catholic Church, which frowns on birth control, and the Filipino male's well-publicised reluctance to use condoms because they sort of spoil the fun. And because the Church is tough on divorce, most married Filipinos take anywhere from one to four mistresses, a cultural quirk rooted in their Malay ancestry. Some 83% of Filipinos are Roman Catholic; the rest — Protestants, Muslims, Buddhists and "others" — are scattered in small communities with the exception of the Muslims in the south.

The Spaniards conquered the Philippines in 1565, overlaying the then dominant Malay culture with Hispanic dynamism and Catholicism. The Americans took control of the islands in 1898 and ruled till 1946, creating the framework for the introduction of Jeffersonian-style democracy, American business culture and a consuming passion among the natives for things originating "Stateside". This socio-political and cultural legacy is worth recalling because it impinges on our understanding of the Filipino brand of culture as well as the brand culture of the Philippines. It will help us mine the Filipino psyche.

The Philippines is resource-rich. It has oil and gas, gold, copper, nickel, chromium, marble, timber, sugar, an abundance of fruit, fine marine life, freshwater fish farms, tobacco, rum, coconut, great beer and possibly unspecified billions of American dollars stashed away in Swiss, European, US and Hong Kong banks waiting to be liberated from the clutches of Imelda Marcos and her kids.

The Philippines is also broke. The country's external debt exceeds $50 billion while its gross international reserves are a modest $14 billion. GNP growth is expressed as being 1.5–3.5%, but these national statistics have over the years been demonstrably unreliable. The Philippines is primarily an exporter of raw materials and an importer of manufactured goods.

People are her other great resource. Filipinos are a very tribal, vibrant lot. They are full of fun, extremely talented in the visual and performing arts, and very ungovernable. The Pacific floor under the earthquake-prone Philippines is very unstable. So is the country's politics.

It is a measure of the Filipinos' relaxed character that the government of President Ferdinand Marcos built the country's first and only nuclear power plant smack on the San Andreas fault line on the island of Luzon. Given the high earthquake risk, the plant was never commissioned. Clearly, less tolerant and joyful folk would have stormed the home of their leader and staged massive demonstrations to protest this pathetic waste of public funds — *over $1 billion, conservatively!* Not the Filipinos; they found the whole episode quite funny in a macabre sort of way. The nuclear power plant became the butt of jokes told with passion in colourful Tagalog and Ilocano, and in hybrid Taglish.

Apart from young radicals and ageing parlour socialists, most adult Filipinos regard America as their homeland, even though most just manage to visit the US a couple of times in their lives. Interestingly, in the 1970s, the Marcos regime coined the term *balikbayan*, by joining the Tagalog words *balik*, meaning to return, and *bayan*, meaning town or nation. A *balikbayan*'s relationship to the Philippines is construed in terms of his sentimental attachments to hometown and family, rather than his loyalty to the nation. At the same time, being a *balikbayan* depends on a Filipino's permanent residence abroad with America the preferred option. It was a marvellous concept, unwittingly perhaps satisfying the Filipino's unabashed longing to be an expatriate.

Reinforcing this curious twist in a people's sense of national belonging is the fact that the venality of most post-Independence Filipino presidents has done little to persuade their countrymen that it is great to be a Filipino. Sadly, there is no strong national ethos. So, against this background, let us focus on what can be created in terms of new global power brands from the Philippines, rather than evaluate tired, existing brands.

Overseas Contract Workers

One of the most promising branding situations is Filipino migrant labour, officially described as Overseas Contract Workers.

The government's official figures (1998–1999) tell us there were 4.2 million Filipinos OCWs working abroad in some 146 countries, with contracts varying from 6 to 24 months.

Their official annual remittances (foreign exchange sent back to the Philippines to support dependants) amounted to $6.2 billion in 1997, according to the government. But NGOs (Non-Governmental Organisations) in the Philippines with a watching brief on migrant workers suggest that this figure should be nearer to $10 to $12 billion, given that many workers use black market channels to send money home, in order to secure better currency conversion rates. Compare this with the annual foreign exchange earnings of the Philippines from exports — officially reported as being in the range of $8 to $10 billion in 1998–1999.

Officially, there are over 500,000 Filipino OCWs in Europe, primarily in Italy, Britain, Spain, Greece, Germany, France, Austria and the Netherlands, but the largest concentrations are in the Middle East and the Asian region. For the 15 years from 1980 (generally accepted as the year in which serious worker migration began) to 1994, the incremental growth of OCWs bound for Asia was over 500%. And this will continue to grow as the more affluent host countries in this region face the prospect of two-income families multiplying.

The preferred destinations of Filipino OCWs are the Kingdom of Saudi Arabia, Hong Kong, Taiwan, Japan, United Arab Emirates, Singapore, Kuwait, Brunei and Qatar.

OCW wage rates vary; monthly wage rates in Europe are around $500, which is also roughly the going rate in the Middle East. Hong Kong's fixed minimum monthly wage for OCWs is $475, plus accommodation and food. The monthly minimum fixed for foreign domestic workers by the Singapore Government is approximately $200, but employers pay a substantial fixed levy to the government for the privilege of hiring a maid; they usually take out health and accident insurance as well. In all host countries, employers are required to provide all OCWs with roundtrip fares.

So, what have we got here? A business which annually generates foreign exchange earnings in excess of $12 billion — but which is not commercially structured or branded. There is a strong case for putting the OCW business on an organisational footing, particularly as the numbers suggest that *one-third* of the Philippine population — the workers plus their dependants at a ratio of 5 : 1 — derives support from it.

Let's look at the existing system. Presently, OCWs wanting to go abroad must register with the Philippine Overseas Employment Administration (POEA), which functions under the Ministry of Labour. It is by all accounts a sloppy, inefficient agency. POEA requires every OCW to pay an exit tax, ostensibly to defray the cost of staffing and running the agency for the benefit of migrant workers. Recruitment for overseas jobs is in the hands of an assortment of employment or placement agencies. Many of them also apparently practise suspect business policies. Their methods are allegedly so cruel and predatory that most OCWs are in debt to their eyeballs before they even leave the country to take up their employment. These debts, which carry usurious interest rates, are paid back in monthly instalments.

Nor are there any recognisably decent training arrangements for OCWs in the Philippines. There are hole-in-the-wall operations totally unqualified to provide any serious training for women who must spend the best years of their lives involved in childcare, cooking, cleaning, washing and serving in a foreign culture.

What has to be done to develop this brand? There are six critical steps, I feel:

1. First and foremost, there must be the political will in the Philippines to do something really constructive for the benefits of these workers and the country. This is best achieved by a foreign consultancy, with sound credentials and branding experience, which will demonstrate to the Philippine leadership — the President, Minister of Labour, Governor of the Central Bank and the Cardinal — what can and should be done.

2. Set up training centres in Manila and the key provinces. This can be done cost-effectively through enlightened Church groups and NGOs. The funding can come from the taxes the government now charges through the POEA. The training programmes should be centrally controlled and developed, preferably using a Robert Powers kind of approach. The head of the training programme should be a foreigner and his expertise

devolved to the training centres. It might be possible to get either the Asian Development Bank or one of the UN agencies to provide and pay for this animal.

3. Create a kind of "Good Housekeeping" badge with sound, intrinsic values, which the training centres will use in their certification.

4. Establish a central placement agency and provincial feeder units, which will be professionally run, with a board of directors drawn from the Roman Catholic Church and minority religious groups — the best way to eliminate graft, exploitation and favouritism.

5. Establish call/help centres in the capitals of all countries where there are large concentrations of Filipino OCWs.

6. Create a benefit fund in Manila which will provide loans to help distressed OCWs, the interest rates limited to covering the cost of administering the loans and no more.

Central to this plan is the need to eliminate the involvement of Filipino government officials and "fixers". This can be done if the political will is established.

Given how much money is currently being siphoned both from government coffers and the exploited OCWs, this new programme can be funded with a fraction of that money. Besides, a soundly structured programme can attract funds from international agencies whose mandates are worker training and care. Host governments, too, can be persuaded to contribute, given that currently they have to deal with socio-economic problems spawned by errant OCWs in their countries.

One final thought: apart from domestic helpers, the Philippines also exports seamen, gifted craftsmen, masons, drivers and mechanics. These groups can be brought under the OCW umbrella organisation, with training tailored to enhance their skills and properly organised recruitment processes.

Philippine Culture

Here is another product crying out to be branded: The Bayanihan Troupe.

Born out of the natural Filipino genius for music and dance, and embellished by the strong Spanish cultural influence, the professional Bayanihan Troupe draws performers primarily from tertiary institutions. Its superbly choreographed folk dances represent the main tribal cultures. If my memory serves me right, it was first set up under the aegis of the Philippine Women's University, a respected educational institution which continues to underpin the survival of the troupe.

Presently, the Bayanihan Troupe mostly performs at home, with the occasional foray to Filipino communities overseas, usually Filipino Americans in the US.

The Bayanihan Troupe should be to the Philippines what the Bolshoi Ballet is to Russia.

Shoemakers to the World

Marikina, one of the 17 cities in the matrix of Metropolitan Manila, is shoemaking country. There, thousands of poor but skilled bootmakers, who themselves go around unshod, turn out hundreds of thousands of pairs of shoes — mostly ladies' shoes — for owners of some of the best brand names in the shoe industry.

Sadly, no attempt has been made to create a global Filipino brand or two, yet all the ingredients are there to do so.

Philippine Wood Products

Good quality timber, a hardwood called *narra* being among the best known, is one of the Golden Assets which God bestowed on the Philippines. Excessive logging, under the patronage of the Philippine armed forces, has done immense damage to this resource.

Over the last 25 years or so, Philippine timber exports — with little or no value added — have been in the form of plywood (usually 4 × 8 sheets) and logs. Japan is the destination for much of this stuff, although Hong Kong imports large quantities of

Philippine ply for the construction industry and to be used as laminates in furniture manufacturing. (Philippine ply also finds itself being cut into 22 million ceiling fan blades in China every year.)

Meanwhile, the skills of Filipino cabinetmakers rival those of the legendary French, Dutch and Chinese craftsmen — but where can one find a single Philippine-produced furniture brand?

Philippine Marble

Here is another great resource, concentrated mostly on the island of Romblon within spitting distance of Manila. The whole island is marble, rivalling the Italian variety for quality, grain and colour. Extracting marble requires power, and therein lies the rub. There is no power grid linked to Romblon. Extraction has to be done manually. It is backbreaking work, often damages the product, and turns out only small-size pieces unsuitable for major commercial applications. Maybe the Philippines should just sell the island to the Italians?

Garments and Fashion Accessories

The tradition of sewing is very strong in the Philippines. Most Filipinas have great embroidery and tailoring skills, and turn out wonderful children's clothes and women's fashion garments. Yet, aside from the *barong*, a loose shirt made of pineapple fibre, often embroidered and worn by men at official functions, and the *terno*, the long, formal, butterfly-sleeved gown inspired by the aristocratic ladies of Spanish courts, there are no garments or fashion products which are branded.

Children's clothes particularly hold much promise, both through the work being done by hundreds of thousands of seamstresses working in Metropolitan Manila and the island of Cebu, which has the only non-agriculturally based economy of all the Philippine territories. Cebu, in fact, is the number one manufacturer and exporter of garments and fashion accessories primarily to Europe, the United States and Japan. With luck, one might occasionally discover a "Made in the Philippines" label, but usually it is more likely to masquerade under a foreign brand name, neatly concealing its national origin.

Seafood Products

With a coastline longer than that of the United States, there is an abundance of marine life in the seas surrounding the Philippines. Tuna, which the Japanese have surreptitiously trawled for decades, crabs, lobsters, shrimps and prawns are part of Nature's bounty. *Bangus*, a freshwater fish unique to the Philippines, is another.

Japan is a major importer of Philippine seafood, but they don't trust the Filipinos to get it right. So they only buy what they can inspect and pack through their own processing facility in Manila. Remarkably, the Filipinos have not only swallowed the insult, but also accepted the arrangement quite happily. Imagine trying that on with the Norwegians, Portuguese or Scots!

Can Philippine seafood products be branded? Yes. But no Filipino company has given it a go because one can't really bring wisdom to bear on those who choose to spurn it.

Agricultural Products

The soil in those parts of the land devoted to agriculture is extremely fertile. So much so that a walking stick pushed into the ground by accident or design will take root and sprout. Of course, Filipinos don't cultivate walking sticks, but they do grow mangoes, young coconuts, king coconuts, oranges, limes, sugarcane, tobacco, breadfruit, jackfruit, pineapples, bananas, betel nut, chikus and a variety of other tropical fruit. With the exception of bananas and pineapples, which are exported under the American "Dole" brand, most Philippine agricultural exports leave the country under their generic names.

Philippine mangoes (for which Japan, Hong Kong and Singapore are steady markets) are excellent in terms of quality and flavour. They're obvious candidates for branding, but they're currently described in all simplicity as "Philippine mangoes" in whichever markets they arrive.

Illustrators and Animators

A fact largely unnoticed is that the American comic book industry uses Filipino illustrators almost exclusively nowadays, as do the Hollywood cartoon producers.

The illustrators are based in the Philippines and the work is outsourced to them from the United States. They are usually paid piece rates, which means of course they are paid a pittance.

Here is a resource that can be organised, branded and marketed very much in the way Indian software writers have moved. For the first decade of the IT revolution, India provided the cheap yet skilled labour — the programmers for the American software industry. Now that the Indians have organised themselves and created companies of their own, they deal with the world abroad as equals and rake in huge profits.

Construction Companies

The Philippines has the critical mass in terms of resources to create large design and construction outfits to rival Turner Construction, Tischman Speyer, Kumagai Gumi and Kajima.

The architectural landscape of Manila and Makati is a tribute to the creative instincts of Filipino architects. It is worth noting that Lindy Locsin was the architect chosen by the Sultan of Brunei, Hassanal Bolkiah, to create his great palace. Apart from architects, the Philippines boasts a good stock of experienced engineers, surveyors, geologists, plus the masons, the carpenters, and so on.

This is not far-fetched. The Construction Development Corporation of the Philippines, which was really a cooperative getting together of a number of small Filipino builders, was one of the most reputable large construction companies in the Philippines. It had projects in several countries in the region including Malaysia, Indonesia, Vietnam and in the Middle East. In the 1970s, CDCP was the subcontractor to Saudi Research and Development Corporation, which in turn was the main contractor building the Port of Jubail. (Under Saudi rules, only a Saudi company can be a main contractor for major building projects in the kingdom.) Sadly, the financial crisis, political misfortunes and

Gaith Pharon — the owner of the Saudi corporation — brought down both his own company and the CDCP. Pharon also reportedly left the Hongkong and Shanghai Bank carrying the bag for some $300 million into the bargain.

Philippine Sugar

This is in demand globally, but is not branded in the manner that Hong Kong's Taikoo sugar is, for example. The Taikoo brand belongs to the Swire Group, which is not a sugar-producing enterprise. It buys its sugar in the international market and successfully packages it for global distribution and sale under the Taikoo name.

Philippine sugar is sold wholesale in the New York market, which presents a problem for any attempt to create a brand that will identify the product with its country of origin.

Philippine Tobacco

The introduction of tobacco leaf to the Philippines is one of those charming accidents of history.

Three hundred years ago the Spanish galleon *San Clemente*, plying the Acapulco–Manila trade route, brought 200 ounces of Cuban tobacco seeds to the Philippine islands. These seeds found their way into the hands of the Spanish missionaries, who displayed the same dedication to sowing the seeds as they did with spreading the faith in the Cagayan Valley of the province of Isabela, a fertile region north of Manila felicitously named after Queen Isabela of Spain. With the climate and soil conditions mimicking those in Cuba whence the seeds originated, the Cagayan Valley became the largest tobacco-growing region in the Philippines and all of Asia.

In 1881, the Spanish tobacco plantation owners in the Cagayan Valley merged their operations to establish Compania General de la Tabacos de la Isabela, "The Flower of Isabela". This consolidation of the Spanish plantations not merely created one of the oldest cigar companies in the world, it also inspired some great Philippine brands — Tabacalera, Don Juan Urquijo, 1881, Alhambra and Calixto Lopez.

These and other brands are popular among cigar smokers in the Philippines to this day, but have never fulfilled their promise in the international market. The quality of the leaf, given its Cuban antecedents, is considered excellent. The tradition of hand rolling has endured for over 300 years and the world's love affair with the cigar has not waned. So why have Philippine cigar brands languished in the backwaters? The explanation may well be in poor marketing and packaging, but the potential for creating new brand value exists and demands a prescriptive framework for capturing its ancient cachet.

THE Philippines has to look outside the traditional resource-based industries to create new products, and therefore new brands. It must avoid the temptation to spin off whims into industries, as it did with its wasteful Philippine Car Manufacturing (PCMP) exercise and an initiative to manufacture Bell helicopters through a licensing arrangement.

The Philippines has other, more wonderful resources. It has a valuable pool of managers in banking, the sciences, media, education, crafts, architecture, graphic design, computer software and the arts. These assets can be leveraged to create new brands, or brands implicit in these resources.

SINGAPORE: ON THE FAST TRACK

The Republic of Singapore is a remarkable land. Born a British colony, it attained self-government in 1959. The first general election for the 51-seat legislature was held in May that year. The People's Action Party (PAP), led by the Cambridge-educated lawyer Lee Kuan Yew, swept to power. A period of co-existence with Malaysia, which began in 1963, ended in 1965. Singapore became a sovereign democratic and independent nation on 9 August 1965.

These bald facts disguise one of the great success stories of nation building anywhere in the world. When the PAP established its first government, Singapore's land area was a minuscule 582 square kilometres. Reclamation has raised this to 682.7 square kilometres today. The country, at its birth, had no industry or agriculture worth talking about. Its busy port was a source of substantial revenue and employment, but hardly adequate to sustain the aspirations of a population that numbered slightly under two million at the time.

There is a story, apocryphal perhaps, that underlines the grievous situation Singapore faced. Prime Minister Lee Kuan Yew reportedly talking to some journalists at the time disclosed that he was aghast to discover that Singapore's gross national product in 1965 was smaller than Sony Corporation's annual turnover. Lee, so the story goes, asked rhetorically, "How do we house, educate, feed and find work for all our people with such little resources?"

The wonder is that Singapore's leaders transcended this major obstacle in spades. Over the last 35 years, Lee — now Senior Minister — and his colleagues in the People's Action Party, in a *tour de force* of planning, hard work and vision, have shown the world what can be achieved if a country is honestly and firmly governed. The government's enormous success in fighting corruption over three decades is all the more amazing in a geographic region accustomed to grease.

Fast forward to the year 2000 and what do we have?

About 90% of Singapore families and individuals own the homes in which they live. Literacy is a high 93%. Foreign reserves are a whopping $80 billion. The Singapore dollar is one of the most stable currencies in the world. Total trade is in excess of $258 billion. Tourism brings in $6 billion and visitor arrivals in 2000 were 7.7 million, 10% more than the 1999 figure. Economic growth for the year 2000 touched 10%. Unemployment is 3.5%. Singapore is a major oil refining centre and boasts one of the largest oil refining and chemical complexes in the region. It is fast developing as the regional hub for telecommunications, finance and health care, and the preferred choice as a regional headquarters for a large number of high profile multinationals.

Today, Singapore must count as one of the most attractive and dynamic metropolitan centres in the world. Its ethnic mix — Chinese, Malay, Indian, Eurasian, Sri Lankan, Arab and a few

Anglo-Saxons to boot — has infused the country's culture with beguiling vibrancy. It is also an exceptional example of success in building a multiracial society.

Extraordinarily thoughtful and creative urban planning has formed a city so green that it artfully disguises the pressure on the land from a growing population. In fact, the illusion is one of great space. Environmental care is an article of faith and its implementation palpable everywhere.

The country's civil service is not simply efficient and corruption-free, but one of the most forward thinking anywhere in the world.

All of these factors have combined to create an affluent, self-confident people. It is a measure of Singapore's success that many of its nationals and corporations are now reaching out across Asia, taking their financial resources, management skills, commercial savvy and strong work ethic to build new businesses abroad.

Singapore is a brand that evokes stability, quality, efficiency and good value (corporate and personal taxes are among the lowest in Asia). It is a brand offering transparency in commercial transactions, the rule of law, modern financial and telecommunications infrastructure and an administration responsive to change and hugely capable of managing change. The fact that Singapore has been enormously successful in attracting some of the best, largest and most technologically advanced foreign corporations to locate and invest over $40 billion in the country over the last ten years is Brand Singapore's best advertisement.

Looking ahead, two interesting things are happening. First, the government plans to steadily divest its investment in a cluster of big conglomerates, thereby freeing them up to operate as independent commercial entities. Secondly, globalisation is a key buzzword, complemented by a language not commonly broadcast in Singapore before — such as, "take a risk", "make a mistake" and "think laterally". All this talk is designed to fire up a greater entrepreneurial spirit, and it is possible that some of the country's best brands are still to come. These will probably be in the areas such as health care, education, the life sciences and finance. One's imagination gets very excited, for example, about a scenario that bolts together a Singapore bank consortium brand to storm the castles of the mighty Western bank brands, or a life sciences brand from Singapore that somehow makes it simple for 80-year-old golfers to out-drive Tiger Woods. In many respects, then, conjuring up such possibilities is as wonderful and endless as peering at a star-filled sky. So, in this Singapore exercise, I'm going to focus my attention on a few, more down-to-earth fixtures that are already in place.

Tiger Balm

The little brown jar is my favourite. A 1994 publication commemorating the 25th anniversary of the founding of Haw Par Brothers International Limited as a public company in 1969 contains the following note: "With humble beginnings from a jar of balm a hundred years ago, heady days under Aw Boon Haw's charismatic leadership, and turbulent transition from family business to diversified public company, the Haw Par story has few parallels in Singapore's history."

It is such a folksy, typically Asian business story. The company name derives from two brothers, Boon Haw ("Gentle Tiger") and Boon Par ("Gentle Leopard"), the sons of Aw Chu Kin, a little-known Hakka herbalist from China's Fukien province who had settled in what we then called Rangoon in Burma. The herbalist set up his own *sinseh* (traditional Chinese medicine) shop and by 1870, had established Eng Aun Tong, the Hall of Everlasting Peace, a place for people both rich and poor who needed medical help. When Chu Kin died in 1908, the future of the business became the responsibility of the brothers Haw and Par.

The Gentle Tiger and Gentle Leopard commandeered their mother's kitchen in Rangoon and turned it into a "cross between a sorcerer's workshop and a chemist's laboratory". They proceeded to put a spin on the recipe for the ointment their father had prescribed to patients. Together, the brothers produced Ban Kim Ewe, "Ten Thousand Golden Oil", a panacea for all ills. They packed the opaque molten cream into little brown jars, added the words "Tiger Balm" as a trademark on the label, and the brand was born some one hundred years ago. Impressed by their undoubted success with the balm, the brothers added a headache cure (an analgesic powder), a laxative (Chin Kwai Chee) and a breath freshener (Pat Kaw Tan) to the product line.

The business was a phenomenal success and the brothers Haw and Par soon became the richest men in Rangoon. The irrepressible Boon Haw, the Gentle Tiger, judged that if it were to grow the business had to spread beyond Burma. In 1926 he set up the Hall of Everlasting Peace in Amoy Street, in Singapore's Chinatown, pushing the Tiger Balm brand into Singapore. His custom-made car, with a snarling tiger head mounted on its front, became a familiar sight as Boon Haw plied the small towns of Malaya. By the start of the Second World War, Tiger Balm was the ubiquitous household medicine in cupboards across Asia, from Batavia to China.

The decade of the 1970s was not propitious for the company. In a bizarre corporate manoeuvre the London-based Slater Walker Securities group headed by Jim Slater became a shareholder in the business, which had been renamed Haw Par Brothers International Limited. Slater Walker was also awarded the management mandate. In a brief six years, through a process of asset stripping, Slater Walker emasculated Haw Par. When Slater Walker collapsed in the mid-1970s, it left behind a troubled legacy. Haw Par, however, slowly rebuilt and reorganised. By the start of the 1990s the company emerged as a lively, diversified conglomerate. Its flagship product Tiger Balm enjoyed a renaissance. With a global awakening to the virtues of traditional Chinese medicine, and the post-war proliferation of overseas Chinese communities in Europe, Australia, the US and Canada, the brand that the Gentle Tiger and Gentle Leopard built is well placed to prosper again.

Tiger Balm is sold in one hundred countries. Many learned marketers classify it as a champion global brand from Asia. If so, why then is Tiger Balm only currently generating an annual global turnover of around $25 million for Haw Par?

I've already mentioned the growing popularity of traditional Chinese medicines, and the expanding Chinese presence in Western continents. Add to this the fact that more and more people exercise daily, and more and more people are living longer, and you've got massive global growth potential for Tiger Balm. The business of warming muscles, of relieving aches and pains, and keeping insects from biting you, is surely a multi-billion dollar global market, and ballooning.

For my money, Tiger Balm is performing well below its potential. A doable global sales target for Tiger Balm should be *four times* its present turnover — in other words, closer to $100 million — *with an annual growth rate of 20%!* Idle thinking? The annual sales of Bengay Rub in the USA alone exceed $45 million, and the global health care market is said to be growing 20% each year.

I feel the brand owners of Tiger Balm need to get onto a faster moving treadmill; they should be significantly more aggressive, and more inventive, in their R&D and marketing. It's plain that Tiger Balm should target a bigger customer base and boost product usage at the same time. In the early 1990s, the brand management of Tiger Balm trumpeted an enterprising mission, "A jar in every household around the world". It's time for Haw Par to put their money where their mission is, so to speak. Only a serious, tenacious programme will elevate Tiger Balm to the premier league of global power brands. And it richly deserves that level of success.

Tiger Beer

This is another tiger I'd like to address. Asia Pacific Breweries Ltd is a joint venture between Singapore's biggest drinks manufacturer Fraser & Neave and the Dutch beer giant Heineken. APB is one of the republic's top ten companies and one of the region's biggest brewers.

Known as Malayan Breweries Limited when it was founded in 1931, the first beer plant opened in 1932. The Tiger Beer brand emerged in 1933 and was the first beer brewed in Singapore.

Today, APB has a turnover in excess of $852 million and 14 state-of-the-art breweries in Singapore, Vietnam, China, Malaysia, Cambodia, Thailand, New Zealand and Papua New Guinea.

Since 1939, Tiger Beer has bagged over 30 international gold medals in Paris, Geneva, Rome, Lisbon and Madrid. In April 1998, it won the big daddy of beer awards when it was judged "The World's Best Lager" at the Brewing Industry International Awards in London. The biennial BIIA event is the brewing equivalent of the Oscars. Tiger's resounding victory was achieved against 191 entries from brewers in 32 countries, notably Australia, Germany, Denmark, the Netherlands, New Zealand, Canada, the US and the UK.

Tiger Beer has been described as one of Asia-Pacific's most recognisable brand names. When the *Washingtonian* magazine surveyed several hundred beer brands in July 1998, it rated Tiger "Positively the best beer in the world".

The chief executive officer of APB noted: "This major achievement adds tremendous value to the Tiger brand in Asia and the rest of the world." He said the achievement has reinforced APB's commitment to developing Tiger into a truly international brand.

A worthy cause. A "truly international brand" is another way of saying a strong global brand. And, sadly, Tiger Beer falls well short of that mark. Its total annual production seems a closely guarded secret, but as far as I can ascertain it's somewhere around 2 million hectolitres, which is dismal when compared to Heineken's 74 million hectolitres, or Carlsberg's 37 million hectolitres, or even Fosters' 8 million-plus hectolitres.

I view it as a case of yet another "Tiger" behaving like a kitten in the global arena. The brand has a proud heritage and has won enough international brewing awards to fill the expansive Singapore harbour. And, indeed, for a lengthy period in the last two decades, it banged the drum about its international reputation. But this was only window dressing, for Tiger Beer has not seriously attempted to penetrate the big Western beer-drinking markets. There are no doubt sound business reasons why the brand has essentially focused just on the Asian region. I just happen to feel that this thinking is too narrow.

In the spirit of globalisation, and Singapore is leading that charge in Southeast Asia, I'd like the Tiger Beer brand owners to take a fresh new look at invading the Western continents with a determination and style not unlike what another Singaporean brand, SIA, did some 30 years ago. The Tiger name is great. The packaging is great. I'd target it to be bigger than Fosters in five to seven years' time. All that's needed is imagination, money and guts.

Creative Technology Ltd

One of those improbable but engaging corporate initiatives, Creative Technology Ltd. was founded in Singapore in 1981 by two ambitious young Singaporeans, Sim Wong Hoo and Ng Kai Wa, who were later joined by Chay Kwong Soon. Their business plan noted that they intended to provide engineering services, but they quickly changed tack, opting instead to build low-end computers for the China market. All too soon the three young entrepreneurs discovered how rough and tough the PC manufacturing business was and started scouting around for something more profitable to manufacture. They underpinned their new efforts by opening an office in the US in 1988 and, in a significant strategic move, opted to manufacture sound cards and other PC enhancements.

In 1989 Creative Technology produced its Sound Blaster sound card, which to this day remains the industry standard — and the market leader. Some 70% of all PC sound systems are built around Creative's Sound Blaster technology. At this writing, Creative had sold over 100 million Sound Blaster products.

Creative strengthened its grip on this sector of PC peripherals by cornering the market for upgrade kits with its own Sound Blaster Multimedia Upgrade Kit (a software package bundled with a high performance CD-ROM drive), the Sound Blaster Pro, and other software applications.

Primary manufacturing is located in Singapore, which is also the company's worldwide headquarters, but Sound Blaster has a global presence. Creative's operational centres are Malaysia, South Africa, Taiwan, the People's Republic of China, Hong Kong, Japan, Australia, the Netherlands, the US, the UK, Republic of Ireland, Belgium, Denmark, France, Germany, Italy and Sweden. Research and development is done out of several overseas locations under the banner of Creative's US-based Creative Labs, Inc.

Sales from sound products accounted for 45% of the group's $1.3 billion turnover in 1999. Creative's product range includes

BlasterKey; MP3 — the first Internet-centric keyboard that drew rave reviews when it was unveiled in California; WebCam Web cameras; NOMAD — a portable digital audio player; LAVA! — an interactive music video player; Sound Blaster Live; and NOMAD Jukebox. The company has also set up Hifi.com, an e-commerce initiative that provides home entertainment products.

Creative Technology was listed on the US Nasdaq in the summer of 1992, the first Singapore-grown company to list on Nasdaq.

Commenting on its business strategy, Creative notes: "With the goal of enhancing the PC experience for its customers, Creative develops and markets a wide array of solutions that complement the diverse needs of its end-users. This includes offering a variety of products that appeal to the senses of sight and sound, as well as the need for effective PC-to-PC communication, including the Internet. This focus, combined with an extensive channel strategy and strong retail presence, has enabled Creative to remain at the forefront of the industry. More than 40,000 retail outlets worldwide currently carry the company's products, including the Blaster® family of graphics and audio cards, as well as Creative's multimedia upgrade kits, speakers, video communications products, PC-DVD solutions and Internet applications."

What I find interesting is to consider how Creative should tackle the *future* branding of its products in order to clinch a position within the world's Top 50 brands.

To date, their branding approach has been similar to that of a traditional packaged goods company. They've chosen to focus on product-as-hero rather than adopt the more corporate focus evident among technology companies like Apple and Novell. This focus served Creative well so long as its range was concentrated in and around sound cards. Sound Blaster is recognised worldwide as the industry standard and has spawned a family of sub-variants.

However, as an outsider looking at some of the company's more recent product ventures, I can't help feeling that there is a growing need for them to do more to allow the company to at least share the pedestal with the individual products. After all, even the mighty Procter & Gamble now makes no bones about overtly identifying the shared parentage of its wide-ranging stable of products in its advertising. In fact, this identification both lends a little magic to each individual product *and* builds the company's overall corporate identity, which in turn makes the endorsement given to the individual product even more valuable.

So long as you continue to produce great products, this is very much a win-win scenario — particularly if, like Creative, you operate in categories where the absolute noise level you can reasonably generate with your marketing communications is more limited than it is for most packaged goods products.

Some might argue that Creative should focus more on exploiting the values inherent in the now extraordinarily well-established Sound Blaster name than on trying to build a more corporate-based brand identity. But to me this seems short-sighted. Who can say just what technological paths Creative will be treading 5 or 10, 15 or 20 years from now? The fact that Sound Blaster stands so firmly for a *single* product type inevitably limits its ability to halo across a diverse spectrum of technological products. *Creative* or *Creative Technology*, on the other hand, can be more or less all-embracing.

From what I've seen of Creative's more recent communications efforts in packaging, advertising and websites, I sense that they are moving more and more to building up the corporate brand. I hope so, because that is almost certainly what I would do were I in Mr. Sim's shoes.

SingTel

The nation's dominant provider of domestic, international and mobile communications and postal services is Singapore Telecommunications Ltd — better known as SingTel.

Over the last decade, SingTel has transformed itself into one of the most modern and efficient operators in the world. The company has built a state-of-the-art telecommunications infrastructure in Singapore, part of the strategy to make the island republic the communications hub of Asia.

Turnover for the SingTel group in 1999–2000 was $2.86 billion, while profit for the same period was $1.09 billion.

SingTel has operations in 19 cities and 14 countries and territories across the globe, including China, India, Malaysia, Indonesia, the Philippines, Thailand, Vietnam, Australia, the UK and the US. SingTel's business objective is to expand operations outside of Singapore through strategic investments and joint ventures. At this writing, it had invested about $2.9 billion in over 80 joint ventures and strategic investments. Its most recent initiative is the purchase of Australia's second biggest telecoms brand, Optus.

A hugely cash-rich company, SingTel says it aims to be the first truly pan-Asian total communications carrier with a reach unmatched by any other telco in the region.

SingTel has just about everything in place to move into the telecoms brand super league in Asia-Pacific, and to be a worthy global brand. A possible vexing issue, however, is its international communications strategy, given the complexity of joint-venture deals and the relentless technological developments that impact on the game being played. Conventional wisdom says that any international branding programme should be focused on the high-end business and government audience, and that the effort should be fairly conservative. Then there's the school that preaches a totally opposite, more ambitious scenario. I think you can guess where my head is on this brand-building issue. In the scale of things, advertising is still the cheapest, most flexible, most effective way to build a brand identity. And in line with SingTel's ambitions to be a highly successful star in its industry, a decent branding programme across Asia-Pacific seems fundamental.

To be a leader you have to look and behave like a leader, and you must always be out there leading the charge. If SingTel does it right, it should become as well known in the world as the SIA brand.

Education and Research

A major new initiative to start up companies in the life sciences underscores the weightage being given to education and research in Singapore.

In June 1999, the government launched a $1 billion "technopreneurship" fund, signalling its commitment to cultivating venture businesses and venture funds promoting research in the life sciences. There is also a $568 million Life Science Investment Fund set up by the National Science and Technology Board and the Economic Development Board to commercialise homegrown and overseas technology in the life sciences. Additionally, Singapore has established a new Centre for Drug Evaluation to assess new drugs based on international standards.

Singapore's game plan is to focus on drugs, medical and food products, and agrobiotechnology. Already, the Singapore Institute of Molecular & Cell Biology has won wide respect. In 1993 it set up a joint venture with the British pharmaceutical giant Glaxo Wellcome to use molecular and cell technology for screening natural products for drugs. In 1995 the Institute spun off Singapore's first life science venture GeneSing, which is developing health care products for the Asia-Pacific market.

Recently the Institute of Molecular Agrobiology, established in 1995, set up a joint venture with Monsanto of the US to commercialise the use in China of cotton that had been genetically modified to fight the boll weevil pest.

At the National University of Singapore, a bioinformatics centre has created a successful spin-off holding company, Bioinformatrix, and a US-based venture, geneticXchange, Inc., which markets bioinformatics software.

There is currently a huge overseas investment interest in these developments. As a result, the Singapore Government is pressing ahead to develop a whole spectrum of talent, including not only researchers and entrepreneurs, but also investment bankers, analysts, venture capitalists and corporate lawyers. It is adopting an open door policy to draw talent from around the world. As the Minister for Trade and Industry noted: "As an industry, the life sciences will grow rapidly in the coming years, worldwide and in Singapore. We hope to make it the fourth pillar of Singapore's manufacturing sector, after electronics, chemicals and engineering. Recently, the government announced plans to expand this industry through investment in R&D and the development of human resources. We are focusing on four main areas: medical devices, nutrition and health care, pharmaceuticals, and biotechnology."

In the more conventional academic sector, the Singapore Government — consistent with its plans to develop high level research and business skills — has set up the Singapore Management University in collaboration with the Wharton School of the University of Pennsylvania. The SMU will be lodged in a $568-million campus and accommodate 15,000 students when it is completed in 2005. Currently it is functioning out of temporary premises.

The government is also investing heavily to modernise and upgrade the National University of Singapore and the Nanyang Technological University. As part of this development process, the government is encouraging the enrolment of foreign students at its national universities. This move is paying off. In 2000, nearly 16,000 foreign students enrolled. The students came from Vietnam, Myanmar, India, Sri Lanka, Hong Kong, China, Taiwan and South Africa.

I'm not quite sure how long it will be before business schools lose their appeal to more esoteric schools of learning, but all the three main universities are gung-ho about their own MBA courses being seen as the best in Asia. Certainly, the one that emerges with the best reputation is likely to be the one with the sharpest brand strategy and publicity programme. In this regard, I'd lean towards SMU. The name helps for a start. It's also totally new and will be consciously more adventurous. And it's driven by an entrepreneur. Not surprisingly, of course, SMU will be hard-pressed to get close to global "Harvard" fame for many years to come. In brand-building terms, this industry is a bit like producing a good red wine — the value of one's reputation customarily gets better the longer you're around.

Singapore's aim to be the seat of education in Asia-Pacific will be hotly contested by Australia. Indeed, the Aussies are clearly in front at present and I see them tenaciously strengthening their position. So be it. The number two slot is a very healthy ranking in a terrain housing half of the world's population.

SOUTH KOREA: CHEAP ISN'T ALWAYS CHEERFUL

It is instructive on occasion to look at the fate of divided countries. Let me suggest South Korea and what was once West Germany. Both were separated — South Korea from its northern half and West Germany from its eastern territories — as a consequence of war. Both have thrown enormous quantities of money and invested a great deal of political will into the process of unification with varying and unspectacular results.

West Germany brought the Berlin Wall down and in one great symbolic gesture heralded the unification of Germany. The Germans continue to pour money to lift the eastern territories by their economic bootstraps to underpin unification.

In June 2000, South Korean President Kim Dae-jung journeyed to the North to meet with President Kim Jong-il, the first step in an attempt to unify the two Korean halves. Over the next few years, this will be the focus of the South Korean leadership, and as was the case in Germany, the South Korean economy will be burdened by the cost of putting the North Korean economy back on its feet.

The question of course is whether the South can afford to pay this price. I for one think that it can and unification will succeed in transforming the Korean economy into a new economic powerhouse.

Today, South Korea is the world's 13th biggest economy. In 1999 and 2000 its GDP growth was 10.7% and 9% respectively, although at this writing its 2001 GDP growth is expected to be around 2.5%, given the global economic downturn.

But beyond these statistics, what is worth noting is that South Korea is to this day the world's largest shipbuilder, the second biggest steel producer and home to the world's leading semiconductor manufacturers. Other major exports are textiles, clothing and agricultural products. South Korea also boasts six major carmakers — Hyundai, Kia, Hyundai Precision, Samsung, Ssangyong and Asia — which with their pricing strategies have penetrated quite a number of overseas markets.

One of the country's biggest auto companies — Daewoo — is, at this writing, broke and has been declared bankrupt. The company's legendary founder, Kim Woo Choong, is a fugitive. Daewoo remains afloat under court protection until a buyer comes along. Daewoo's collapse with debts exceeding many billions of dollars has undermined almost every financial institution in South Korea.

The story of Daewoo underlines the strengths and weaknesses of the Korean business structure. In the 1920s and 1930s, the Japanese colonisers introduced the *chaebol* system. These were large corporations inextricably linked to the government and enjoying all types of preferential treatment. The *chaebols* were in fact clones of the Japanese *zaibatsu* which in a cosy relationship with the government transformed post-war Japan.

The *chaebols* prospered hugely under President Park Chung Hee in the 1960s and 1970s. There are several *chaebols*, of which four are referred to as *superchaebols*. These are Hyundai, Samsung, Lucky Goldstar Electronics and the now crippled Daewoo. Between them, these *superchaebols* employ over half a million South Koreans and control the lives and jobs of many millions more.

The close relationship between the *superchaebols* and successive governments has stood in the way of corporate and financial system reforms. Most Korean experts believe that this is acting as a brake on innovation and economic growth. It has also polarised relations between the corporations and their workforce, which could in turn seriously undermine the economy.

Professor Byung Nak Song of Seoul University is one of the more bullish observers of the Korean scene. He does not subscribe to the gloom and doom scenario. He believes that these enormous conglomerates will continue to grow. He has no doubt that the *chaebols* represent Korea's future.

How will the *chaebols* change the direction and image of South Korean business? Let us step back and look at where South Korea is today.

Second only to Japan in its production of electronics and automobiles in the Asian region, South Korea has nevertheless scored weakly compared with Japan in establishing its own global power brands. Only *one* Korean brand, Samsung Electronics, made it to Interbrand's Top 50 Brands in the World, and even then it only managed to scrape into 42nd position. What happened to names like Hyundai and LG?

Korean companies have never taken seriously the *business need* for creating powerful brand identities for their products. Instead, they've banked on lower pricing vis-à-vis their Japanese competitors. Fine, as a prime selling point it will cut for a while. But when the quality of South Korean and Japanese products is arguably *in*distinguishable, why keep playing the role of the cheaper alternative? Why permanently cast yourself in the role of the cheap cousin?

Japanese brands have always kept well ahead as global brands because of their commitment to R&D programmes, their global marketing knowledge and their consistent brand building and advertising strategies. It's time for Korea to do some healthy catching up on several fronts.

Not only have the Koreans not connected with consumers to communicate brand values other than price, they have let their products lag behind on design. According to an investigative report in 1998, the Korea Institute of Interior Design (KIID) concluded Korea is 40% behind leading nations in design competitiveness, losing to Japan, Taiwan and Singapore. Against the marketing downside, South Korea is still an economic heavyweight. Factor in the emotional impact of reconciliation between North and South and who knows how far they will go.

In 2000, total exports were valued at $172.6 billion. Consumer and industrial electronics accounted for 36% and textiles 5%. Half of Korea's exports go to Asian countries, Japan being their largest customer. But outside of Asia, the US is their biggest market.

The year 1999's exports of semiconductors reached $19 billion, with South Korea carving out 40% of global sales of DRAM. Despite the fact that global sales have taken a battering in most recent times, the Korean Semiconductor Industry Association confidently predicts the long-term demand for DRAM will rise. Samsung had 18.6% of the world's DRAM market in 1998 and 21.7% in 1999. In 1998, Hyundai had 11.4% of the market, and LG Semicon, recently bought by Hyundai, notched up 7.9%; by 1999, they held 21%. *By 2000, Samsung and Hyundai Semiconductor made up to half of the world's memory chips.* Not surprisingly, South Korea is the most wired country in Asia and aims to be the most computer-literate country in the world. The government plans to provide 470,000 personal computers to schools in two years' time; it hopes to have seven million housewives owning PCs by 2002.

Smarter *chaebols* like Samsung and LG are already leading innovators in Web-related businesses and the leading buyers of startups. Serome has become the world leader in Internet telephony through its DialPad. New startups are trying to remain independent of the big *chaebols*; a lot depends on pressure for funds.

In 1995, South Korea was the first country to adopt the CDMA (Code-Division Multiple-Access) digital mobile phone network. As a result, it is the world leader in CDMA mobile phone production with 70% of the global market led by Samsung and LG. US-based Qualcomm developed CDMA. Despite its advantages over the entrenched GSM system, CDMA was slow to gain global acceptance. South Korea took the gamble early and it's paid off; global demand for CDMA handsets has risen 70% to 70 million in 1999, and Korea's exports have risen 232% to $3.5 billion. The amount rose to $4.13 billion by end-2000. South Korean CDMA handsets now hold 40% of the global mobile phone market. (Interestingly, Singapore's M1 closed down its CDMA network in September 2001 and customers reverted to GSM.)

South Korea leads the world in day trading. On-line equity lending is a high-risk activity, to put it mildly, but it does resonate with the entrepreneurial spirit of the young, the educated unemployed and women in general. As far as the South Korean punters are concerned, why work for a *chaebol* when you can work for yourself from home? Day trading is a national obsession. One in three adults trade on-line. Two years ago, only 3.7% of trading on the Korea Stock Exchange and Kosdaq was on-line; by January 2000 the amount had grown to an astounding 44.6% of all trading, the highest in the world. Web trades placed by Korea's top five securities firms totalled $89.2 billion. For the rest of Asia, it will be another five years before regional on-line trading reaches 20% of retail securities turnover.

If several South Korean brands are to rank in the global top 50 within the next two decades, the route map looks like this:

Automobiles

The global industry is worth about $2 trillion. Japanese makers have 30% of the market with South Korea holding just 5%. Korean auto brands are working to a template of early Japanese car-making strategies. But having now gained a basic level of respectability with consumers around the world, Hyundai should set its sights on shifting from 3% of the global market to 10% by year 2020. How?

1. Hire or steal the world's best design talent. Lead, don't follow.

2. Drive the strategy from home base with R&D, marketing and synergised communications that travel across all borders. Learn from Mercedes, BMW, VW, and have an appealing, single-minded brand personality around the world. Build connections with consumers.

3. Behave like a world leader by coming up with a unique vehicle idea, something that will change the way people relate to motor vehicles. It might be a *shape* perhaps (like the VW Beetle or the Mini), a unique *function* (what's the next concept after a people mover?), a unique *engine* that does something different or differently (works underwater or runs on solar energy), or a unique *safety feature* (something as amazing as the Mercedes-Benz A-Class engine that drops on impact). This idea must be daring otherwise it's not worth doing. South Korea's appetite for business risk is legendary; use it now to take *creative risks* and drive faster growth.

Electronics

World turnover in electronics exceeded $956 billion in 2000. South Korea has big opportunities in both the white goods and air conditioning segments. The recognised Korean brand is LG. In

India, LG beat top domestic brands like BPL in the consumer durable goods category by changing the perception that Korean brands are just cheap brands. In China, where foreign electronic brands find it hard to thrive, LG holds the second largest market share for microwave ovens with sales of $1.4 billion. LG has attributed its success in India and China to its "localisation" strategy and is now stepping up its presence in Asia. LG's reported net profits in 1999 were $2.8 billion; beyond consumer goods, LG is a leader in semiconductors with a 7.9% share of the global market and produces mobile phone handsets and other Internet-related businesses.

The target for LG is to challenge the likes of GE and Whirlpool (and potentially Haier) as the world's number one brand in white goods and air conditioning. Currently, LG is sitting around tenth position. LG has to programme a world leader attitude into everything it does; when you walk taller, it's amazing how much more you see. I feel that LG's brand communications strategy needs some fine-tuning. Don't attempt to be too slick. Moreover, I suggest that one thing needs urgent attention — the LG logo design. I think the present one does not match the quality and stature of this global brand.

Mobile Communications

The worldwide mobile phone market was worth $129 billion in 2000. Annual growth to 2001 was 44%.

In the early 1980s, so I'm told, AT&T asked a consultancy to estimate how many cellular phones would be in use in the world at the turn of the century. The story goes that the consultancy took note of all the problems that existed with mobile phones at that time — absurdly heavy handsets, batteries that kept running out, patchy coverage, exorbitant cost-per-minute call rates — and promptly concluded that the total market would be about 900,000 units. Small wonder that AT&T decided to pull out of the market, although they changed their mind later. These days, 900,000 new subscribers join the world's mobile phone service *every few days!*

And the mobile phone does more than phone calls, like

sending and receiving e-mail. WAP (Wireless Application Protocol) allows mobile phone users to connect to and browse the Internet and access their bank accounts, even switch their lights and alarm systems on and off at home while they are elsewhere.

Clearly, Samsung is South Korea's mobile communications champion in the global fight for consumer loyalty. Samsung should aim to shift from its present fourth position to outright world leadership by year 2010. A big issue to resolve in the consumer's mind is specialisation. All the major mobile phone makers are dedicated telecommunications companies, whereas Samsung's name pops up on everything from rice cookers and consumer appliances to memory chips. For some marketers, the concept of having the same brand name across a variety of different product categories has not been such a problem — Virgin, for example, is bolted onto airlines, colas, record shops, books, even railways. Samsung lacks the madness of Virgin. It is at war against incredibly professional brands, each possessing concentrated experience in telecommunications. One strategic scenario could be for the Samsung brand to be bolted solidly to mobile phones at the high, infocommunications end, and for Samsung to play a more subdued branding role in its other manufacturing categories, for example:

1. Step up the advertising budget for the next five years and pump the bulk of funds into promoting Samsung mobile phones.

2. Progressively relaunch and promote only the top Samsung products in other categories, under sub-brand names. The owner is present, but takes a back seat.

DRAM Memory Chips

South Korea's stranglehold on the memory chip industry should be leveraged with the same gusto and madness that the Americans have brilliantly demonstrated in IT areas. While the two biggest brands, Samsung and Hyundai, should be given some recognition, the chips themselves should have a special brand name and hero status of their own. Again it's a case of developing brand names that are perceived as *specialised to the category*. While world demand for DRAM memory chips has recently taken a dive, I think it will recover and in the years to come, as other makers challenge South Korean market share, the global ownership of the category will be an exhilarating battle.

TAIWAN: FROM POORHOUSE TO POWERHOUSE

Taiwan is a 36,000-sq.-km island located 100 miles east of the Chinese mainland. Beijing claims Taiwan is a province of China, while the Taiwanese believe they are an independent country.

While relations between China and Taiwan remain prickly, Taiwan itself has undergone a remarkable change in the intervening 50 years. Three developments underscore this change:

One: Taiwan has built up one of Northeast Asia's most robust export economies. Today it is one of the world's largest trading economies, ranked between 15th and 18th. For readers who keep a close eye on such claims, it is perhaps instructive to point out that the downturn in the global economy which surfaced in the second quarter of 2001 will temporarily put a crimp on Taiwan's exports, particularly personal computers and computer chips. Disruption in exports of semiconductor devices, which appears certain in the face of declining demand in the United States because of the recession, will over the next 18 months at least grievously impinge on the export forecasts of Taiwan's individual manufacturing houses.

Two: Taiwan has transformed itself into a working democracy, shedding the ideological and autocratic underpinnings of Chiang Kai-shek's KMT.

Three: The shape of Taiwan's economy is undergoing a major change and it is becoming a key player in the new global economy. Moreover, despite the election in May 2000 of the pro-democracy candidate Chen Shui-bian as president, investments in China by Taiwanese businesses are rising significantly, adding a whole new dimension to the unification debate. Nowhere is this more in evidence than in semiconductor manufacturing. Rather interestingly, Winston Wong, son of a top Taiwanese industrialist, is building a $3.6-billion semiconductor fabrication plant in Pudong, Shanghai. His partner? Jiang Miancheng, son of China's President Jiang Zemin.

I sense that these developments will have a major impact on relations between China and Taiwan. No less, with Hong Kong and Macau already functioning as Special Administrative Regions of China, what we can anticipate is the emergence of a strong Greater China geographic and economic grouping with a shared business culture.

The flow of capital, technology and skills across this geographic area will elevate China, Taiwan, Hong Kong and Macau into dynamic manufacturing and service centres. They will be highly competitive, modern and innovative, and slowly we could witness the breaking down of the ideological barriers between Taiwan and China.

Meanwhile, Taiwan's 23 million people haven't done badly since Chiang Kai-shek fled Mao's victorious troops in 1949. The current global economic slowdown and some domestic political instability, which is expected to persist through 2001–2002, have slowed economic achievement a bit, but certainly not to crisis proportions.

While subject to change without notice these days, Taiwan's economy is forecast to grow by 3.4% in the year 2001 and 4.7% in 2002. Consumer prices will rise by an average 1% in 2001 and 1.8% in 2002. The country's current account surplus will fall from $9.3 billion (3% of GDP) in 2001, to $5.9 billion (1.7% of GDP) in 2002. Taiwan's foreign currency holdings reportedly stand at around $85 billion, one of the largest in the world. Not bad for a nation that 39 years ago was classified as a poor, agricultural country, qualifying it for foreign economic aid.

Remarkably, for such an economic powerhouse, there are very few celebrated Taiwanese product or service brands. The world's third largest manufacturer of semiconductors, and the second largest manufacturer of personal computers, remains an almost *anonymous* maker of electronics cornucopia.

Part of the problem stems from the role Taiwanese manufacturers chose for themselves right from the 1950s — making products so others could put their corporate logos on them. Taiwan is the classic OEM (Original Equipment Manufacturer) and ODM (Original Design Manufacturer) country. IBM, Dell, Compaq and HP all have their PCs made in Taiwanese factories and badge them for export. Taiwan offers extremely competitive OEM and ODM arrangements, unquestionable quality, and reliable delivery schedules.

Another explanation for Taiwan's absence from the world stage of brands? It's apparently all a question of focus. As one of my Taiwanese colleagues told me, Taiwanese businessmen regard China as their global stage because of its market size and their own cultural advantage.

Computers

Taiwan's only high profile PC brand is *Acer*, which was established in 1976. You would be justifiably puzzled why Acer — already a strong global brand — is highlighted in this study. I'll explain why.

Acer Inc. is among the world's top producers of PCs. Stan Shih, founder and company chairman, says: "Our philosophy is to make it possible for everyone everywhere to enjoy these technologies by driving down costs and making PCs easy to use." The technologies Shih is referring to are not only those that create PCs; he has in mind video game players, computers for kids, DVD players, video telephones and intelligent consumer products.

In 1999, Shih disclosed that his strategy was to develop the Acer Group into a $15-billion giant by the end of the year 2000. This dream remained unfulfilled because of the slowing down of the American economy and its impact on Europe, Latin America, South Asia and Southeast Asia.

Stan Shih's plan to build Acer into one of the world's top five computer companies was not far-fetched, but in the prevailing global economic climate Shih was compelled to switch horses in midstream as it were.

Previously, Shih's branding and marketing strategies allowed

Acer to dominate many hot-growth emerging markets from Malaysia to Mexico, Moscow to Manila. It also has one of the most efficient global manufacturing organisations in the industry. Acer's manufacturing empire, *BusinessWeek* noted as long ago as 1996, "includes 39 just-in-time assembly plants scattered from San Jose, California to Subic Bay in the Philippines". In that year Acer plants pumped out 4 million PCs, 1.7 million CD drives, 3.5 million monitors and 52 million memory chips, reported *BusinessWeek*.

Acer's best-known PC brand is Aspire, a line that has been a big consumer hit in the US and many key Asia-Pacific markets.

But on 21 June 2001, Acer announced that it was transforming itself from a purely manufacturing-based organisation into a marketing and services-based company, even as it disclosed year 2000 group revenues were $4.5 billion and profits were $534 million.

The June 2001 reorganisation, in the words of Stan Shih, means that "Acer is reacting to the changing nature of the global economy, moving from the IT era to the era of the knowledge-based economy; and in terms of corporate culture, Acer is going from a technological innovation focus to a user-centric focus. Acer has led the way in Taiwan, helping the island nation become a global IT leader, and is now leading the way as the knowledge-economy pioneer of Greater China and beyond."

Shih's success, both as an independent computer maker and OEM/ODM player in Taiwan, and now as a player in the knowledge-economy sector, should encourage other Taiwanese computer and electronics manufacturers to consider moving away from faceless manufacturing primarily focused on personal computers.

Acer is creating a new road map for itself through its reorganisation. First, Acer is separating the Acer-brand side of the business from the manufacturing side. To achieve this, Acer has created a new enterprise — Design, Manufacturing and Services (DMS). The Acer Brand Operation (ABO) will in future be responsible for Acer Inc.'s traditional Acer-brand PC and IT marketing operations. It will also have responsibility for the company's Greater China business and the development and execution of its e-business-related initiatives.

"Separating the DMS business from the Acer-brand business will allow both ABO and DMS to remain focused and therefore more competitive," says Shih.

Acer has also created a separate Holding and Investment Business (HIB) to support its new e-business efforts through aggressive investment and mergers, consolidation and acquisition of strategic e-business resources and partner companies.

So, given the huge reputation Taiwanese have established for quality and reliability, will we see other Taiwanese manufacturers involved in PCs and electronic products follow Acer's lead?

The jury is still out on this one. Cautious industry gurus suggest that opting out of OEM/ODM to create new, proprietary brands may not be the answer. Some point to *Twinhead*, once a highly successful OEM/ODM notebook PC maker that tried to cover both branding and OEM bases. It ran into trouble and floundered.

However, many Taiwanese firms in the computer and electronics products business refuse to accept Acer as the exception that proves the rule. Let's look at three other industries involved in faceless manufacturing and as a result have no known branding...

Semiconductors

Taiwanese semiconductor manufacturers are among the biggest in the world, but we would be hard pressed to find a recognisable brand. Taiwan is the world's third largest chip maker, but where, for instance, is Taiwan's equivalent of Intel?

Chintay Shih, chairman of the Taiwan Semiconductor Industry Association, says Taiwan's plan is to capture an 8% share of the global chip market by 2005. This translates to $66 billion in semiconductor revenues.

Industry leader *Taiwan Semiconductor Co. Ltd.* is Taiwan's largest publicly traded company by market value. TSC was founded in 1979. Apart from plants in Taiwan, TSC also built two large plants in China in 1995 and 1996 to boost production.

Despite the slowdown in the industry, Taiwan Semiconductor chalked up sales of $4.8 billion in 2000, and its profits were equally impressive. Looking ahead, TSC feels the market will be relatively uncertain in the short term, but expects the semiconductor industry to regain its footing within the next 18 months to 2 years. Given the continuing growth of products which are developed around chip sets and the quantum leap in the production of communication devices, shouldn't Taiwan's savvy chip producers brand their products? After all, *intel inside* is now an obligatory badge on any decent PC, but where is Taiwan Semiconductor?

Now, at this point allow me to press the pause button and to get a little theatrical about an issue that I suggest is getting more daunting each passing day — China.

Common sense tells us that the People's Republic of China will suck increasingly large chunks of unskilled and semi-skilled manufacturing business away from other parts of East Asia. This will force the affected nations to move up into more highly skilled industry sectors with less vulnerable growth opportunities. While Taiwan has been taking this route for some time, I feel it is still vulnerable. Why?

Notwithstanding my earlier commentary that China and Taiwan will move to a more comfortable business and political relationship, this development will clearly take some time to mature. In the immediate term — the next five to ten years or so — it seems to me that China has a bigger axe to grind with Taiwan than it has with others in Asia, and my guess is that it will work harder and more passionately to undermine Taiwan's manufacturing strengths at *all* levels. One positive way for Taiwan to help counter this assault is through a strong stable of powerful global brands. Acer, and particularly now because of the clever way it has transformed itself to respond to change, is the obvious role model. It patently demonstrates that intelligence is transportable and that the whole world can be your factory and your marketplace. But even Acer has to be more aggressive, as mainland Chinese brands will unquestionably challenge its ranking in years to come. I'd appoint Acer's chairman as the leader of the "Taiwan World Brands" crusade. Moving from essentially a faceless manufacturing force to a dynamic global brand force will achieve all sorts of wonderful benefits for Taiwan. Don't wait a second longer!

NOW, let's relax a little and turn to a few other branding opportunities that are more classically "Old Economy" in character.

Boat Building

The building of yachts, sailboats and trawlers in Taiwan began sometime in the 1970s as Taiwan's economy shifted from agriculture to manufacturing. Even though their construction quality was not outstanding the early boats from Taiwan sold reasonably well, primarily because they were low priced and lavishly embellished with teak. Today, following a shakeout in the industry in the late 1980s, Taiwanese boat builders are recognised for their technological and design innovations, excellent building and competitive pricing.

There are reportedly some 50 boat builders in Taiwan. Their yards boast modern facilities, use advanced technology for design and construction, and employ skilled craftsmen. But the industry is facing serious competition from Singapore and Malaysia. For example, *Grand Banks* trawler yachts and *Eastbay* fast cruisers were previously manufactured in Taiwan for the American firm Grand Banks Yachts. No more; these boats, which are extremely popular in America, are now made in Singapore. The Taiwanese yards are switching from volume production of smaller boats to building bigger craft of higher quality. The average yacht built in Taiwan today is in the 48- to 55-footer range and priced around $350,000. Taiwanese yards also have the capability to build larger 80- to 100-foot yachts.

Taiwan's annual export of boats is around $100 million, most of it going to the US (67%), followed by Hong Kong, Spain, Australia and Japan. Recognising the threat to Taiwan's boat industry, Taiwan's Ministry of Economic Affairs set up a fund in 1995 to support research and development in the industry. The Taiwan authorities are also setting up a special boat building zone at Tamsung Harbour in northern Taiwan.

Despite its export success, *Taiwan has no identifiable boat brands.* Taiwanese-made boats parade under code numbers. Typically, H.S. Code 89031101000–8, one of five H.S. codes used in the industry, identifies yachts and other pleasure or sports vessels, rowing boats and canoes as being made in Taiwan. The reason? They are OEM-type deals. As a result, a boating enthusiast in Australia, say, buying an Aquasport 215, a Bertram 46 Convertible, a Glacier Bay 2640 Renegade or a Blackfin 33 would hardly be expected to know that his toy was "Made in Taiwan". Boats, in fact, are branded by the companies that sell them, not the builders.

And here's a little secret. Companies that brand and sell boats disguise the country of origin quite smartly. Here is a typical example from a boat brand owner's website: "Welcome to our world of luxury yachts and cruisers. Here you will find descriptions and photos of each model and size *we build*..." The bold italics on "we build" are mine, to flag the point. One wonders why no mention is made that these boats were previously built in Taiwan and that production has now been switched to Singapore.

So can Taiwanese boat builders brand their products? I would venture to think they can, particularly in markets such as Japan, Australia, Hong Kong and Europe. The US is tough, however, because American brand names have survived the ages, ever since rich folk in the States between the two wars started buying expensive toys and floating gin palaces.

NOW let's turn to another fascinating field of big branding opportunities.

Textiles and Apparel

Taiwan exported $14.18 billion of textiles and apparel in 1999 (the last available figures) — and exports are rising. This is Taiwan's second major export industry, penetrating over 50 countries.

No less remarkable is the fact that Taiwan does not produce cotton or wool, while production of silk is minuscule. What it does produce though, and in spades, is polyester filament (2.7 million tons in 1998) and nylon (3.2 million tons in 1998). Taiwan is the world's second and third largest producer respectively.

As it is with semiconductors and boats, apparel in Taiwan is a massive OEM play. You name the brand and chances are a lot of the high-end products of international fashion, leisure and sportswear are made in Taiwanese factories. Higher labour costs in Taiwan as opposed to those in China, Bangladesh, Vietnam and Sri Lanka are transcended by modern technology — spinning, weaving, cutting, sewing — and super product quality. Small wonder then that Taiwanese factories serve as OEMs for Nike, Adidas, Tommy Hilfiger, GAP, Liz Claiborne and huge retailers such as J. C. Penney. In 1998, this business was worth $2.5 billion.

But there is hope that Taiwan might soon be producing some really high fashion brands of its own. It made a significant push in that direction when it hosted the Taipei International Textile & Apparel Show — TITAS 99. The show focused on high quality fabrics and *haute couture*. Foreign buyers from over 50 countries flocked in, and judging from published reports, were very impressed. To pursue the brand end of the garment business, Taiwanese factories are shifting their lower-end operations to neighbouring countries while retaining their design studios and sophisticated, high-end manufacturing at home. It is going to be a slow transition from OEM to ODM and finally to OBM, but the signs are strong that the world will soon be able to choose from some high quality Taiwanese fashion brands in their own right.

Here are three companies that are preparing to brand their creations:

Eagle Garments is Taiwan's leading house for men's formal wear — suits, jackets and tuxedos — and has been in the business for 33 years. Eagle is widely respected by buyers in Taiwan and visiting firemen for the high quality of workmanship and zero defects. Eagle also scores heavily for design and creativity, and a high level of professionalism and reliability in fulfilling orders. Eagle has its priorities right and could well be the first of Taiwan's high fashion men's brands to hit the international market.

One of Taiwan's oldest textile companies, *Diamond Hosiery & Thread*, is an integrated textile operation involved in spinning, dyeing, knitting and garment production. Its annual production capacity is 180,000 garments and 120,000 kilograms of knitted fabric. It is now focusing on men's and women's sports and leisurewear.

Regarded as one of Taiwan's leading producers and exporters of knitted sweaters and pullovers, *Silver Knitting* has been in business for 30 years. Silver has built long-term relationships with major retailers worldwide, particularly in Japan which accounts for 50% of Silver's output. Silver has a strong in-house design group and produces two annual collections, winter and summer. Industry experts believe that Silver is well positioned to brand its knitwear lines that have already achieved acceptance in large retail stores worldwide.

Food and Beverage

Something more down to earth now, a food and drink brand that is spreading through Asia, and on to Chinese communities in the West (especially America) under the not-so-felicitous name *Want Want*. The brand is owned by who else than Want Want Holdings, headquartered in Taiwan. I think it is a fantastic name. It's fun, light hearted, easy to remember, and offers a ton of creative opportunities.

Want Want is big on rice crackers, confectionery and beverages. There are some 50 products in all. Although Want Want is a Taiwanese-owned company, 28 of its 32 major production plants are in mainland China. The other three are in Taiwan mostly turning out around 52,000 tons of rice crackers a year, Want Want's core business. Rice crackers account for 55% of group turnover, snacks contribute 29% and beverages 13%.

Want Want has 90% of the rice cracker market in Taiwan. In China, where it dominates the rice cracker, snack and biscuit categories, it has elbowed out Uni President and Tingyi, which are both Taiwanese companies, as well as competitors from Japan and Korea.

For all the simplicity of both its name and products, Want Want is big business. In 1999 the company's profit was $65 million, a jump of 8% over the previous year. Want Want is currently planning an assault on markets in the United States, Europe and selected Asian countries. It plans to achieve this through acquisition of related businesses or interests. This expansion strategy is critical to the company's future, particularly for pushing its core brand — rice crackers — which has reached saturation point in Taiwan and China.

Given that the brand owners are as keen about this brand as I am, there should be no reason why it will not rank among the top five global brands in its field within the next ten years. The whole world will Want Want.

THAILAND: TIME TO BE BOLD

A strong, monarchic, Buddhist nation, Thailand has a population in excess of 60 million. It is a stable and prosperous country, and until the economic crisis hit in the 1990s, enjoyed rapid economic growth. The fallout from the 1990s appears to be contained and Thailand entered the new millennium pursuing a new agenda of economic and commercial growth. A commentary on Thailand notes: "Thai society is characterised by a rich blend of cultural traits, an openness to new ideas, and a high degree of adaptability to new situations."

Despite a certain amount of diversity, Thai society is bound together by three basic tenets: Theravada Buddhism, unquestioning support for the Thai monarchy, and pride of citizenship in the only nation in Southeast Asia to have maintained its independence throughout its history, including the heyday of European colonialism.

However, the image of Thailand that endures today derives not from its three basic tenets, but from *The King and I*, an amusing celluloid fantasy about an English governess, Anna Leonowens, and Thailand's King Mongkut circa 1862. Successive Thai governments have judged *The King and I* to be neither amusing nor historically accurate, and the recent Twentieth Century Fox remake, *Anna and the King*, failed to impress the Thais who suggested it was full of historical and cultural distortions.

Be that as it may, the foundations of modern Thailand were established by the Chakri dynasty that came to power in 1782. At that time the country was known as Siam and it was only in 1939 that the name Thailand was adopted. Thailand's early modernisation was the legacy of King Chulalongkorn (1868–1910). He westernised the institutions of the State, introduced a Cabinet-style government, and created a standing army and a modern civil service. Thailand is politically one of Southeast Asia's most stable countries with strong economic underpinnings.

In spite of the fact that there is Chinese blood in a third of the population, the Thais see themselves as an ethnically homogeneous society. Thai Chinese, mainly second or third generation, make up slightly over 14% of the population and they play a dominant role in economic development, as indeed those of Chinese extraction do in many countries in Asia.

Thailand's current economic framework is built around the country's eighth Five-Year Plan (1997–2001). It emphasises development of the private industrial and service sectors; further deregulation of trade, finance and industry with tax revisions to encourage domestic competitiveness; introduction of national environmental protection and pollution policies; increased government expenditure on infrastructural development and health care; and land reform, improved education and government decentralisation. However, the economic crisis of 1997 impinged grievously on the Thai economy and planned targets have had to be revised in its wake.

Thailand has a labour force of over 32 million and a GDP of $388 billion. Primarily an agricultural country, its enterprising, independent small farmers have consistently given Thailand food surpluses. About 54% of the country's total labour force is engaged in the agricultural sector, and nearly 80% of the population is dependent on the land for its livelihood. Agriculture is where you will find Thailand's Golden Assets — rice, maize, cassava, rubber, sugarcane, coconuts, cotton, kenaf and tobacco. Fisheries are also an important export industry.

Manufacturing industry is of recent origin and mainly in food and beverages, textiles and apparel, and wood and mineral products. The majority of these modern industrial enterprises is Thai-owned, but a significant number of foreign ventures also help to drive Thai industry which is largely concentrated in Bangkok and the city's immediate hinterland. Industry accounts for between 30–43% of GDP, and 30% of total exports. Mineral resources like tin, tungsten, fluorite (or fluorspar, whichever you prefer), antimony and precious stones contribute about 2% of GDP and are important foreign exchange earners.

Thailand's energy sources include small oil fields, large lignite deposits, natural gas in the Gulf of Thailand, and hydroelectric power. Extensive, largely unevaluated oil shale deposits have recently been identified. Thermal power generation — using oil, natural gas and lignite — accounts for 70% of the total 18,000-megawatt installed generating capacity with hydropower accounting for 30%. Actual power production runs at around 15,000 MW.

Thailand's major exports are primary and processed agricultural products, tin, clothing and a range of manufactured consumer goods, quite a bit of it OEM manufactured. Clearly, agri-business — agriculture and fisheries — is where the country must look to create new and successful brands. Thailand is a net food exporter. In fact, *it is the fifth largest global food producer.*

With a fleet of 50,000 vessels, Thailand is one of the world's largest seafood producers. It also has a large prawn farming industry. Frozen fish exports, mainly prawns, are valued around $3 billion annually; canned fish exports net an annual $450–500 million.

Thailand is a major chicken producer for both domestic consumption and export. The Charoen Pokphand Group is probably the world's single largest chicken producer and animal feed miller with extensive international operations; amazingly, the CP Group is the largest private foreign investor, in dollar terms, in China.

Thailand is also a leading producer and exporter of natural rubber (accounting for 12% of total agri-revenue), pineapples and prawns, besides rice and a harvest of seafood such as squid, clams, crab and tuna. Interestingly, Thailand is the world's largest supplier of canned tuna. Her two million tons of pineapples represent roughly 20% of the world's total annual crop. Then there's some 18 million tons of fresh cassava roots annually, giving Thailand about 11% of the total global output.

With so many positive fundamentals, Thailand should be able to supply a bumper crop of agri-business global brands.

The kingdom's other great revenue earner is tourism. Visitors to Thailand contribute between $8 to $10 billion annually, attracted by its wonderful cultural offerings, bargain shopping, beach resorts, temples, and of course Bangkok's exotic night life. In 2000, Thailand welcomed 9.5 million visitors.

Jim Thompson Silk

Without a doubt, one of Thailand's most celebrated brands is Jim Thompson Silk. It derives its name from the man himself, Jim Thompson. A retired American OSS officer, architect and entrepreneur, Thompson settled in Bangkok after the Second World War, a city he knew quite well during his days as an American intelligence operative.

Silk has been produced in Thailand from very early times. Then, as now, it remains the occupation of poor farmers living mostly in the northeastern part of the country. These peasants cultivated the silk worms, produced the silk yarn, spun and wove it, and used a variety of dye materials, primarily lac and indigo, to create the red and blue colours typical of Thai silk fabrics.

When Jim Thompson looked at creating a serious business out of Thai silk, the craft was in decline. He turned it round by introducing colourfast chemical dyes, improved weaving techniques, and vibrant new fashion designs and colours. Thompson's impact on the Thai silk industry was substantial. Designers from New York, Paris, London and Tokyo discovered the magic of Thai silk for their *haute couture* creations, while interior decorators found the fabric indispensable for furnishings and accessories. Thompson himself led the charge through his Thai Silk Company, producing and marketing a remarkable range of ready-to-wear silk clothing, handbags and purses under the Jim Thompson brand. Not surprisingly, he added bedspreads, cushions, curtains and tablecloths.

Thompson's business was already a success when he literally vanished from the scene; while on holiday in the Cameron Highlands of Malaysia, he went for a walk one afternoon and was never seen again. His disappearance remains a mystery to this day, but his silk and the brand he championed go marching on. Even his Thai-style home in Bangkok has become a "must-see" for tourists.

The Thompson company maintains four retail outlets in Bangkok and tourist hangouts such as Phuket and Koh Samui. The company has agents in 35 countries including the United States, United Kingdom, Japan, Switzerland, Taiwan, France, Germany, Hong Kong, Argentina, South Africa and Turkey. Exports contribute 30% of the company's annual turnover. Domestic sales of Thai Silk Company's products derive from purchases by foreigners visiting the country; the company says only 10% of its business comes from Thai customers. Thai Silk Company annually produces two million yards of Thai silk and Thai cotton, two million yards of finished products and printed fabrics, and one million individual items of clothing and accessories. Also grouped under the Jim Thompson corporate umbrella are two major subsidiaries: Thai Printers and Finishers Co., producing dyed and printed Thai silk products, and SKK Manufacturing Co. Ltd., which produces neckties, clothing, handbags and fashion accessories.

Successful as it has been, I think the Jim Thompson brand is substantially underleveraged in the global theatre because it is perceptually linked to Thai silk and worldwide interest in Thai silk is relatively narrow. It is clear that this brand should be synonymous with the finest and most beautiful things made in Thailand, with special focus on personal fashion and accessories, as well as home furnishings, broadening the offerings to include furniture and tableware. Jim Thompson should be a fashion as well as a cultural statement of Thailand, ever evolving on one side, and never changing on the other. Once the brand owners get this right and the message is spread widely, they'll have a great enduring global brand.

Singha Beer

The name Boon Rawd Brewery Company Limited may not ring a bell, but Singha Beer usually does. It is Thailand's most famous beer brand, universally available in the kingdom and served with pride among Thai communities overseas.

Phraya Nhirom Bhakdi founded Boon Rawd in 1933. It sells its beer domestically through 400 dealers. Its most popular brand, Singha (Sanskrit for "lion") is a lager. Other brands are Singha Gold Beer, Singha Draft Beer, Leo Beer and Super Leo. Non-beer brands are Singha Soda Water, Singha Drinking Water and Singha Fresh, a range of fresh fruit juices in cans.

Boon Rawd's executive director says its three breweries command 49% of the total Thai beer market, with the lager accounting for 23%. Competing brands are Heineken, Carlsberg, Kloster and Chang, a recent entrant that is also in the spirits business. Boon Rawd has an annual capacity of 500 million litres, but production is running at roughly 60–65% of that.

Singha beer and the company's associated brands have plenty of room to grow. Indochina, notably Vietnam, sitting on Thailand's doorstep as it were, has to be a prime target market. Elsewhere in the world, you'll find Singha Beer wherever you find a Thai restaurant. Not a bad customer base.

However, total exports still only represent a fraction of total consumer sales, which clearly signals where the marketing priority has been focused. I have a problem with this risk-averse style of play. Very simply, the opportunity to vigorously expand Singha's global business should not be missed. To give you some perspective of global beer consumption, if Singha *doubled* its total sales this year it would still only represent about 1% of the world market. So let's get even more adventurous and target to put Singha on the global power brand map within five years — with just a 2% market share. *This would enlarge Singha's business by four times its current size.* Worth shooting for! Certainly the marketing investment will be substantial, but the return on investment should be excellent.

Thai Rice

As is the case with most agricultural exports, Thai rice yet remains to be effectively branded. Oddly, the most popular export variety is rather blandly described as "Fragrant Rice".

Thailand is a significant global rice producer; production for 2000–2001 is estimated to reach 24 million tons. More importantly, Thailand is *the world's largest rice exporter*, about 25% of her annual production going primarily to Asian countries — Indonesia, Japan, Hong Kong, Sri Lanka, Malaysia and Singapore. Other export markets are Nigeria, Iran, Senegal, South Africa, the United States and Iraq. So the opportunities exist to create some meaningful brands. Take Thailand's high quality Thai Hom Mali variety, previously known by its more felicitous name, Jasmine Rice; it has considerable potential and is currently the focus of the government's rice export promotion strategy. Exports of Thai Hom Mali until recently stood at around 1.3 million tons annually, roughly one-sixth of total rice exports.

The export of rice is a crowded industry in Thailand with some 121 companies involved. The most successful is the *Capital Rice Group*, with 20% share of the export market. Capital Rice is one of the two exporters which meet the Hazard Analysis Critical Control Point (HACCP) standard, a food safety control set by the US Food and Drug Administration. So this should be a boost to its efforts to establish a beachhead in Europe for Thai rice. The other HACCP standard bearer is *Siam Grains Co.* It exports between 70,000 to 80,000 tons of fragrant rice annually under three brands — Ko-Ko, Camel and Siam Grains — and focuses on the European Union, the United States, China and Hong Kong. Interestingly, China currently allows up to 200,000 tons to enter the country; however with China's membership of the World Trade Organisation, Thai exporters — particularly Siam Grains — expect to be able to lift exports to China significantly.

One could rightly argue that Thai rice is already a respected, well-known brand, so why complicate things by fostering other special brand names? Well, remember that for all sorts of good reasons, the game plan is to expand the base from selling commodities to also selling clearly defined exclusive brands. Certainly, foreign companies using Thai rice in *their* products are encouraged to flag the relationship — for example, Nestlé Thai Rice Pudding. However, the brand driver is Nestlé and that brand calls the tune. (Who knows, next season there could be a switch to Nestlé Australian Rice Pudding!) Which is why the concept of Thailand's rice-producing companies building their own strong individual brand identities is paramount to long-term survival. The specially branded rice should be the best quality, premium-priced rice. As well as providing better revenue yield, the specially branded rice will raise the bar for the perceived quality of all Thai rice. If this marketing exercise is handled with flair, I see no reason why distinctively branded Thai rice should not enjoy the world's best rice reputation within the next decade.

Wacoal

And now for something feminine ... the Thai Wacoal Public Company Limited is a small Thai manufacturer of women's clothes ranging from fashion to casual wear to maternity wear for a number of famous labels, including Wacoal, Guy Laroche and Louis Fortain. One speciality, however, is what goes *under* them — bras. The worldwide women's undergarments industry has always been prosperous, but in recent times — thanks to the imagination of some leading brand owners — it's literally bursting at the seams. This Thai producer of other people's labels should join the fray and embark on a vision of establishing its own brand and besting the best in this category.

Why not? The Thais are extremely creative. They are naturally comfortable with sensual things. And their workforce is skilled to handle virtually anything from high-tech productions to cottage industries. The immediate task is to identify the brand name that will crusade the global drive for this company whose corporate name unfortunately is the same as a famous foreign bra label. While I'd be inclined to choose a brand name that feels international, I wouldn't be shy about promoting its birthplace either.

Thai Union Frozen Products

Next, a return to the more predictable...

Thai Union Frozen Products is a highly successful operation that just needs a brand strategy consultant to get its branding act together. It unquestionably has the pedigree to be a significant global player.

The company reported sales exceeding $600 million in 2000 and annual growth of about 20%. It exports yellowfin and skipjack tuna to canning companies around the world. It also manufactures frozen shrimp and sushi. Fish fillets are manufactured using red snapper, yellowfin sole, Alaskan pollock, hoki, cod and flounder. Leftovers from the company's own tuna canning operations are used in its pet food lines. Canned tuna accounted for 34% of 2000 revenues, frozen shrimp 27%, canned pet food 18%, frozen tuna loin 6%. About 95% of Thai Union products are exported.

Thai Union offers a marketing opportunity that brand builders usually only dream about. Not only has it some great goodies for two-legged folk, it also has a strong product range for four-legged customers. Thai Union could potentially have not one but *two* global power brands within the next decade.

Celadon

I'd like to conclude with a more esoteric thought: a few words about Thai celadon. This glazed stoneware has been around since the 10th century. Celadon was originally a product of China; the green glaze was popular because it simulated the green of auspicious jade. Today the celadon kilns in Chiangmai are extremely active, turning out exquisite tableware, decorative vases and lamps and other artefacts. They are produced in the traditional celadon green, and as an extension of their ancient craft, the craftsmen today turn out some marvellous stuff in hues of brown, blue, black and white.

I personally think there is a lot of potential in Thai celadon. A learned commentator on the craft recently noted, "Ten centuries of artistic development have altered the product in only the most positive ways. Even a 350-year hiatus in Burma did nothing but bring about the restitution of the ancient craft in Thailand. Through this entire historic period, Thai sensitivity to artistic warmth and proven traditions in authentic Thai celadon have never lost their unique flavour and unusual vitality."

AND THE WINNER IS...

Finally, let me really stick my neck out and predict which Asian country will ultimately emerge with the most global power brands. *China* or *India* — which will take the crown?

It would be easy to say China. After all, it has been slated to be the world's leading economy by 2020. Both China and India have introduced a raft of economic reforms and China, much earlier than India, extricated itself from the embrace of state capitalism. Both China and India are encouraging free enterprises to drive economic growth and create national wealth. And following in the footsteps of post-war Japan, hopefully both China and India will unleash a catalogue of brands onto the world.

China, however, is struggling with its hundreds of loss-making state enterprises that defy all efforts to make them efficient and profitable. Nicholas Lardy, senior fellow at the Brookings Institution, Washington DC, is not impressed with China's record in generating growth and improvements in productivity, as opposed to simply accumulating capital. "It is difficult to foresee how, in the next 50 years, China can move to an economy where technological innovation — a knowledge-based economy — generates a large portion of its growth."

The slow transformation from an agricultural to an industrial economy creates massive upheavals. Population shifts bring with them all the accompanying socio-economic distortions that impinge on the economy. Corruption still bedevils provincial, state and central governments. Old Economy platforms like building roads, constructing the Three Gorges dam, producing steel and coal, and manufacturing cars, ships and barges are gobbling up huge investments. As Zhang Yunling, director of the Chinese

Academy of Sciences in Beijing, sums up: "I think you will see continuous globalisation and technological innovation in the future. China's economy will be based more on high technology. However, since China is such a large country, vast areas will be relatively backward. In the next 50 years, 80% of the population will move to urban areas. They will not rely on agriculture for their livelihood. That's a fundamental change in society: 500 million people will move, changing their lives, changing culture, changing values…"

India, meanwhile, has a few things over China. India's talented, highly skilled workforce is educated and trained in the new technologies. A measure of what India can achieve is underscored by a McKinsey study that tells us India's exports of info-tech products amounted to $50 million in 1991, $4 *billion* in 1999, and will hit $50 billion in 2008. In fact, entrepreneurs in the New Economy have left the regulators behind. The new technologies and the products and services they create don't quite fit into the rulebooks of civil servants. Nor are these creators of new wealth impeded by India's historic infrastructural shortcomings — congested ports, bad roads, antique fixed telephone systems and dilapidated public transport. They are operating in a borderless world. Satellites connect them to their global markets. Venture capital is flooding in to bankroll new info-tech startups. Overseas listings are creating overnight millionaires. Meanwhile, about 25% of the Mumbai Stock Exchange's capitalisation resides in 120 technology stocks. *BusinessWeek* said, "There's a Gold Rush energy level in many Indian cities."

Another strong point in India's favour: English, the lingua franca of today's global business, has been widely used for generations. The truth is, many Indians speak better English than the English and have a habit of snitching the Booker Prize for Literature from under British noses. The country employs internationally-recognised accounting and auditing practices. The rule of law is enshrined in the Indian constitution. A judiciary renowned for its feisty independence dispenses justice; it lost no time in convicting former Prime Minister Rao on corruption charges. British law and Indian barristers, it seems, were made for each other.

China, on the other hand, presents a sharp contrast.

Andy Xie, the Asia-Pacific executive director of Morgan Stanley Dean Witter suggests that "the most important development in China's future will be the movement towards the rule of law. It's the foundation of a modern economy in which people with ideas create wealth, not the people who have control over capital. This transition is not going to be an entirely smooth one. Too many people in China are still focused on capital-intensive industries".

And therein lies the rub. Is China still a long way from accepting the rule of law? How long will it take for its accounting and auditing practices to conform to international standards? And will the English language still struggle to find its voice in the Chinese workplace ten years from today?

Objectively, conditions on the ground in India favour a more dynamic transformation of enterprise in the context of the New Economy. Everything, it would appear, exists for the emergence of ideas, products and services that are on the cutting edge of new technologies. It seems to me that India will win the global power brand race initially, while China will still be wrestling with all the bricks and mortar stuff, very much as a function of the change from a command society to an enterprise society beneath an authoritarian leadership structure.

My 20-year "Wishlist" Projection for the World's Top 3 Brand Owners in Selected Categories

Category	2000	2020
automobiles	2 western; 1 japanese	1 asian; 1 japanese; 1 western
beverages (tea/coffee)	2 western; 1 asian	2 asian; 1 western
beverages (beer)	3 western	2 asian; 1 western
bottled water	3 western	1 asian; 2 western
white goods	3 western	2 asian; 1 western
IT hardware	3 western	2 asian; 1 western
software	3 western	2 asian; 1 western
alternative health care products	n.a.	2 asian; 1 western
wooden furniture	1 western	2 asian; 1 western
top-quality hotels	3 western	1 asian; 2 western
packaged foods	3 western	1 asian; 1 japanese; 1 western
sportswear/ sports equipment	3 western	2 asian; 1 western

Note: Definition of Asian Brand ownership: a brand that is owned and controlled by Asians (excluding Japan), with the seat of global marketing power residing in Asia. Remember, too, that in the context of this scenario, Australia and New Zealand are included in the Asian team.

Part four

THE WORLD CONQUERS ASIA

CHAPTER 11

WHEN GIANTS ROAMED THE EARTH

Why are giant global brands going through rougher weather these days?

One of the most memorable communications in advertising history happened about 30 years ago when two hundred young people sang *I'd like to buy the world a Coke....* That was the defining moment for the world's best-known global brand. Today, Coke is going through some serious rethinking as a result of unsatisfactory earnings. Where is this giant missing the plot as a great global brand?

McDonald's, P&G, Gillette and Levi's have also been experiencing troubled growth. And yet, as world markets increasingly deregulate, opening up *billions* more customer opportunities, the picture should be the reverse. What's the key problem?

Some experts suggest that local cultures in large emerging regions such as China, India and Eastern Europe are deeply resistant to Western influences; in fact, their less Westernised — even anti-Western — values are more solidly entrenched than might have been expected. These people take great pride in their national identities and prefer domestic products (which are also generally cheaper). The multinationals have responded by trying to build or buy more local brands, and this of course doesn't help the "global" brand crusade.

The shakedown on big global brands has also extended to mature markets, and the likes of Coca-Cola and McDonald's have been feeling the pressure in the USA. There, the explanation put forward by seasoned observers is different — a story of consumers becoming more individualistic, or developing different taste buds, or going the health route, or a combination of all these things.

Whatever the rationale, some of the biggest and best-known global brands have been feeling more vulnerable, and diversification into a larger menu of regional and local brands or sub-brands may witness a steady decline of the giant global brands themselves.

A consumer backlash against global power and control puts another spin on it to confuse us more. In a book titled *No Logo*, author Naomi Klein sets out to show that environmentalists, human rights campaigners and labour organisers have joined together, via the Internet, to fight the same cause. Their enemies? Transnational corporations and neo-liberal globalisation. This is heavy stuff and challenges the whole marketing game. Frankly, the author is pushing a concept that's been around for years, and I don't believe that cutting edge technology will accelerate support for her idea. Nonetheless, it deserves close monitoring. One aside: the notion of replacing brand names of goods and services with generic titles or numbers begs the question of why Naomi Klein specifically identified herself as the author.

The concept of branding is fundamental to the culture of all urbanised societies in the world (and has been since Adam and Eve, who might otherwise have been called "man" and "woman") and the benefits of competitive branding to the consumer need no supporting explanations from me.

Hindsight tells us that the hiccups being experienced by the big global guns are not too unexpected. While the new, potential growth markets of very recent times — Eastern Europe, India and China — are huge in numbers of people, they are also huge in terms of investment costs. Reports signal that establishment expenses to date have far exceeded budgets in these territories, thus impacting on global financial performance.

Expenses are one thing, but revenue projections have also been tough figures to pin down in a new, bigger global arena. The largely less educated, less aware consumers have had relatively little exposure to Western values and influences. Then there's distribution, another interesting nightmare, and also the very interesting business practices in new emerging markets. (For example, how would you like a deal where you as the Western partner agree to finance 100% of a 50/50 joint venture?)

OVERALL, the business and marketing strategies for global brands in these new emerging regions of the world have produced disappointing short-term financial performances and certainly have bruised the confidence of some of the key global brand decision-makers.

But having gone this far, the message is clear to the toughened brand owners: *stick to the mission.* Western-cum-global values will gradually prevail. Life for the global brands will get better and better and the global brand will triumph, *so long as the connection with the consumer is seen by the consumer as relevant, genuine and friendly.*

This view applies globally, in the West as well as in the East, perhaps even more so in the West. In my view, McDonald's doesn't connect with the consumer these days as empathetically as they did in past decades. McDonald's seems to believe that everyone, from a 3-year-old to an 83-year-old, buys only on a deal. At least, that's the way the ads come through to me. Way back, McDonald's put out its hand and heart and touched everyone, and everyone returned that love. I'm not advocating that "deals" are henceforth disqualified; rather, I'm saying that McDonald's should step up to the plate again with a lot more warm stuff that caresses its customers.

The same applies to Coke. Get back to some strong, compelling, emotional work. Give me a 21st century version of *I'd like to buy the world a Coke,* and I'll bet this communication would win the hearts of people of all ages and races on this planet.

CHAPTER 12

WHAT MAKES
ASIA TICK?

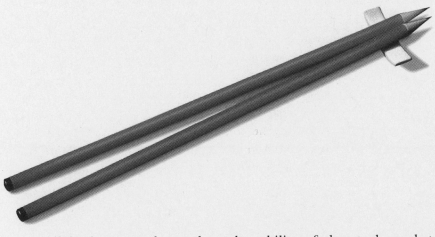

All businessmen know the vulnerability of the stock market. Something happens in the press and millions and millions of dollars can be wiped off a stock's value in no time. Yet few businessmen acknowledge that precisely the same thing can happen to the value of their brands as a result of their marketing mismanagement. If a brand doesn't maintain a certain style and credibility, as well as a certain level of awareness, its value declines. How much it will cost to restore brand equity, to put it back on the pedestal again, is anyone's guess.

Statistics tell us that scores of Western brands have not put a foot wrong in their penetration of Asia. But for all the Western successes, there are no doubt numerous Western brands that have not yet effectively established and consolidated a power brand position in Asia because of their stubborn arrogance and, sadly, their ignorance.

Let me share with you some branding mishaps I've experienced in an industry where the brand is highly sensitive to the whims of its brand manager. I refer to the luxury watch business.

In the late 1970s, we relaunched Tissot in Singapore. As a result of strong pressure from the local distributor, a company called Silvaroyal, the Swiss brand owner agreed to upgrade the styling of the Tissot range and reposition the brand as a contemporary fashion statement. We got all excited and put together an integrated package that included a small black ball attached to each watch; swishy point-of-purchase displays; and media advertising featuring black men with blondes, and fair-haired men with black women, all having fun doing unusual things. The theme line was *Next time...Tissot,* and the strap line said, *The best selling watch among the Swiss.*

The campaign worked like a dream. The first year's sales exceeded their entire 3-year sales target!

We happily envisaged the youthful Tissot fashion statement spreading right across Asia. A great case history was evolving before our eyes. And then we did a double blink. The new watch designs coming off the Swiss assembly line in year two did not meet our fashion positioning expectations. Sadly, we couldn't convince the Swiss brand owner to get the styling back on the fashion rails. The entire strategic platform collapsed dramatically. Tissot is still around, but it's not like the power brand it could have been in Asia.

Wordsworth wrote, "Grieve not, rather find strength in what remains behind", or words to that effect. I think Silvaroyal supported this sentiment because they bravely came back to us a year later asking for our help on yet a bigger challenge — the Omega brand.

As an Omega distributor for Southeast Asia, Silvaroyal had a growing concern that Omega was moving away from its position as the prime prestige competitor to Rolex. However, the Swiss guardian of the brand seemed to be ambivalent about the brand's decline in identity. We shared Silvaroyal's concerns so we developed a rather good speculative global advertising campaign. Together, we hurried off to Switzerland to present the initiative to the Omega brand owner.

We should have stayed at home. A committee of grim-faced Swiss gentlemen gave us a negative response. (In Switzerland, egalitarian principles are practised in business with an almost paranoid fervour. I was later told that the top man in the voting committee supported our campaign, but six of the ten members were against it, so it died before birth.)

The Omega brand subsequently went through a dark period in its life, but since its change of ownership and a ton of advertising support it has regained some of its old swagger and stature; apparently sales growth has been healthy. However, I am not an admirer of the present, poorly crafted endorsement campaign. The Omega soul rightly deserves a lot more class. If only the Omega owners of the early 1980s had run a consistent global campaign like the one we proposed, I think the brand would have achieved higher acclaim for its quality; Omega today would have been on the same pedestal as Rolex. The financial implications of this "What if?" scenario still boggle one's imagination. Methinks that Switzerland's practice of the democratic referendum in business has its defects.

We were not fated to have a serious creative connection with a watch account again until the mid-1990s. And once more we were dealing with the Swiss.

Only this time, the brand was the youthful, highly successful Swatch brand. The brand owners had developed an ultra-thin watch, and our agency was lucky enough to be chosen to compete against some of the best creative ad agencies in Europe and the USA for the global launch creative of this model.

We pitched in Switzerland to the brand owners. The ubiquitous committee of grim-faced Swiss gentlemen was on hand, reminiscent of the time we presented to Omega some 15 years before, but with one difference. This time there was only one genuine decision-maker, and he was Mr. Hayek, the owner. He opened the meeting by making it bluntly transparent that he had little time for advertising agencies and viewed them with the same respect a water buffalo has for a frog. Having grown up in the hard-knocks school of Asia, our chaps knew how to handle bullies. His huffing and puffing only strengthened their resolve to win the business.

And win they did. The agency created the name of the ultra-thin watch — Skin — as well as the logo design. The print ads featured some of the world's top models, naked except for the almost unnoticeable watch. The theme line was, *Am I naked or am I not...?*

As much as I have problems with Mr. Hayek's view about ad agencies, I find dealing with clever, autocratic clients is a much more efficient way of doing business. And, in telling you the campaign was a great success, I also have to tell you that it wasn't easy to produce.

When it came to shooting famous models in the nuddy in the studios of famous New York and London photographers, the client's key production delegate stepped up to the plate and insisted on close involvement. And we couldn't protest — he was Mr. Hayek's son! So we decided to send a clever, wildly passionate and theatrical agency creative director to the shoot with the view that he'd overwhelm Hayek Junior with his lateral and rather hypnotic behaviour. And off he went.

But we had overlooked one thing. This agency creative bloke had a habit of sometimes going walkabout and turning up at places not in the brief. True to form, he led us a merry dance for several days. We simply lost contact. The client's son was raising the roof, and just as we started to panic our agency creative man phoned in, from Venice, complaining that he couldn't find the photographer's studio. Correct, we said. The studio is in New York, not Venice.

Fortunately, there was a positive end to this story. Confused and as late as he was, our agency chap finally got things sorted out and everyone lived happily ever after.

Some of our watch brand work in the 1970s.

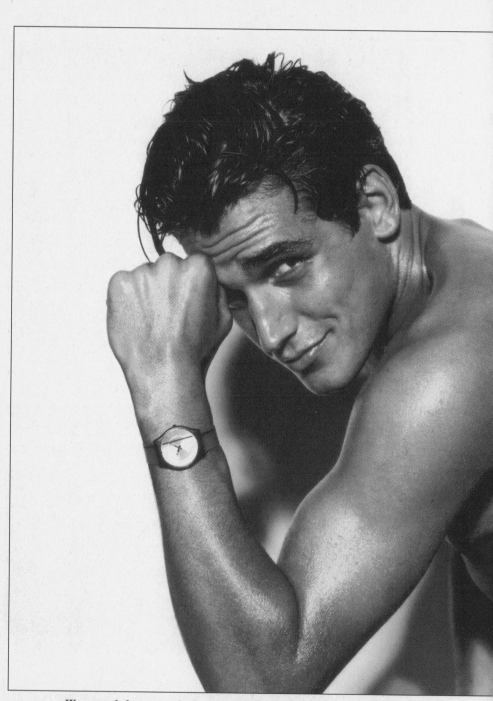

We created the name, the logo, and the global launch creative work…

CHAPTER 13

MAMASAN KNOWS BEST

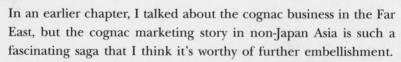

In an earlier chapter, I talked about the cognac business in the Far East, but the cognac marketing story in non-Japan Asia is such a fascinating saga that I think it's worthy of further embellishment.

At one stage in the 1970s, Hong Kong accounted for more than 50% of Remy Martin's total export sales worldwide. The rational view why cognac was in such demand was because it went extremely well with Chinese food. Some seasoned marketers pointed to a different consumer motive: cognac represented a badge of great affluence. Whatever the reason, it was not uncommon at Chinese banquets to see many patrons sipping a glass of vastly expensive cognac topped up with ice cubes and water! Importantly, the opened, well-branded bottle stood like a proud emperor in the centre of the table.

Western marketers have found it difficult to precisely pin down the relationship between cognac and the Chinese community. And they've experimented with all kinds of brand values in their communications programmes. But there's no argument on one point: the Chinese nightspots are the critical battleground.

Every big city across Eastern Asia has a string of nightclubs and bars. And to a Western observer, the majority of these places are a mirror image of the sort of venues one pictured existing in America in the 1920s and 1930s — the sort of scene that would make Humphrey Bogart feel right at home. Everything is dimly lit and every nook and cranny filled with tobacco smoke. A live band is bashing out something Western in the background, or is it canned music? Then again, it might be the karaoke section letting it rip. It's hard to know because what you can discern seems to indicate a dark cluster of rooms and cubicles of various sizes mixed in with some open spaces and hallways, and the noise level of human chatter and clinking glasses is close to damaging your eardrums. Male patrons fill the tables, the hallways, the restrooms. And young, beautifully manicured feminine creatures in long, clinging dresses glide around like swans, gracing the tables, sharing time and drinks with the customers. To a visiting clergyman from Ohio, it might all appear somewhat depraved and lack a sense of propriety. To a Chinese adult male brought up the hard way in Asia, it's a mix of pleasures: it's relaxing, highly rewarding, a great *macho* experience. Besides, Chinese happily embrace noisy, crowded environments.

All these clubs have a chief priestess, the *mamasan*, who controls the important action in the place. In the sale of cognac at such venues, the *mamasan* is the key client. In Taiwan, for example, there are literally thousands of karaoke clubs where businessmen entertain. A bottle of Hennessy X.O. could cost around $250, and a comfortable night out for several clients — with young ladies also imbibing and refilling the glasses — could cost the businessman host five or six bottles. Which is not a big concern; it's part of standard business expenses. The *mamasan* ensures that the selected cognac brand — in this case Hennessy X.O. — is continuously consumed throughout the evening. And she does more. If the businessman host chose to give his client's ego a boost, he might negotiate with the *mamasan* to release a young girl to leave with the lucky client before closing time. But not to do what you might think. It's a demonstration of face. The middle-aged client would be seen leaving with the young siren on his arm. Once they reached the kerb, a taxi would whisk her home — alone.

And so cognac reigned supreme in Asia's male nightspots until the early to mid-1990s. More than half the global revenues earned by cognac producers were derived from Asia. Then, seemingly almost overnight, whisky came in and took over.

Whisky marketers had been trying to get it into the nightspots as the favoured spirit for years without success. They had tried everything; advertising, merchandising, below-the-line. Then, so we're told, they went below-the-belt. They staged a *whispering campaign*. They spread a rumour that cognac contained sugar, which added weight, whereas whisky did not make you get fat. Parallel to this, the dynamics of changing demographics and psychographics of the alcohol-consuming market were starting to kick in. And the *mamasans* were converted to the whisky cause through the pressures of consumption, the mounting negative image of cognac as a yesteryear drink and, quite naturally, better financial incentives. The cumulative impact of whisky has been awesome, and cognac is now trying to reinvent itself to stay seriously in the game in Asia.

(There's a postscript to this story. My friends in Taipei tell me that businessmen now prefer to entertain their clients in golf clubs. *Sayonara, mamasan!*)

REVIEWING the liquor brands in Asia, it mystifies me why some pan-Asian brand owners insist on taking drinking so seriously. The breweries are among the worst offenders. Drinking is supposed to relax you in a social or business environment. Drinks are supposed to be enjoyable, fun companions. Yet a lot of advertising runs counter to this. Another thing I find difficult to understand is why some pan-Asian marketers think it necessary to develop different campaigns for their brand in different Asian countries, clearly supporting the view that their brand is consumed for different rational and emotional reasons in each of the different markets. And they certainly couldn't have made it so bewilderingly complex without the security blanket of loads of supporting research!

Well, I'd take a match to all that kind of research, and simply get the offending brand managers to go and get drunk with a group of people of mixed demographics in each Asian country. I think they'd find that after a few drinks, people in one market are much the same as people in any other market. There must surely be one creative idea, one campaign that happily connects the brand with its consumers across Asia.

Another thing about Asian liquor advertising is how it attempts to reach out and focus on young people — yet still tends to communicate with them in a young, naïve manner. I'm talking here about the 21- to 29-year-old segment. To start with, every popular brand worth its salt is trying to win more favour with this age group. So it's a pretty noisy battlefield. Secondly, this target group is remarkably aware of what's going on around it and is tuned in to the cutting edge of just about everything. While the gulf of knowledge between a 21-year-old and a 29-year-old is probably sizable, it's narrowing by the hour.

What should be of greater interest to global or pan-Asian brand owners is the growing view that this young adult market — right across the world — connects with much the same emotional values, even though socio-economic statistics may vary quite a bit. It is therefore fundamental that all advertising (liquor brands, fashion brands, and others) should address the young adult segment in a highly intelligent, mature manner. But don't neglect the fun, and keep things sharp and fresh.

This view also signals that *one* single creative idea can impactfully connect with this target audience right around the world.

AS more young Asians discover liquor, more changes come into focus. Sophisticated Asians are now much more comfortable with wine. In Singapore, the young especially are taking up wine. New wine bars are a dime a dozen. Wine has become such a new Asian status symbol that Singaporeans have been participating in London wine auctions and snapping up cases of rare wines for several thousand pounds each. Red wine has had a terrific boost after a medical report suggested that drinking it was good for one's health. The Asian palate is becoming far more discerning. French wines, once perceived as superior to all others, now vie for favour against wines from California, Australia, Germany, Chile and other wine-producing nations.

But do Asians really love wine or is it merely a badge? The answer lies in the evolutionary trek from being one kind of society to another. The journey into an affluent, middle-class society calls for all kinds of new social experiences and learnings. Wind back the clock in Britain or Australia and you would have seen consumers experimenting with cheap red wine, better known as Red Ned or Rouge Edward, the bottle concealed in a brown paper bag, while their mothers kept a discreet flagon of cooking sherry hidden under the kitchen sink. In America, a white wine called Blue Nun conquered but could not quite destroy everyone's taste buds. Going back a few years to the early 1960s, a symbol of social "maturity" was *Chianti*, a dry red Italian wine. It was *de rigueur* to have these round, string-bound bottles exhibited somewhere in your "pad", either with a candle burning in them or slung from the corner of a ceiling to indicate you were either a peasant or a poet, or both. Preferably, of course, the bottles would be empty. Asians have missed these pleasures; their middle-class societies have emerged at warp speed and while their pace of development is hectic, one gets the impression — judging by the rocketing sales of wine in Asia — that they're enjoying the catching-up process.

Indeed, right across the entire spectrum of the liquor industry in Asia, the growth opportunities for global brands will continue to be very bright — even for cognac, *if* it rewires its thinking.

CHAPTER 14

FROM STUTTGART WITH LOVE

At the last count in my records, there is one car for every two people in the USA. There is one car for every 1.9 Germans, while not to be outdone, the French have one car for every 1.9 of their citizens, too. Non-Japan Asia can muster one car for every 36 people, and China tops the scale with one car for every 180 people.

To put it mildly, Asia offers amazing growth opportunities for those in the car-making business.

The basic emotional reasons for owning a car in Asia are the same as they are in the West. Ownership is a significant statement that you have made it, and that you managed to elevate yourself above the economic situation that your parents or grandparents might have been in.

And the better the car, the better you have made it. It's on this point, however, that Asians tend to be more ostentatious than their Western counterparts in demonstrating their wealth and success. They passionately love the more expensive, more luxurious brands. Mercedes-Benz is the ultimate automobile icon, but it hasn't always been that way.

In the 1950s, in places like Singapore and Malaysia, Mercedes-Benz did not exist. In those days one saw hardly anything except British cars — Humbers, Rovers, Vauxhalls. The prestige car in Singapore was a big American sedan, the Chevrolet. For a while, Australian Holdens marketed by General Motors did well in Asia, until the fuel crisis hit. British cars generally had a decent market position in Asia; then the first Japanese cars arrived. By all accounts they were initially horrific. Yet unbelievably, not unlike their disastrous Second World War capitulation of Singapore to the flag of the rising sun, Britain gave its entire car business away to the Japanese. As the Japanese improved their product, the British cars seemed to adopt an inferiority complex. They were not as well trimmed nor as reliable as their Japanese competitors. Within a few years, Japanese brands had reduced the British brands to a shadow of their former selves.

As the years rolled on, and affluence in Asia started to blossom, more expensive automobiles from the factories of Europe appeared on Asia's highways. At the forefront was Mercedes-Benz, with its lofty aristocratic pedigree. Asians embraced the brand with a passion not witnessed before, and the bonding between the brand and successful Asians has steadily strengthened ever since. Not that it's been an easy ride. While Mercedes-Benz is the brand leader in its field, it always behaves like a challenger in the business. By the mid-1990s, the brand owner had managed to move the brand in

Asia to the enviable position of an "institution". But the focus was narrow. Looking ahead, they wanted to broaden the brand's appeal to add value in terms of connectability with new consumers like the younger families, the younger motorists, and the career woman.

But it had long been a "given" that if you were rich and successful, you ended up with a Mercedes-Benz. The *towkays*, the bookies, the hawkers were the faithful converted. In one sense, they worked *against* the brand. A newer, younger audience with subtler aspirations seemed to question such conspicuous show of wealth; making a statement of individuality, being "different", topped their agenda. They admired the brand's engineering, but not necessarily its badge value. This, in turn, brought about a watershed for the brand.

Clearly, Mercedes-Benz enjoyed enormous respect but had become "one-dimensional". Few Asian consumers, for example, knew how seriously Mercedes-Benz took its responsibilities as a corporate citizen; it was a huge car maker that had pioneered some amazing measures to save the environment. Nor was the market aware of just how "young" and sporty the brand could be. The C-Class, particularly, offered virtually endless ways to personalise the car. Some were very radical; tasteful, of course, but revolutionary in terms of the general perception of the brand. *Your Mercedes-Benz didn't have to be white!* So two new complementary mandates arose in marketing communications: to reach broader marketing opportunities and to take on board environmental issues.

At the same time, the launch of the new E-Class demonstrated how complex life gets when you are a brand owner trying to satisfy global needs. When you sit in Stuttgart, you have to take account of all the different marketing dynamics. You have to look at the European base, then America, and then the Asian market, and produce cars that cover all those taste buds. You're running a global brand, but human nature being what it is, there's no shortage of people telling you "that-won't-work-here". Your designers have to work with all those considerations, satisfy all those needs, transcend all those cultures, and provide enough options to appeal in every market. And just when you think you've cracked the design of a sensational new E-Class, you run up against the Chinese businessmen in Taiwan!

This "little" market is probably a fraction of the brand's world sales. But when you look at it as over 10,000 Mercedes sold in a market of 23 million people, it's not insignificant. So when the word got out that a totally new, totally different E-Class was about to arrive, panic struck the Taiwanese market. We don't want it, the Taiwanese said. If it doesn't look like a Mercedes-Benz, forget it! The same message started to feed back into distributors in other Asian markets. How dare Mercedes-Benz change the E-Class and make it look like something else! Where was the sense in that? Where is the prestige in driving a car that doesn't look like a Mercedes-Benz? At which point the most successful model run-out in history began. Conservative Mercedes-Benz diehards snapped up every available "old" E-Class. Of course, once the new car had arrived and its beauty was appreciated, common sense prevailed and everyone fell in love with it.

And while it is amusing to reflect on incidents like that, they underscore the potency of the Mercedes-Benz brand in Asia. For generations, paper effigies have been burnt as offerings at the old traditional Chinese funerals of Southeast Asia. The most common effigies are still a house and a Mercedes-Benz, so that the deceased will have the best creature comforts in the next life. Sometimes the models are intricately crafted; others are just crude red paper cutouts with the three-pointed star inked on the front. What is significant is the fact that no one has ever been known to burn an effigy of a BMW.

In China, however, the rich cadres were more concerned about having a Mercedes-Benz in *this* life. A vast undersea smuggling operation battled to cope with demand. It worked like clockwork. When someone valet parked their new Mercedes-Benz in Hong Kong, the attendant might make a wax impression of the key. When the car was reclaimed, a motor cyclist would follow it home. A few days later, the gang would swoop. They would simply put the key in the lock and drive the car away. It would then be secured inside a big inflatable bag and towed *underwater* into China.

In Taiwan, parallel imports of Mercedes-Benz challenged the authorised distribution network. A Mercedes-Benz, intended for delivery in the States, would suddenly pop up in Taiwan or a province of China requiring its official warranty service. Even though the distributor didn't sell the car, it was nevertheless a Mercedes-Benz that its owner had bought in good faith and had to be serviced in accordance with the usual warranty.

EVERY brand owner with regional or global aspirations can learn from Mercedes-Benz. Here is the living proof that *great global brands should never be changed to suit one or two markets.* The brand, its values and its voice must never be compromised. Mercedes-Benz is the same car, representing the same excellence and offering the same motoring experience, wherever it goes in the world. It is what it is. Frequently though, most brand owners are faced with a challenge where they feel they have to change key pillars in their brand communications strategy in order to succeed in a certain market. Which, in reality, means not just changing the brand packaging, but also changing the whole personality of your brand, the whole culture of your thinking. Rather than sacrifice a brand on the altar of expediency, it is better to develop a totally new brand altogether to cope with these situations.

Mercedes-Benz, like other great global brands selling top-quality goods or services, is singularly focused wherever it goes. It takes the brand's soul and personality all around the world and people have to like it for what it genuinely is. While the affluent global consumer tribes have varying tastes and varying purchase motivations, goods and services of exceptional quality transcend those differences; nevertheless, the brand owner must not be coy in consistently comforting his admirers with communications and physical expressions that mirror the brand's special place in life.

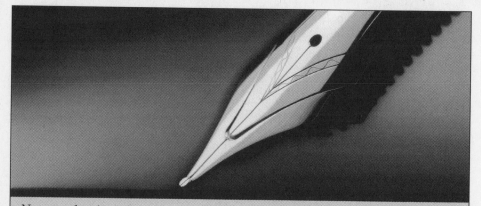

How we helped broaden Asia's respect for Mercedes-Benz.

In Germany, we chase the police.

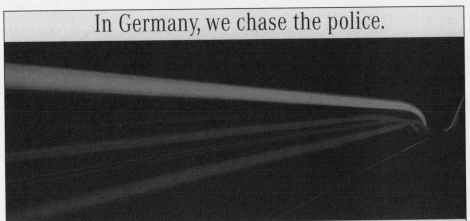

▶ Actually, it's a good deal more serious than it sounds.

Since 1969, thanks to the co-operation of the German police, our engineers have been travelling to major road accidents in which a Mercedes-Benz has been involved.

Today, we have the benefit of 25 years of experience in accident research behind us.

▶ This year, our Accident Analysis teams will study the causes of up to 160 accidents.

And their effects.

One team has even received additional medical training.

▶ We now have over 2,900 cases of unique accident data stored in our archives.

In 1959, we did our first crash test. And we still conduct over one hundred such tests every year.

Painstakingly, we compile all the evidence, and feed it back to the engineers who are working on the next Mercedes-Benz models.

▶ As you would imagine, the results are well worth the effort.

In 1949, we performed the first safety car door which neither pops open nor jams shut on impact.

In 1956, we introduced the glovebox which safely concertinas into half its size on impact.

And, in 1982, we developed pedals which pivot away on impact, rather than crush the delicate bones of your feet.

As you can see, our pursuit of safety is a day and night affair.

In fact, you might even say our cars are designed by accident.

★ Mercedes-Benz
Engineered to move the human spirit.

Stopped by Mercedes-Benz.

▶ At Mercedes-Benz, we believe that safety is something every driver should take for granted no matter what car he drives.

That's why we chose not to patent so many of our safety inventions.

▶ Like the anti-lock braking systems, or ABS, which allows you to steer away from danger even when your brakes are fully engaged.

Or the crumple zones, large tensile sections of the car designed to deform upon impact to absorb the forces of the collision.

Or the safety cell, a rigid passenger compartment structure that protects the occupants in the event of an impact.

▶ We feel that in any accident, the chances of survival should be the same for everyone. Better.

Even if they are not driving a Mercedes-Benz.

▶ Fact is, we've been conducting safety research and development for well over 50 years.

All the while, sharing our new-found knowledge with the rest of the motoring industry.

And that, we're quite happy to add, is a gesture that will never be stopped by Mercedes-Benz.

Mercedes-Benz
Engineered to move the human spirit.

CHAPTER 15

COMMUNICATING IN CHINA

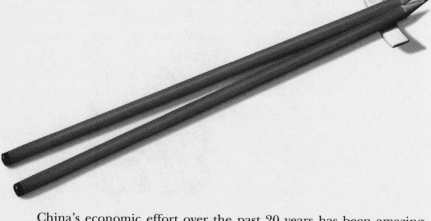

China's economic effort over the past 20 years has been amazing. The once-closed economic power ballooned the annual value of its foreign trade 12 times, from $38 billion in 1980 to $474 billion in 2000. And while doing this, it has steadily improved the quality of its manufactured goods and expanded its export reach to almost every country on earth.

China's entry into the World Trade Organisation will provide a further boost for exports, and also open the door wider for foreign brands to penetrate the domestic market. Some observers say this challenge is like putting your hand into a wild bees' nest, but I suggest that the huge bounty of honey is worth the painful risk.

There's a lot of stuff written about marketing in China these days, so I'll confine my commentary to a few communication-related things that scratch the surface of this exciting new consumer society.

Chinese consumers, for example, still tend to read every word of text on a pack. They are hungry for information, even for basic stuff like what the product will do.

It was not so long ago that Made in China products actually had barcodes printed on them, not because Chinese supermarkets had the technology to read barcodes (at that stage, most didn't), but so consumers would think they were foreign-made products of superior quality and, presumably, would pay more for them.

Packaging designers are still hamstrung by the old "black-equals-death" myth, prevalent among older Chinese in less sophisticated communities; being black, however, hasn't been a setback for mobile phone sales.

But the times they are a-changing. The target market in the near-term is clearly identified: the younger Chinese, the 16- to 35-year-old segment, in the urban areas. In late 2000, *Time* predicted that more than 600 million young people under the age of 24 in China are "pushing the boundaries with their numbers, needs and ambitions". *China's youth exceeds the total populations of North America, Russia and Australia — combined!*

The younger Chinese are surprisingly sophisticated. Stroll down the main streets of Beijing and Shanghai, and you could be in New York or London. The contemporary, fashionable clothes, the colours, the amount of English spoken — it's all quite overwhelming. Young China is on the move, hungrily absorbing more and more global values and trends like an army of locusts storming a huge prairie of corn, and this accelerating force is, I believe, unstoppable.

Connecting with younger Chinese is a fairly complex affair. The national media includes 3,240 television channels (double the number of stations in the US), serving China's 1.1 billion viewers; some 2,160 newspapers with a total circulation of 26 billion; and 1,200 radio stations. In 2000, 6.5 million Chinese computers were linked to the Internet, and 22.5 million Chinese were surfing on them. And if all that isn't enough to numb your brain, the unreliability of individual media statistics will. Then there's poor reproduction in print media to contend with, and whether or not your advertising will survive the bureaucracy of the "censorship" system.

But things are getting better by the day. Come 2005 this whole scene will be as streamlined and sophisticated as it is in Western markets, so they say. I suggest you don't hold your breath. However, what's immediately more exciting are the creative advertising opportunities.

When the domestic market seriously started to open up to foreign brands in the late 1980s, major multinational companies from all sorts of industries moved in to establish bases. And, like the happy camp followers that they are, the multinational ad agencies servicing these corporations quickly followed suit. In those days, the indigenous advertising industry was predictably still in the dark ages. Nevertheless, there were legal constraints on foreign ownership, and the local practitioners were more experienced in local ways than the smart foreign professionals, so all sorts of joint ventures and collaborative arrangements occurred for a while. After the dust settled, the big global ad agencies took charge and because the local creative talent was as scarce as hen's teeth, it became a common practice for Chinese-thinking, Chinese-speaking creative people to be parachuted in from nearby countries to help out on project work. Some of them became more permanent fixtures. The same "recruitment" practice has been followed for senior account service management.

No one expected the China ride to be an easy ride. And China has not let anyone down on this point. It's been a case of trial and error, and a need for very deep pockets. And, despite the healthy growth of the advertising industry (measured media growth rose from $532 million in 1990 to $9.6 billion in 2000) there are still several tough years ahead before many global brand owners and their multinational ad agencies start reaping a decent return on their investment. Such is the game.

However, I see much more potential joy in the immediate future on the creative front. The domestic creative talent is now starting to bloom, stimulated by the foreign teachers and a creative environment that is steadily emerging in the urban areas of China. And, most critically, the younger Chinese urban audience is ready and enthusiastically waiting to connect and bond with creative brand advertising. This target market has patently demonstrated its sophistication, intelligence and international mindset. If you have a top-quality or lifestyle "want" brand, don't hesitate to communicate with this target audience in the way you'd talk to the same age group in Sydney or San Francisco. And, if you have a catchy English language jingle, or a sharp English language pay-off line, communicate it in English. Young China is remarkably savvy.

Let me tell you one story that supports my commentary on this topic. Ericsson wanted to secure a stake in China's telecommunications future (and sell a few mobile phones in the process), so they decided to run a special advertising campaign to lobby their cause. While their competitors were running ads about technology, our North Asia creative director at the time, Mike Fromowitz, took another route. He crafted a campaign of television scripts about family life in China. The plots focused on the importance of communication between people — communication, naturally enough, is Ericsson's game. The legendary Chinese movie director Zhang Yimou was persuaded to shoot them. The end result was highly sensitive in its emotions, intelligent in its simplicity, and sophisticated in an international context. It was highly successful, winning not only the hearts of young China (and others as well), but also achieving top recognition at several international creative award events. It was a stunning victory for Eastern and Western creative talents combined. And speaking of awards, the nectar that keeps creative hearts pumping, I will be disappointed if advertising created in China does not consistently carry off the top trophies at international creative award shows within the next decade.

CHAPTER 16

FOOD FOR THOUGHT

Sesame Street's Miss Piggy once remarked, "Don't eat more than you can lift", and judging by the level of food consumption in the USA, Miss Piggy's advice is religiously observed in her home country. While Asians have nowhere near the same ravenous appetite of their American friends, it is impossible to spend any time in Asia without becoming keenly aware of the huge importance that all Asian cultures place on food. It is a love affair that begins young and continues throughout life — a love affair characterised by frequent eating out, by remarkable knowledge of the finer points of cuisine, by intense curiosity about new types of food and new eating establishments, and by an unflagging commitment to fresh, quality ingredients.

But the extent of this passion for things gastronomic was not fully brought home to me until 1999 when our intelligence unit, the Batey Research and Intelligence Centre, joined forces with Reader's Digest Asia to conduct a study into how Asian consumers approach the business of shopping for food. We called it Asia Food Mind. So the rest of this chapter is a pretty hearty meal of statistics and their rational assessment.

The methodology involved a self-completion questionnaire inserted into all the various language editions of the February 1999 issue of *Reader's Digest* in Singapore, Malaysia, Thailand, the Philippines, Hong Kong and Taiwan. The readership profile of *Reader's Digest* has too much of a middle-class tilt to be truly representative of a country's population spread, but it does tap into the heavy buying end of the consumer base so this makes the information very useful.

The questionnaire was immensely detailed — five separate sections asking about such things as how individuals prepare to go shopping for food, the key factors influencing food purchases, their spontaneous purchasing behaviour and attitudes to a variety of food-related issues. These questions were asked in relation to four main types of food shopping venues and 33 different food items covering a good cross-section of all important categories. And if that wasn't enough, there was also a detailed section on demographics, allowing numerous different demographic breaks to be used in tabulating the data.

All in all, anyone who wanted to complete the questionnaire was faced with a process that required consideration of over 350 different possible response choices.

And just to make it even harder, they had to pay their own postage to return the questionnaire.

The response was extraordinary. Almost 40,000 questionnaires were returned, *a response rate approaching 5%*. This, of course, is not only eloquent testimony to the tremendous appeal of *Reader's Digest* in Asia, but also to the singular importance of food among Asian communities.

Some of the findings from Asia Food Mind were predictable, reflecting trends seen in various other parts of the world.

This was particularly evident in the important role supermarkets now play in food shopping in Asia. Even though wet markets were still very important, with 70% of shoppers visiting one at least once a week, supermarkets weren't far behind, at 64%. (For

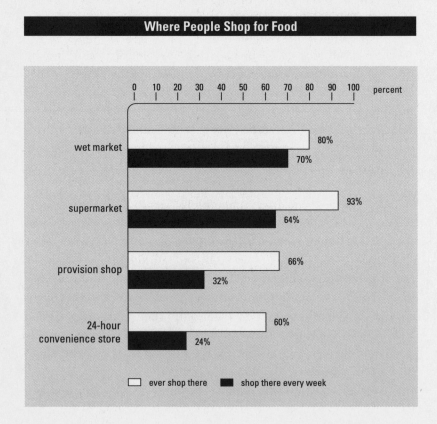

Where People Shop for Food

Base: 4,200 respondents.

my foreign readers, wet markets are big, communal markets specialising in fresh meat, fish, vegetables, spices, and so on. They are called "wet" because chickens and other creatures are slaughtered on the spot for Asian housewives insisting on *really* fresh food!)

The average time spent in supermarkets on each visit was about *twice* that spent in wet markets, reflecting the fact that people look to supermarkets for just about everything other than fresh meat, fish and produce — although supermarkets were clearly also beginning to make inroads even there. Meanwhile, local provision stores and 24-hour convenience stores were relegated to a very

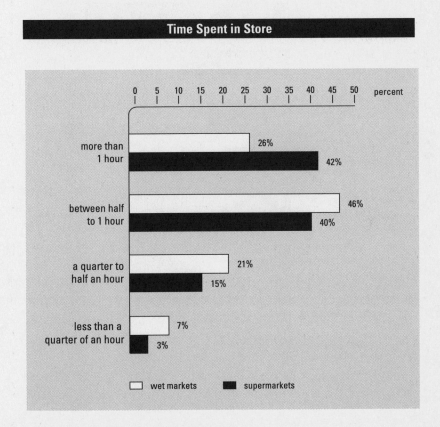

Time Spent in Store

- When shopping for food, normally would take.

Base: Those who shop at the specified store types.

secondary role indeed — that of a convenient place to buy urgently needed items.

What was more surprising was just how much time and effort goes into food shopping in Asia. Our study showed that the typical

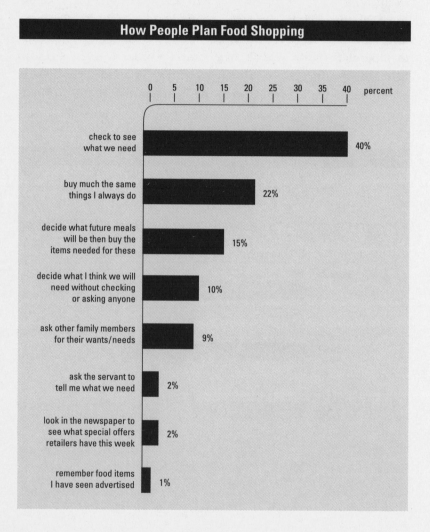

How People Plan Food Shopping

- Preparations done prior to going shopping for food.

Base: 3,547 respondents (84%) – those who do plan beforehand.

food shopper in Asia makes *at least* three major food shopping trips each week — about as many trips as the typical American makes each week for *every* type of shopping! And these trips involve a considerable time commitment; better than four in five shoppers actively pre-plan each shopping trip and, on average, they are spending more than half an hour in the market on each visit to the wet market, and more than an hour in store on each visit to the supermarket. Add on the time spent travelling to and from the shopping venue, multiply it by the number of shopping trips made each week, and the total time spent on this activity is considerable.

IT was interesting to see just how important brands are in food shopping in Asia. Better than nine in ten shoppers prefer branded food items over unbranded (a category which includes generic and commodity items as well as "own brands").

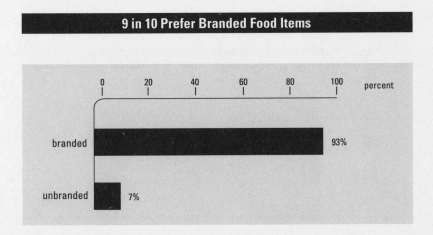

9 in 10 Prefer Branded Food Items

percent

branded   93%

unbranded   7%

• Brand choice made (18 product categories).

Their loyalty to these brands is high — 60% would delay purchase rather than buy an alternative if their preferred brand is not available; 71% were willing to pay a premium for a well-known brand, with a full 15% willing to pay more than 20% extra.

On the face of it, international brands enjoyed considerably

Most Will Delay Purchase When Their Usual Brand Is Not Available

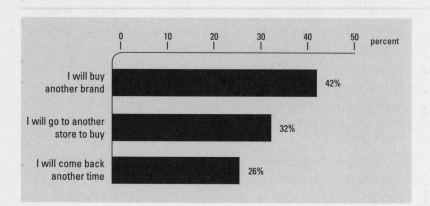

- Brand choice made (18 product categories).

Well-known Brands Command a Premium

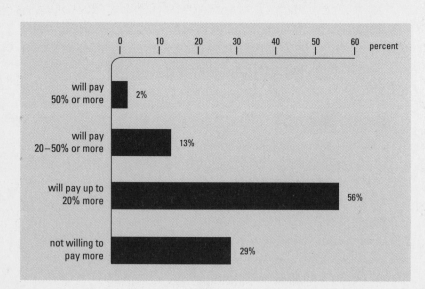

Base: 4,200 respondents.

greater cachet than local brands. By substantial margins they were seen as being of better and more consistent quality, more likely to be made from the best ingredients, and more likely to be free from harmful ingredients.

But international brands were also seen as being less readily available, less widely advertised, and far more likely to cost more than local brands. All of which goes some way in explaining why actual purchase preference was for local brands notwithstanding the perceived quality advantages of international brands, even though on value for money — as opposed to price — local and international brands were at parity.

Probably even more importantly, international brands are, by definition, not local. So they are less likely to be totally attuned to the local taste, to the local cuisine. Consequently, shoppers still prefer to buy the product that they identify as local — with preferences for local brands being strongest against products most closely identified with the local cuisine and palate.

It seems to make common sense for those global food brands focusing on deeply-rooted parochial taste habits to be clearly seen as local in the taste proposition and enjoyment attitude, while at the same time identifying the pedigree of the brand and its international standards of product quality and know-how.

This is something best done by being linked with a recognised international brand — using "brand" in the broadest sense to mean anything from the name of a country (like, for example, New Zealand milk or Australian beef), to the name of a specific manufacturer or brand (like an "ownership" line, *Another product from the Coca-Cola Company*).

AMONG the wealth of information in Asia Food Mind, I thought three other findings were extremely interesting and had potentially high significance for food brand owners.

The first was how willing our food shoppers were to admit being receptive to advertising. *More than 90% said that they were influenced by advertising at least some of the time*, with more than 20% claiming to be influenced quite often or very often.

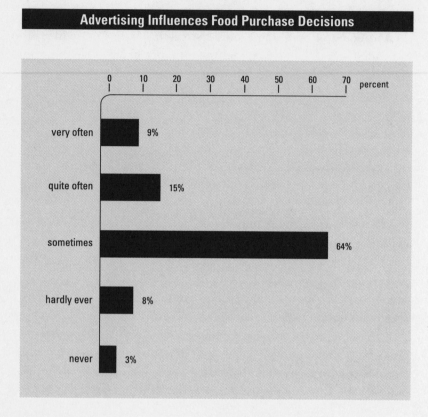

Advertising Influences Food Purchase Decisions

	percent
very often	9%
quite often	15%
sometimes	64%
hardly ever	8%
never	3%

Base: 4,200 respondents.

These figures are markedly higher than those found for responses to similar questions in the West, which in turn suggests that our consumers have not yet developed the cynical attitudes towards advertising that are now so prevalent in developed Western markets.

The second was the importance of on-pack information — 90% said that they looked at the pack for information about ingredients and use-by dates at least sometimes; 67% said they usually look on packs for this information. On-pack information was particularly important for more highly-processed foods and for fresh produce, but in *none* of the seven categories respondents were asked about did the total numbers claiming to look at on-pack information fall

Attitudes Towards Health-related Food Issues

I am trying to eat less fats & oils than I used to

| 40% | 51% | mean 1.6 |

I eat healthier food now than I used to

| 44% | 47% | mean 1.7 |

I am trying to eat less sugar than I used to

| 43% | 47% | mean 1.7 |

I worry about my diet more than I used to

| 47% | 42% | mean 1.7 |

I am trying to eat less salt than I used to

| 45% | 41% | mean 1.8 |

I prefer confectionery containing healthy ingredients like milk, fruit or fruit juice

| 44% | 41% | mean 1.8 |

■ disagree strongly   ▨ disagree somewhat   ▧ agree somewhat   ▢ agree strongly

- Base: 4,200 respondents.

below 70%, nor did those claiming to "usually" look on the pack fall below 50%.

Interest in on-pack information was not just because of concerns about use-by dates. Food shoppers were in general agreement that they "pay attention to ingredient information on labels", giving this the *third highest measure of agreement* out of a total of 20 attitudinal statements. It seems clear that this level of agreement also suggests a degree of interest *higher* than would be accounted for by religious dietary restrictions alone.

And this is confirmed by the third finding that especially interested me: the high level of concern about health issues revealed by Asia Food Mind.

Going into this study, we were aware of the growing importance of health issues in developed Western markets and wanted to measure the levels of concern in Asia. We therefore included a number of questions related to health in the 20 attitudinal statements which respondents were asked to score on a 4-point agree/disagree scale.

The results indicated that as it is in the rest of the world, health is becoming a hot button item in Asia, with food shoppers keenly aware of the health message and attempting to adjust their food intake accordingly.

Six of the twenty attitudinal questions dealt with health-linked dietary issues. Mean score for these six was 1.7, where 1 is *Agree strongly* and 2 is *Agree somewhat*. Mean score for the remaining 14 questions was 2.1.

By any standard, these differences are meaningful, but it is also clear that Asia has still some way to go before it is walking the walk as well as it talks the talk. The statement, *I go out of my way to buy healthy foods*, got the lowest measure of agreement of any of the health-related attitudinal questions.

Eloquent proof that human nature is the same the world over!

Part five

WORK IN PROGRESS

CHAPTER 17

THE NEW
ASIAN
RULEBOOK

In the blink of an historian's eye, the non-Japan Asian region north of Australia has emerged on the world stage with a sprightly marketing culture, a decent (but vulnerable) advertising industry, and a certain notoriety. On one hand, Asia is product-focused, globalisation-driven, the happy hunting ground for commercial princes. On the other, it is perceived as too unimaginative in its thinking, too bound to a trader mentality, too loose in international business practices and too autocratically governed.

Asia is all those things, and more. But as the new century slowly gathers momentum, Asia will witness changes that will alter its landscape more dramatically than ever before in its history. And many of the new rules that will come into play will be made by consumers, not governments. In line with the sweeping developments to come, it is now timely for Asia's advertisers and the advertising industry to bond closer together as business partners and jointly focus on the only real client in the game — Joe Public.

What will the sweeping developments be in the first quarter of this century? I've already signalled several changes earlier in this book, and in this section I'll attempt to cover a few more topics that I think will have a significant impact on Asian society and the Asian communications services industry over the next generation.

LOOSENING GOVERNMENT CONTROLS

In the business arena, this development is already in train. Some countries are moving faster than others, but this trend will continue with the foot on and off the throttle, depending on the economic and political weather.

There will certainly be no foot on the brakes, because there's a common firm commitment to globalisation. And the globalisation agenda calls for more liberal and flexible trading arrangements, more tax and monetary incentives, more transparent business practices, more imagination and flair — things that are important for the potential fast track growth of entrepreneurial commercial enterprises. And the leading governments are enthusiastically deregulating and reinventing the rules to support the total programme.

The success of this mission will expand the size and prosperity of the Asian middle class, and irrevocably impact on the cultural identity, general behaviour and lifestyle of the local populations. A more individualistic, urbane, liberal, creative environment will emerge. This prognosis suggests that Asian respect for authority and deference to societal interests will significantly decline. Certainly, I feel that governments will have little choice but to happily embrace the intelligent, educated, more mature 21st century Asians for what they want to be. *And they will not be Western.* I think senior Japanese diplomat Akio Kawato hit the spot when he commented that each Asian society will find its own equilibrium between traditional and contemporary values.

The loosening of government controls and the growth of Asia's globalisation programmes will also be breathtaking for the region's communications services industry on two fronts. First, the size of the industry could feasibly rocket beyond the moon as a result of the Asian global brand evolution-cum-revolution. And secondly, the convergence of Eastern and Western values and taste buds will continue to escalate; pan-Asian or global campaigns, created in Taiwan or Malaysia or Singapore, will become regular fixtures.

THE GREYPOWER OF ASIA

About half a century or so ago, Eleanor Roosevelt remarked that "beautiful young people are accidents of Nature, but beautiful old people are works of art". Her view implied that old folk were small in numbers and good-looking old folk were a rare commodity.

I can't answer to how many are good-looking these days, but how things have changed in the *size* of the senior citizens' world since Eleanor's time! In 2000, more than 424 million people in the world were aged 65 or over. Come 2050, that figure will approach *1.5 billion.*

What happens if you reduce the age level a little? Well, for starters, come 2050 you'll find the 60-and-overs will account for *33% of the population of developed societies.*

Already in Japan, more than 20% of the nation's people are 60 and older, and this will rise above 30% by 2025. Looking around Asia, and taking the same age group as a percentage of local populations by 2025, we get 29% for Hong Kong, 18% for Singapore and 12% for Malaysia.

On average in Asia there are estimated to be about 11 people in the workforce for every retired person. Come 2050, the number of workers will fall to just *four* to every retiree.

Another daunting projection: by 2025, 20% of China's population will be 60 years old or over. And by 2050, 7% of them (or 99 million, to be exact) will have celebrated their 80th birthdays.

Most of these figures have been well publicised. What is less trumpeted is the impact the future seniors market will have on the economy and on lots of brands. As Asia moves past 2020, the 55s and over will have the money. It is expected that in the most developed Asian societies they will control *40% or more of the total disposable spend.*

Projecting ahead, Asia's 55- to 75-year-olds will be healthier, more active and more youthful in spirit than previous generations of seniors. They'll dress and behave younger than their dads and mums; they'll certainly travel a lot more and their more enquiring, educated minds will make them more adventurous, comparatively speaking. They'll be more sympathetic to environmental and ecological causes and will genuinely support them with greater passion. They'll be more outspoken, more confident citizens of the world.

The implications of this projection are extensive, and all sorts of hypothetical marketplace scenarios spring to mind. The obvious ones relate to personal looks and health care: the leading brands in these categories are going to have a field day, and the life sciences business will be huge. Other strong performances will be seen in holiday travel, sea cruises, casinos, and equipment linked to family entertainment. The seniors of 20 years' hence will be far more independent, intelligent and highly IT-literate. *And firmly brand-centric.* They'll be mature and wise, and have a clear view on what is good and what is not so good. So in this respect they won't be all that different from the present seniors market. Despite greater sophistication and other enhancements, the seniors market in 20 years' time will follow the basic law of human behaviour — they'll still be creatures of habit, not change.

The seniors will essentially stick with the brand friends they got to relate to and liked in earlier years, and the bonding to the brand will be fairly deep and entrenched from middle age onwards. Which brings us back to the game of brand building. The message for brand owners is fairly clear: work the streets as best you can right now with the classic 20- to 50-year-old age group and keep up a consistent dialogue with this group year after year. Your task is not only to garner short-term sales; it is also to build a long-term bonding with the all-powerful seniors market of the future. Remember, brand loyalty is a state of mind among senior citizens, but it's *not* a given. You have to earn it.

Think into the future as well as the present — keep knocking consistently on the door of the identified target audience (no long silences, please).

DEATH OF A SALESMAN?

With sophisticated on-line information will we need to go to the local GP so often? Will we work out our legal problems without going to lawyers? Will we figure out the sums without the accountants? Will the whole education system for children be totally overhauled — no need to go to a physical school in order to be instructed by a teacher? Will the choice of learning topic be optional for young people? Will they sit for their exams in the confines of their own homes? And so on...

In his book *Roaring 2000*, Harry Dent predicted pretty accurately that the Internet would transfer power and place it firmly in the hands of the consumer, and that this empowerment would be awesome. Dent interestingly illustrated the process of change in the past century. At the beginning of the 20th century, the assembly line revolutionised production. The traditional craftsmen were replaced and costs dropped dramatically. Today, only 20% of the purchase price represents the cost of production, while the balance goes for administration, distribution, marketing and retailing. According to Dent, direct producer-to-consumer commerce on the Internet replaces the middleman, the retailer. The new network organisation consists of leaders guiding entrepreneurs and self-managing teams in a real-time process that is organised around the ever-changing needs of individual customers.

Dent's thinking is now being practised across the world. In cutting out the retailer, we have cut out the *human influencer*, the salesman. And with the passing of the salesman, trade advertising could also be a thing of the past. Marketers heavily committed to the e-commerce trail no longer have to buy the loyalty of sales staff in retail outlets.

Branding, predictably, will be more important in the e-commerce world than it ever was before. The brand's relationship with the consumer must be stronger than it ever was before. The conventional percentage of advertising spend to sales turnover will need some serious rethinking (and serious upweighting, generally speaking) because the game now includes a different playing field.

HAVING said all that, there is an argument that the Internet will *not* take over our lives. Remember the forecasts of radio's demise when TV hit the stage? Certainly cinema went through a trying period, but has emerged smarter than ever!

There is a view that because humans are the most enquiring, gregarious and tenacious of all animals, we will take the Internet on board with all the passion of a Latin lover, enjoy it immensely for a few years, and then gradually treat it as yet another plaything in our stable of playthings. The theory is that we like the flexibility of buying a sack of potatoes at the press of a button, or by voice instruction, or taking a stroll down to the store for a social connection with other humans and buying the potatoes when we're there. Or, we can even take a ride into the country for the charm and romance of buying the potatoes from a roadside stall. (Besides, it's a good silly feeling to get your hands grubby every now and then.)

I support that theory. I feel the Internet and all its power will *expand* our way of living and *expand* our options rather than significantly change the way we live. We're told that we only

seriously work about 10% of our brain's capability, so who knows —
the Internet might expand our use of our brains *by another 50%*. If
it does, that will take us up to about 15% of our brain's capability,
maybe…

HOW SMART WILL WE GET?

It's likely that the most personal form of information technology
that we'll have will be the smart card. Already widely popular across
Asia, these cards will eventually contain all the data imaginable
about ourselves in digital form.

Some versions already hold personal financial information such
as banking and investment accounts and credit limits; credit history
will soon be added. Then there's your medical data; things like
records of your health history, your allergies, your doctor contact
details. Information on insurance — details of your policies,
premiums, renewal dates — will also be packed onto your smart
card, not to mention legal stuff like wills and tax returns. Clearly,
all the numbers and codes you use to access your bank, your airline,
your frequent flyer mileage and all sorts of other fundamental data
will be on your card. The plan is to use one smart card to interact
with any digital hookup any time of the day, anywhere in the world,
without obstruction.

This tiny piece of personal plastic is likely to evolve into a
commonplace toy and may even replace your driver's licence,
identity card and international passport.

But, for all its incredible talents and potential, the future smart
card will reduce the user's connection with quite a number of
service units to that of a faceless, soulless communication. Those
brand owners affected will clearly need to step on the brand pedal
to effectively counter the downsides of the cold and silent
relationship created by the smart card. As the empowerment
technology programme takes wing, so must branding get stronger
and more seductive.

CHAPTER 18

FUTURE
TRUTHS

Before 20 or so of the world's top 50 global brands can reside in non-Japan Asia, it is transparent that fundamental changes will have to be made to Asia's management, marketing and advertising methods, and the Asian mindset.

While Asia will unquestionably continue to learn from the West, the changes will reflect the new Asian reality. They will come about as Asia reshapes its global brand building and marketing. They will be Asia-centric changes, the ripples from which will travel in a Westerly direction.

HOW CLIENTS WILL GET THE BEST ADVERTISING

There is a well-worn old saying that "the client gets the advertising he deserves". And this sentiment is still relevant.

Look at the brands that have consistently good advertising — not just consistent for a year, but over several years. Nike, Absolut, Rolex, SIA, Levi's are just some examples. Now look at the clients behind that advertising. In every case it will be a strong, prosperous organisation. A focused, dynamic, *confident* brand owner and his agency generally have a close working relationship in which the agency is encouraged to explore and expand creative boundaries so long as the brand's core values are nourished rather than reinvented. Strong clients know their own brand disciplines. So do their agencies. They work as one in building the brand's relationship with consumers. Over time, the consistency of emphatic and empathetic advertising sweetens the bonding.

Sounds too good to be true? Nowadays, unfortunately, the above is actually the exception rather than the rule. It is very tough to keep focused. More brand owners are starting to jump around in all directions, championing the need for change. And the process of change to some brand owners means different brand values, different New Age advertising, and so on. In some cases they may well be correct; but in most, they are not. They are merely confusing themselves.

There is a fine line. The brand's core values need not change, whereas the creative delivery of those values should constantly be at the cutting edge. Somehow brand owners get that confused; then they confuse their advertising agencies, and their final advertising reflects the lost path and confuses the consumer as well.

Brand building and advertising mean taking responsibility and committing oneself in public. Someone has to sign off on the corporate promise. This explains why a lot of advertising is exceptionally bland and rather evasive in what it does promise. This advertising inertia was exacerbated by the abdication of responsibility in the boardroom. Too many decisions are financially driven; too few are brand driven. Which is a dichotomy, because the brand drives the bottom line.

Now that the world acknowledges the enormous value of a strong brand, and with the Internet driving consumerism to greater heights of empowerment, it is imperative that the CEOs of worthy companies become seriously brand-centric. In the future mass-consumer marketing environment, the brand owner will constantly have his head down in a gale-force wind trying to come up with inventive product and service ideas while he satisfies his shareholders with a decent profit. To meet this challenge, the brand owner's operation in the mass-market category has to be retooled in order to survive.

Traditionally, CEOs have come from the ranks of accountants or engineers or administrators. There is a glaring absence of CEOs with marketing skills both in the West and in Asia. If the top 100 companies in Asia were surveyed, probably no more than 10% of them would have a CEO with a marketing background. And within that 10%, most CEOs would be from a sales background as opposed to pure marketing. This needs to be corrected. Asian CEOs are often younger than their Western counterparts. They must get themselves highly tuned into brand building, rather than delegating that responsibility. And because marketing systems are newer in Asia, they should be easier to change.

In the quest to develop Asia's global power brands, the CEO — as the brand owner — will need a new corporate *modus operandi.* Two teams of sharp, creative brand-oriented people will flank him. One team will think and act very quickly, very nimbly, in the present context. The second team will think ahead and create ideas that no one has ever thought of before, ideas that will give the brand owner a competitive edge and higher profits long before the competition catches up. So, the question of which dynamic drives a mass consumer organisation is closed: marketing is the clear winner.

The obvious critical and sensitive area that will demand the brand owner's personal attention is what the brand is saying to consumers through its advertising. One must henceforth question the power vested in marketing directors, commercial directors or marcom staff in dictating how the brand should present itself to the public. It is not because they lack good judgement; many of them are very clever people. It is simply because the importance of the brand is such that the CEO should now take *final responsibility* for the way the brand connects with consumers in advertising. The CEO should be the brand champion as he is, in fact, in companies like Nestlé, Virgin, GAP and Sony. (I'm told that one prominent British ad agency now offers a discounted fee to clients if the agency only has to deal with top management.)

In line with this imperative, advertising agencies must move back into the advertiser's boardroom. Thirty-five years or so ago, agencies presented campaigns in the boardrooms to the client chief, together with the sales manager responsible for the advertising. The agency was unquestioned as the professional in charge of the communications programme. The campaign had to be rationalised to the chief executive officer or his number two at board level, the men responsible to the shareholders for the bottom line. Once approved by them, the sales manager would handle the processing. Then some smart alec changed "sales" to "marketing", and as marketing evolved, the marketing departments grew bigger and bigger, stronger and stronger, and advertising agencies stopped having boardroom meetings with the client. They became suppliers. Nowadays, the ad agencies might see the top men when they pitch for the business, but rarely after that. And we know why. But all that needs to be changed — along with the conventional advertising agency service delivery.

THE AGENCY IS DEAD.
LONG LIVE THE AGENCY!

The non-Japan Asian advertising industry is a relatively young entity, having only seriously been around since the turn of the 1970s. It has enjoyed decent growth, but in recent times has been stumbling.

One basic problem is the quality of its leadership. We're too weak-kneed. Advertisers in Asia, with their natural aptitude for bargaining, consistently squeeze remarkably low compensation packages out of their agencies, and agencies seem to relish the massacre. Frankly, it's difficult to criticise advertisers for driving agency revenues into the ground. After all, the products or services they sell are constantly under yield pressure from the marketplace, so they look in every nook and cranny to trim costs. The advertising budget, as a flexible cost centre, always looms large and enticing in their sights.

Trouble is, this heavy mauling sets up another problem for advertising agencies — their quality of service. The old "you-get-what-you-pay-for" saying is put to a severe test. On one hand, the advertisers still cheekily seek what they perceive to be good service — good creative, good ideas, all delivered on time. While on the other hand, the agencies often struggle to meet quality expectations from a thin income base.

Sadly, it's been like this in Asia for several years. And now there's a big, Western-created trend towards a different servicing structure whereby the ad agency focuses its responsibilities solely on media creative and production for which it gets paid a fixed fee, with the advertiser separately sourcing media planning and placement and non-media advertising. This re-engineering potentially offers further savings to the advertiser, and hopefully more specialised attention will generate better quality results.

For the advertising agency, the conventional fixed fee model is direct agency staff costs multiplied by 2.5. This is a sound, sensible compensation deal, and some savvy advertisers add in an incentive bonus scheme. True to form, however, there's a growing tendency for advertisers to test the standard compensation model and I regret to report that some Asia-based ad agencies have yet again demonstrated their mettle by caving in to heavy pressure from their advertiser clients.

Interestingly, while championing savage cost-cutting measures, quite a number of respectable advertisers are significantly swelling their own fixed costs with the expansion of in-house marcom staff, and the employment of more high-powered, high-priced marketing managers. I guess it makes sense for advertisers to have a lot more people to deal with the bigger stable of different communications services consultants. Somehow though, I can't help but see this development as one that encourages umpteen round-table meetings to sort out agendas, umpteen more meetings to monitor the process, and umpteen more meetings to address brand value issues about which everyone has a different interpretation. Importantly, I think this development is at odds with the way I see the marketplace battlefield is behaving and will continue to behave for quite a long time. Underpinning everything is the edgy product, sensitive pricing, daunting distribution and the right brand strategy. These are the critical fundamental pillars. Then there's the mindset: you must have creativity, courage and confidence. Furthermore, consistent high-powered success will be reliant on the sharpness of an advertiser's 3Fs: the game is *Fast track, Flexibility and Flair.*

Margins are thin and always under siege. Fixed costs have to be lean. So I venture a scenario that postures no fat in the brand owner's internal marketing team — each member is a leader. But a tight internal team is not just a cost-cutting measure; more critically, it enables the advertiser to respond to the 3Fs with much more agility, professionalism and purpose. The lean, mean advertiser's senior marketing team would *exclude* a marcom department. There would be no advertising manager. And yes, marketing directors (as such) would possibly disappear. No layers would separate the advertiser's decision-makers and their professional external consultants. The brand owner's team would outsource most of their marketing support services and deal direct with their chosen partners. And accountability would be everything.

Parallel to this exciting development I see the best move for Asian-based advertising agencies is to retool themselves into *Brand Marketing Consultants (BMCs)*. Asian advertising agency people have been gazing at their own navels too long, and losing credibility in the process. As well as being media advertising professionals, many have engaged in the total communications menu, and certainly the majority of the experienced hands have a good understanding of marketing and what makes a brand tick. In the shifting sands of the playing field out there, it's time for advertising professionals to get off their backsides and leverage these talents for all sorts of self-evident reasons. It's not a heavy-duty change. As brand marketing consultants, the delivery will include the ubiquitous bundle of integrated communications services, which could be offered as a total package or in separate parts. And clearly, creative solutions remain king. Brand strategy development should rise to the surface as a prominent fee-based service, together with the emergence of a business strategy capability that focuses on the *creation and development of totally new brands in a business plan context.* This gem of a service will compete with the likes of PWC, Accenture and McKinsey on certain briefs.

Arguably, however, the most prized service offering will be the BMCs' intimate knowledge of the consumer's mind. The consumer is the owner of this century, and the BMCs' sensitive understanding of the feelings and emotions of multi-layered consumer segments across the globe should be the envy of the commercial world.

The contract between brand owners and their Asian brand marketing consultants should be fairly conventional, I sense, based on retainer fees and performance incentives and, of course, everything must be fully accountable.

No other force will match these brand marketing consultants on how best to connect and bond with the ultimate client — the consumer. In the retooling of advertising agencies into BMCs, our industry will recapture the high ground of communications. And once this happens, I feel we will witness an explosion of wonderful creativity and a quality of imaginative advertising not seen before in Asia, nor in the world since the 1960s. Advertising will be back in the hands of those who believe it is both a religion and an art.

Additional to servicing brand owners, the BMCs should aim for revenue opportunities in other related businesses. Some agency owners already play this game. For example, the franchise of a TV programme, a joint venture in a magazine, the part-owner of a consumer brand, and so on. Way back in the early days of advertising, the agency owners did this sort of thing quite regularly. Let's bring back some of this entrepreneurial spirit, and boost our margins in the process.

Speaking of which, you can bet London to a brick — which was the beloved saying of a famous Aussie race caller — that the mighty global communications services groups of today will consolidate down to the two American giants Interpublic and Omnicon, the great British brand WPP, and the Japanese icon Dentsu. And this will happen within the next three to five years. It's a case of margins. Down the road a bit, however, there lurks a huge threat to this cosy league of global giants. I will be bitterly disappointed if China and India fail to create a few of their very own great communications services entities. Indeed, one of them may well end up owning the likes of WPP!

TURNING ADVERTISING IDEAS INTO INTELLECTUAL PROPERTY

Unlike every other industry in the world, the advertising industry has never placed a value on its product. Woolgrowers don't give away wool. Oil companies don't give away gas. But advertising agencies give away ideas without a thought.

An advertising idea is like a song, a poem, a story, or any other intellectual property; it does have a dollar value. And that dollar value is not related to how long it takes to "get" the idea, but how strong the idea is in terms of its persuasiveness and memorability. Everyone agrees that *Marlboro Country* is a big, enduring idea. Everyone agrees that the Volkswagen *Lemon* ad was a turning point in print advertising. But if Leo Burnett or Bill Bernbach confessed that they first got their idea in a bath, or on a toilet, or they had scribbled it on a table napkin at lunch, would their idea be devalued accordingly? Very likely. Some advertisers, and certainly many agencies, would take the view that ideas are "worth nothing" until they have been executed and brought to fruition. Nothing could be further from the truth.

The truth is, advertising ideas are *so* valuable that advertisers never actually legally own them. Advertising ideas remain the property of the advertising agency that created them and *not* the advertiser. The fact that the advertising industry has never expressed this truth in a public forum speaks volumes about the industry fear syndrome. ("*We'd better not tell the clients, they won't like it...*") Basic copyright law states that the author is the owner, or in the case of salaried ad agency employees, the author's boss becomes the owner. Even if the advertiser has spent millions on production and media exposure, the idea is still the property of the agency, unless the agency assigns the copyright to the advertiser in writing.

Copyright law is often unpalatable. Copywriters and art directors employed on a full-time basis by an agency don't own the copyrights to their work by virtue of their salaries. However, *freelance* copywriters and art directors do retain ownership of their ideas unless they specifically assign the rights to the agency, in writing, upon receipt of their fees. The "idea" that a creator owns is just that, the idea, the written or visualised form of it. When the idea is photographed or filmed or recorded, more copyrights are *automatically* created. The still photographer owns the copyrights to his shots. The production house owns the copyrights to its films. The music composer owns the copyrights to his jingles and sound designs. The recording studio owns the copyrights to its recordings. Even though a client has paid a million dollars for a commercial to be written, shot, and for music to be specially scored for it, none of the copyrights are vested in his company.

Smart advertisers appreciate the value of the ideas they "buy". They insist on having rights assigned to them. And they add copyright symbols to protect their advertising. The Service Mark (SM) symbol or the ® symbol often follows famous slogans or corporate signature lines. Any advertising agency wishing to clearly protect its copyright ownership needs only to rubberstamp every piece of copy and artwork with these words:

COPYRIGHT © 2002 AGENCY NAME & CITY.

Likewise, any advertiser possessing an assigned copyright should make the fact public with a small line across the base of every advertisement:

COPYRIGHT © 2002 ADVERTISER NAME & CITY.

Advertising copyright ownership is a can of worms that should be publicly debated by brand owners and agencies. Many companies calling pitches expect to freely pick and choose from all the ideas submitted; public exposure of copyright issues would quickly scotch that form of creative theft. When agencies pitch their ideas they still own their ideas, win or lose. The trouble is, the agencies are too weak-kneed to own up to it.

Once creativity is seen in a legal context, once ideas become *negotiable property*, the agency-client relationship will be strengthened. Putting a copyright assignment clause into the standard agency contract would become a bargaining point. Creativity would be recognised and delineated. And not before time, because brands are properties and so are the advertising ideas that build them.

AWAY WITH AWARDS

Is the best advertising award-winning advertising? Rarely, and there are several reasons for this. Effective advertising is often reassuring stuff. It's like a friend who meets up and chats with you frequently. Award-winning advertising, on the other hand, is usually chosen by creative judges who love anything different; work that has no discipline, work that is more outrageous, work you don't see around that much except in the award books.

Significantly, some of the newer cutting edge advertising

agencies in London, whose work is *truly* different and pioneering, have declined to enter award shows. Chasing awards can become a trap for creatives. When they come up with ideas, the first thing they ask themselves is "what will the judges think?" rather than "what will the consumer think?"

Creative people would do well to close the award books they bought, switch off their computers and go out and explore the incredible beauty of nature more often. The world's greatest symphony performance is but a humble whisper against the theatre of a lavish electrical storm dancing along the peaks of the American Rockies. The work of Renoir, Monet, Picasso is pedestrian compared with the diversity of colours and shapes of trees in a forest, flowers, butterflies and other creatures in this world. No Louvre or Tate or Met will ever match the art gallery of Nature. Yes, man *has* achieved amazing things in the past five thousand years. He is seen by many as the driver of just about everything creative on this planet. However, compared with the awesome brilliance of Nature, he is still a creative minnow.

Having said this, creative awards excite many brand owners. And I personally see nothing wrong with the idea of creative contests. Madness pumps up our adrenaline. We love to win prizes. But we must keep perspectives right. The greatest thrill is clearly shaping a brand, seeing it grow from childhood to maturity, watching it win more market share, applauding its triumphs. And this is where the advertiser-agency relationship works at its best, when the brand owner treats the agency like a business partner, when the business targets and revenues are transparent, and when they share the sales successes and failures together. This is the richest relationship. It is more than a marriage. It is a long, binding, passionate love affair.

THINKING *AHEAD* OF CONSUMERS

If someone had said, 20 years ago, that families would one day delight in driving around in little vans called people-movers, colleagues would have said, what are you talking about? If someone had predicted, 20 years ago, that grandmothers would happily go to the supermarket in running shoes, people would have laughed in your face.

In 1927, H. M. Warner of Warner Brothers said: "Who the hell wants to hear actors talk?"

In 1943, Thomas Watson, chairman of IBM, said: "I think there is a world market for maybe five computers."

In 1962, Decca Records rejected the Beatles, proclaiming: "We don't like their sound and guitar music is on the way out."

In 1977, Ken Olson, president, chairman and founder of Digital Equipment Corp., said: "There is no reason anyone would want a computer in their home."

In 1981, Bill Gates said: "640K ought to be enough for anybody."

Marketing is one of the last great entrepreneurial arenas. No research can give you *all* the answers, and quite a lot of research can't give you any, particularly if you're thinking ahead. If someone hasn't done something before, or seen something before, how can they intelligently comment on it? So much innovation is blown out of the water by research. We *have* to take risks now and then and scorch the earth. Nobody can quantify imagination. Nobody can qualify intuition.

What's evolving in an Asian's mind, and where is that mind travelling? According to the highly talented Maslow and his *Hierarchy of Needs*, human development goes from survival to belonging to self-esteem to self-actualisation. Humans tend to develop as their standard of living advances. In Asia, millions of people in newly developing countries are enjoying middle-class living standards for the first time ever. They have leapfrogged from survival, past the belonging stage, and are moving into self-esteem faster than Man ever did in the West. They are industrialising faster and individualising faster than ever happened before in human history. They are daring to dream. They will self-actualise earlier, too.

The new paradigm of the right-brain revolution is the individual who determines, through introspection and personal evaluation, how he or she best fits into society. Traditional authority has little to do with this process. More and more, our customers are inner-directed people. As brand builders, we ignore these new Asian consumers at our peril.

They may not become as cynical as Western audiences, but that does not mean they are naïve or unsophisticated. They are better educated and mature enough to spot a con. Asia is evolving from tribal structures to nuclear families, liberalised and urbanised.

Like the West, Asia has Yuppies and DINKs (Double-income-no-kids). And now, it seems we will have BoBos. In his book *BoBos in Paradise*, David Brooks coined this term to describe a new phenomenon in society, the merging of the Bohemian and the Bourgeois into one upper middle class in America. The convergence has produced a new, sensitive, open, more confrontational generation; a BoBo has one foot in the Bohemian world of creativity and counter-culture and the other firmly planted in the bourgeois realm of ambition and worldly success. They are elitists who live in highly expensive lofts in Bohemian downtown areas or sip espresso in arty coffeehouses in upscale suburbs while listening to alternative music. Says author Brooks, it's harder to separate the educated anti-establishment renegade from the educated pro-establishment company man. BoBos thrive on change. They are the lateral thinkers who can turn ideas and emotions into products. And if any Asian brand owner cares to investigate BoBos in Asia, they can be found in Hong Kong, Singapore, Kuala Lumpur and Bangkok, wherever the college-educated population base is exploding, wherever moral and commercial values are being reconsidered, and wherever IT is growing at warp speed.

The bottom line looks fairly clear to me. And it's exciting. There's an urban middle-class society burgeoning right across non-Japan Asia, as interested in new creative ideas and product innovations as the smartest folk in the West. In fact, this Asian tribe is likely to be more responsive than its Western counterparts to experimental, breakthrough concepts because of its younger, fresher, more enquiring mind.

I confidently predict that by the year 2020, Asia's urban,

middle-class society will be universally recognised as the most adventurous, most sophisticated of all middle-class tribes in the world.

A CAUTIONARY NOTE

There are quite a number of wise, experienced global business people who feel there's a lot of old garbage to clean up, and a lot of readjusting to do, if non-Japan Asia seriously seeks to be a prominent global player in the 21st century.

Jock McKenzie, worldwide chairman of Caltex, is one of those people. And Jock is closer to the issues than most other global businessmen — his worldwide headquarters are in Singapore. In Jock's view, expressed in a *Straits Times* report, the West had evolved its own distinctive ethos, emphasising individual rights and freedoms, and education that placed a premium on individual thought and expression. This open culture had bred entrepreneurial thinking, and an understanding of *the benefits of failure as well as success.* Asia, he said, had generally upheld a totally opposite view, with compliance and social obligation taking precedence over individual rights and creativity. He ventured the opinion that business leaders should move away from the traditional "command and control" organisational structures where top-down decisions rule; instead, they will have to create an environment which has a more open and challenging culture for employees.

Other critics close to the trench warfare of marketing in Asia say that a number of large corporations in the region are adopting the more open, empowerment management style recommended by business leaders like Mr. McKenzie. They are entrusting their brands to younger, highly intelligent, well-educated Asians — but the results to date are mixed. Too many good brands are now in dangerous hands; these younger people are totally inexperienced in marketing, in marketing communications — and in human relations generally.

The challenges of reshaping business cultures to create a healthier environment for creative expression, and the challenges of fostering competent talent to handle the big future picture, are, I'm sure, topics high on the agendas of global-centric government and corporations across Asia.

In an earlier section of this book I've touched on many of the obstacles, but I'm consciously raising these hurdles once again to remind us all that the road ahead for non-Japan Asia in its globalisation thrust is no gentle jaunt. However, I'm firmly convinced that Asia has the fibre to succeed.

A GREAT WAY TO FLY

As well as a recognisable part of this book's title, I think that *A great way to fly* is an appropriate caption for my closing comments.

Most of you are aware that this statement has been Singapore Airlines' slogan since the company's birth. And the airline has consistently demonstrated to the world that non-Japan Asia can be highly successful against the biggest in the West; indeed, Asian brands can be the best in the world. The airline is a fine role model for non-Japan Asia's globalisation dreams, and its slogan could well be Asia's spirited battlecry.

But first, let's recap on other key topics.

If you wish to create a reputation for yourself, whatever you do, **branding** is the name, branding is the game. The brand comes in two parts: body and soul. The body is the change engine; the soul can often remain unchanged forever.

Every single communication that exhibits your brand logo or trademark is a brand advertisement, be it on a T-shirt or on a bus ticket. Recognisable aspects of the core values of the brand must be evident across all communication vehicles. It is a tough discipline. Skilled brand guardians are essential.

Branding has always been the major bugle player in the marketing battle. With the invasion of the Internet, the smart card and other technology, branding is now the Napoleon in the battle.

The brand is no longer just a marketing concept. The brand is now a financial concept; *it is a company's most important financial asset.*

On the topic of Eastern and Western values, these definitions are far too broad. At best, there's a national cultural model. In countries like India there are dozens of culturally different permutations; but, in the same way that the grand old English game of cricket connects so positively across all religious and cultural tribes in India, so too there are increasingly common attitudes and values permeating the urban middle-class societies of Eastern and Western countries. The continuing spread of the Internet, education and prosperity in Asia will see the taste buds and behaviour patterns of this middle-class group converge strongly with those of the West over the next two decades. I'm wagering that *the Asian middle-class society will be sharper and more globally sophisticated than its Western counterparts by 2020.* And don't fret too much about the less attractive Western influences. The 21st century Asian society itself will intelligently find the equilibrium between traditional and contemporary values.

If you get nothing else out of this book, I sincerely hope you retain the message and play some part in rocketing 20 brands from non-Japan Asia into the World's Top 50 Brands by the year 2020.

Asia's globalisation commitment is firm and the leading Asian governments and commercial enterprises are fully aware that *entrepreneurship and creativity have to be fostered, and some attitudes and regulations need to be rewired.* But the repositioning of the goalposts does not have to be significant, I feel. The 21st century Asian is a savvy, well-educated individual.

In the short term, import the best Western coaches one can find to train up the Asian teams to beat the West at the game the West invented. Don't be coy about the level of imported talent. The world's most successful soccer brand is Manchester United. It is owned by the British, controlled by the British, it is British through and through. Yet about half the key players are foreigners!

As long as the guidelines outlined earlier in this book are observed, success in this ambitious but doable global mission will have a monumental impact on the marketing and communications services industry in Asia. To put it modestly, it will change Asia's industry into a superpower. *The sum of measured global advertising created and managed from Asia could eclipse $400 billion annually in the next two decades.* It would not be uncommon, for example, to hear about advertising shops in Mumbai or Kuala Lumpur directly controlling global budgets of Asian brands worth $500 million.

And as this picture unfolds, so too should advertising agencies take up their rightful roles as Brand Marketing Consultants. The true advertising professional is a gifted marketing all-rounder. He knows the consumer better than anyone. He is highly qualified to have a big say in brand-building programmes from the birth of the strategy, through to the marketing plan, and on to the creative solution — even to monitoring the results, because accountability will be a *tour de force.*

In line with the 3F game — Fast track, Flexibility and Flair — Asian brand owners should unshackle themselves from layers of internal marcom and marketing process people, and *just have the brand's decision-makers work direct with independent brand-marketing professionals.*

As well as mind-blowing technological advances, several other interesting things are predicted to happen this century, but I can only be supremely confident about two of them. First, this will be the consumer's century. Secondly, this will be Asia's century.

So aim high, you Asian global entrepreneurs — it's a great way to fly.

Appendix

Here are some more of my favourite Batey Ads print campaigns from over the years…

RAZOR REEFS CROUCH UNDER SWIRLING

CURRENTS, HELL BENT ON RIPPING THE LIFE

OUT OF ANY... WHAT DARES PASS. NOW,

500 METRES ABOVE THE WHITE CAPS, AN

AUSTRALIAN INVENTION CAN PINPOINT NEW

SHIPPING CHANNELS THROUGH WATERS WHICH

HAVE DEFIED NAVIGATORS FOR CENTURIES.

Inventive Australia ... an Australian Government initiative to raise the nation's commercial stature in Asia.

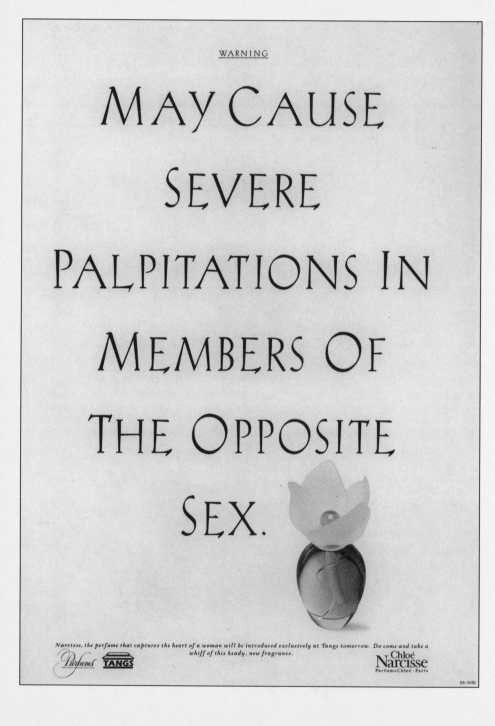

VISA GOLD. He who has the gold makes the rules.

VISA GOLD. He who has the gold makes the rules.

VISA GOLD. He who has the gold makes the rules.

VISA GOLD. He who has the gold makes the rules.

You won't be the only one to appreciate your Sony HiFi.

The Sony FH-G80 really is a clever little box of tricks. It can deliver 1000 watts of power with perfect clarity. Its revolutionary Music Express Dial offers easy one touch control of CD, timer and tuner.

And its Dynamic-Bass FeedBack allows selection of different bass levels for different music. What's more, its sophisticated graphic equalizer can choose from five preset modes. While its five user

memory files let you select and store your own acoustic patterns. In fact, about the only thing the FH-G80 can't do, is go unnoticed.

You won't be the only one to appreciate your Sony HiFi.

The Sony EX10 really is quite an ingenious little thing. It delivers 1200 watts of power with total clarity. Its Electro-Static Tweeters can capture the beauty of high frequency tones such as orchestral instruments. While its Dolby Pro-Logic produces true movie theatre sound. Just connect it to your video and you'll feel as if you're right there in the thick of the on-screen action. What's more, its Motional Feedback Woofer creates bass intensity that defies its size. In fact, about the only thing our new EX10 can't do, is go unnoticed.

SONY

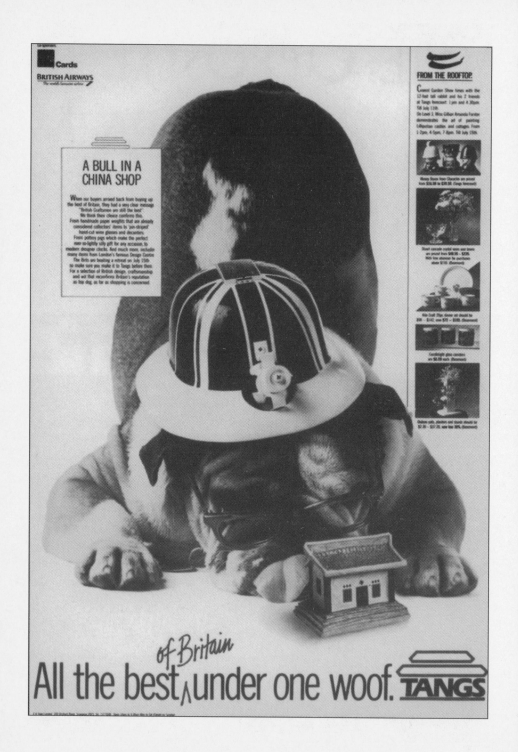

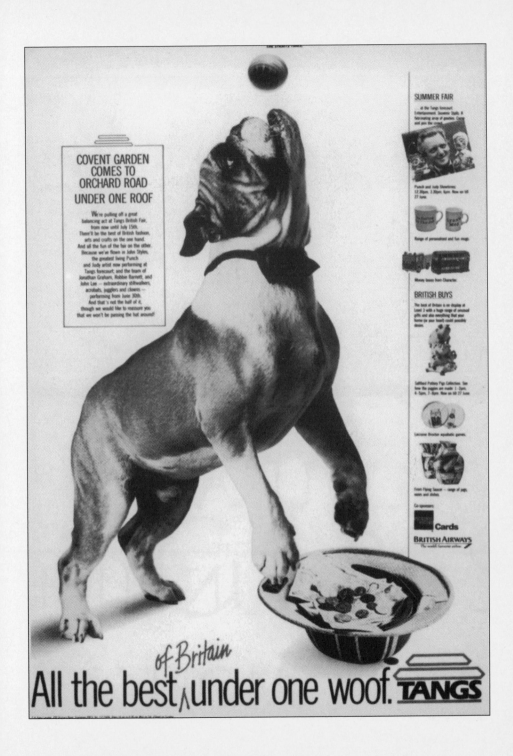

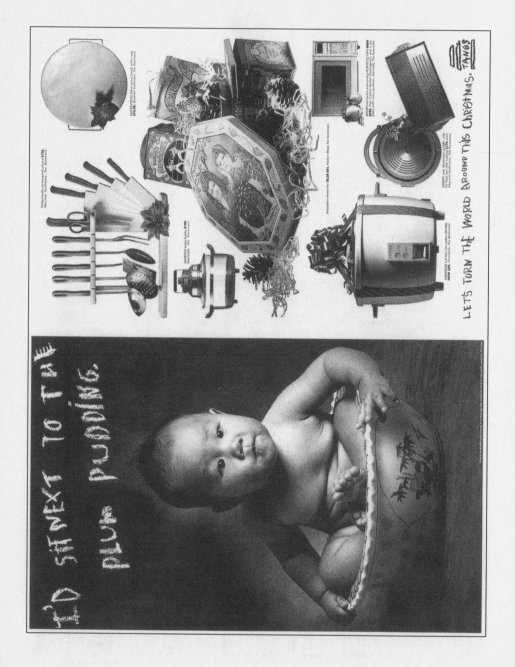

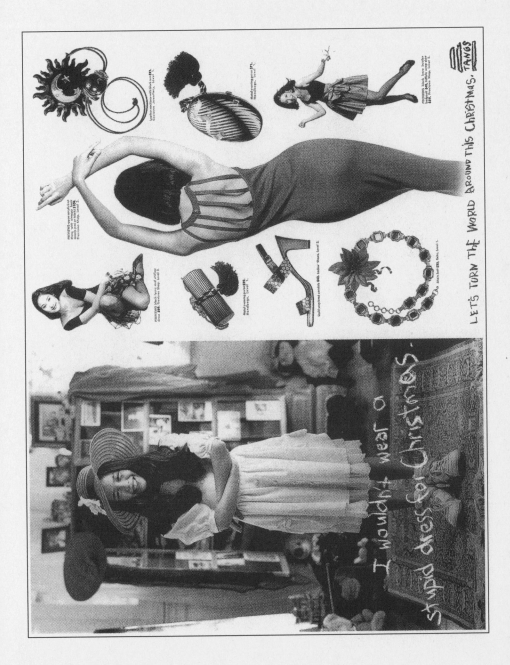

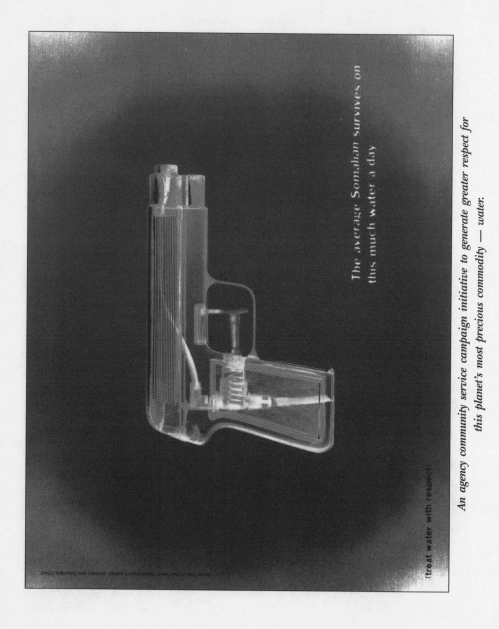

The average Somalian survives on this much water a day

(treat water with respect)

An agency community service campaign initiative to generate greater respect for this planet's most precious commodity — water.

(treat water with respect)

Another agency community service initiative in the early 1990s
on a topic that needs no explanation.

Thanks to Tog Ward, David Lancashire Design, The Printsetter, Columbia Offset and Newsweek.

Most office workers spend more time at their place of work than they do at home, yet for some reason they don't think of it as somewhere to start saving the world. How short-sighted. An enormous amount of resources are consumed at the office, and much could be saved with just a little effort. Apathy and the belief that there is little they can do about the state of the world is to blame when in fact nothing could be further from the truth. Every single action we take affects the wellbeing of our planet. You just have to work at it a little that's all.

APPENDIX

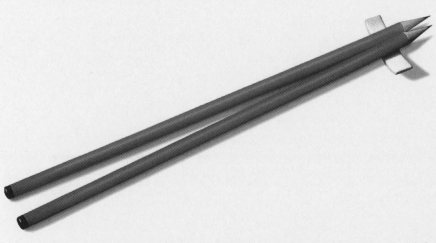

There's just space to include some documents, which I hope might interest and even inspire you in all the madness of brand building and advertising.

10 TIPS FOR YOUNG PEOPLE WHO ASPIRE TO BE SUCCESSFUL ACCOUNT SERVICE PROFESSIONALS IN THE ADVERTISING INDUSTRY

The game is changing rapidly. You have to be quick and smart. But it's great fun!

1. Aim to establish yourself as a brand communications consultant.

2. Position the advertiser as your business partner, and the consumer as your *real* client.

3. Get to know your consumer like he's your closest friend. If you don't understand your target prospects better than your advertiser partner, best look around for another career.

4. It is essential to develop strong, imaginative strategic planning skills.

5. Always provide written creative briefs that a 10-year-old would understand and get excited about. It's not that your creative people are dumb — rather it's because a creative brief should always be sharply singular and simple in its focus.

6. Developing and managing strong annual communications programmes is fundamental. Throwing additional pro-active ideas on the table *every week* is also fundamental.

7. Think and practise integrated communications.

8. Never forget that advertising is an art. And be prepared to die for the art.

9. Commit to a steady 60-hour working week. And love it.

10. Don't hesitate to exhibit a little madness every now and again. It'll keep you sane.

HOW TO RUN AN ADVERTISING AGENCY (OR ANY BUSINESS INVOLVING PEOPLE IN REASONABLE NUMBERS)

It's a loaded topic, because just about all private companies are run by people whose style of doing things only works well in the culture they've created within their own company. So in telling you a bit about my way of running an agency, please keep the culture point in mind.

When I started the agency back in the early 1970s, I had absolutely no knowledge about running a business, and I sadly did not have any mentor to guide me. So I had to rely on some gut feelings to get things off the ground, and I applied a number of key fundamental values as the company evolved.

1. **Identify and secure great senior talent**

   From day one, I chose a number of highly talented leaders for our Singapore HQ — leaders in creative, account service, finance, production and media.

   To secure their long-term loyalty, each leader was made an equity partner in the company. This "equity partner" philosophy was extended across other offices and subsidiaries as the years rolled by.

2. **Strict application of a special "Triple Energy" model**

   I'm not sure where I got this idea from, but I'm a firm disciple that the success of any business comes down to the energies of three forces — the Entrepreneur, the Administrator and the Antagonist.

   - The Entrepreneur leader — the creative madman, the lateral thinker, the great salesman, always upbeat.

   - The Administrator leader — the manager of the systems, the process genius, the person who gets things done on time at the right price. Always a positive, pragmatic attitude.

   - The Antagonist leader — highly efficient, but consistently provides a negative scenario to any idea or issue; always sees the dark side of the equation.

While the three dynamics usually come from different people, it is possible that the Entrepreneur and Administrator could be the same person.

Critically, the Entrepreneur and Administrator leaders play complementary roles, and one of them is the final decision-maker in the company. Equally as important, the Antagonist — while never given the power to make the final decision — has a big voice in keeping everyone's eyes on the bottom line and providing an intelligent counterbalance to the fantasies of the Entrepreneur. You guessed it. The Antagonist is usually the Finance Director of the company.

3. **Encourage lateral dialogue and confrontation**

I have some views about life, and I can get fairly passionate about my views. And I certainly get tough about responsibilities and accountability of senior managers. But if you were a fly on the wall at one of our regular management meetings you might describe it like a political debate in the Australian Federal Parliament about a beer tax. OK, maybe it's not that bad. But everyone, from despatch clerk to managing director, is encouraged to air their views on any issue. And I encourage this attitude to extend externally through to client sessions. Sadly, some of the more defensive clients interpret this attitude as arrogance, rather than a healthy way of finding a better solution to a challenge. So be it. I will continue to encourage our people to be open and confrontational, both internally and externally, as there's no doubt in my mind that it's an effective way to achieve better solutions for the brand owners and their shareholders. I think the "21st Century Asian" will happily embrace more open, confrontational relationships.

4. <u>Articulate your company's philosophy in writing</u>

We're all so frequently absorbed in writing strategies and the like for clients, that we often forget to do one for our own company, our own brand. I certainly was sloppy in this area, and it wasn't until I was chastised by one of my subordinates that I penned out a "What we believe" credo. And I'm so glad I did.

All multinational agencies have truckloads of this sort of stuff, but I suspect there are many independent shops out there who haven't yet penned a decent philosophy about themselves, and to help you Independents get some idea on how to do this, I've reproduced the details of the Batey credo here. All our offices have it framed on their walls. And it features in most presentations to new or prospective clients. I guess, above all else, this best summarises how we run our agency.

THE BATEY CULTURE

As an organisation founded in Asia in October 1972 by a bunch of Caucasians and Asians, we're a rather odd mob, as we're driven by a seemingly incompatible mixture of feelings and values: the strong work ethic, shrewdness and pragmatism of the East ... and the passion, naïvety and gregariousness of the West.

What sort of culture has this created in the Batey Group?

Several years ago, I penned out 19 points on why we are what we are. This "What we believe" credo hangs in all our offices.

I've now been asked to distil what I see as our culture down to a few paragraphs. It's a tough call, but here goes, with focus on what I consider to be the key qualities.

First, my definitive summary of our culture:

KILL FOR THE ART.
DIE FOR THE CLIENT.

AND ALWAYS BE
BRIEF, DIRECT, HUMBLE.

We abhor waffle, fat documents, long-winded speeches, overworked rationales. In short, we're disciples of brevity.

And when we talk we're direct, outspoken, always prepared to challenge the client's opinion, and only prepared to do work we feel we can do well. But we don't talk or challenge things like we're auditioning for the role of Dracula's mother. Instead, we always project an open, engaging face, and a good belly laugh is frequently on our agenda.

When it comes to our creative product, however, we get quite serious. We put art firmly before profit. We believe that if we do good creative for our clients, money will come to us without us having to think about it too much.

And we're equally tough on ourselves in all other departments. We always believe we can do better next time. Because doing things better and better for our clients is what we're all about. We don't just want to make clients happy with us, we want to make them feel they can't live without us!

For those few among you who don't know by heart the 19-Point Credo of the Batey Group, here for your enjoyment is the unabridged text.

What We Believe

Our Craft

We believe in advertising that tickles the toes as well as the head.

We believe in creating ideas that endure rather than one-off ads that win awards.

We believe in never sacrificing the art for profit.

We believe raw concept testing of advertising ideas was invented by a frustrated Tasmanian transvestite.

We believe that the most important rule to follow in developing an idea is not to have any rules.

Our Personality

We believe we're lucky to be in such an exciting industry and hopefully it shows in the energy and passion we apply to every task.

We are more like hawkers than suave admen.

We believe in being fair to the point of being boring; frank to the point of being disruptive; cheerful, always cheerful — to a point.

We believe that a little madness helps keep us sane.

Our Business Attitude

We believe the best clients are the ones we have: it's more important to develop existing business than to continuously chase new business.

We believe we must seek to know as much about our clients' business as the clients know themselves.

We believe there's no such thing as a bad client, just bad judgement or salesmanship on our part.

We believe the most effective client relationship is when we're seen as a business partner, not just a provider of advertising.

We believe forward planning is next to godliness.

We believe in treating the bottom line like grandma: with reverence.

Our Staff

We believe in sharing our financial rewards solely with the most deserving: our staff.

We believe in open door management, delegating responsibility and making everyone responsible for their actions.

We believe every single person on staff, from office boy upwards, should think, eat and sleep creatively.

We believe that hard work makes Jack a bright lad.

FURTHER EXCERPTS FROM THE 1970s GUIDEBOOK
HOW WE PLAY THE GAME

Attitude Towards Non-media Advertising

This section essentially covers consumer and trade sales promotions, plus sales aids/mailers to both target groups. The complexities of non-media are such that, for this paper, my comments are confined to directional brush stroke thinking. But it's a start.

As you all know, this is the blood-sweat-and-tears part of the account. Quite a lot of work for a fairly small return. Yet SIA is a keen supporter of non-media advertising, seeing it as an economical means to support mainline programmes; to increase more widespread awareness of the airline; to spread the word against segmented pockets about a certain development; and to enrich relations among selected clients.

Frankly, SIA is not really fussed who does the non-media work, so long as the work is competent, the price is competitive, and the ad agency coordinates the action. This point is emphasised because, from my experience, some advertising agencies are not too comfortable when it comes to crafting sales promotion ideas or sales aid gimmicks, yet spend endless weeks trying to come to grips with the challenge.

If you don't think non-media is your bag, sub-contract the job to an independent specialist.

Needless to say, all non-media activities must relate to agreed advertising objectives — be they strategic or tactical.

Indeed, non-media advertising is sometimes the sole promotional force in serving an objective, e.g. sustaining awareness and/or building relations among cargo agents.

Sales Promotion

Probably the toughest nut to crack effectively.

At consumer level one inclines towards cooperative deals to obtain extra mileage, and control elements can get severely bruised. Be it a sports sponsorship or a contest or a 10-second clip in a Hollywood movie, one often has to pray that things will work out the way everyone said they would.

Desirably then, when developing a consumer sales promotion with other partners, think of one partner only and nail him down firmly at negotiation stage.

Think also of the administrative logistics. You should avoid any scheme that requires heavy SIA staff admin involvement.

As with all key consumer sales promotions, the planning should start well ahead of the promotional period — say, six to nine months in advance.

Travel trade sales promotions can be even more challenging. You know these people are exposed to all sorts of fancy promotions, and to burst through the fanfare with a blockbuster can be tougher than getting a smile out of a Thatcher joke.

Fortunately, most sales promotions against the trade are totally controllable, so we simply look for a flair and imagination, not to put too fine a point on it.

As a general principle, be it trade or consumer, SIA favours one or two "Big Idea" promotions that achieve several months' recall rather than a series of rifle shots.

Sales Aids/Mailers

In markets where SIA has stature and is well entrenched, we can be quite relaxed in the tone of the sales aids/mailers to both consumers and the trade. They can be light hearted or serious, gimmicky or classy. So long as they're always well finished to reflect the quality of the brand.

In markets where SIA is still climbing the reputation ladder, we would tend to be more serious in tone — both in the way we talk and the way we look. A top-quality presentation is of paramount importance.

Consequently, the unit cost of items in less established markets will generally be more expensive than in well-established markets.

One last point: we favour giveaways/mailers that offer residual value.

INDEX

ABOUT THE AUTHOR

Ian Batey was born in Britain and bred in Australia. Batey and his advertising agency are Asian legends. Singapore Airlines was his first client in 1972. He has campaigned for many causes, including the arts, education, the environment and served on Singapore's National Council Against Drug Abuse. In 1990, the *Wall Street Journal* nominated Batey as one of the leading advertising personalities in Asia. In 1997, Asia's leading advertising trade magazine *Media & Marketing* chose him to receive its inaugural Asia's Top Ad Man of the Year award. In 1998, his agency was hailed Asia's most creative by *Campaign Brief*. In 1999, he received the very first Lifetime Achievement Award bestowed by the Institute of Advertising Singapore. As the agency's Chairman Emeritus, Batey now has time to indulge his passions: travel, art, grandchildren and advertising.